F JAPAN

APAN

AOMORI

L. Towada

AKITA
MORIOKA

R. Kitakami

Sado Is.

YAMAGATA

NIIGATA   SENDAI

FUKUSHIMA

R. Shinano

AZAWA

TOYAMA   NAGANO

Mt. Yari △ KARUIZAWA   NIKKO

FUKUI   *JAPAN ALPS*   MAEBASHI   UTSUNOMIYA

R. Tenryu   *R. Tone*   MITO

GIFU   KOFU   URAWA   *L. Kasumigaura*

SU   NAGOYA   TOKYO

△ *Mt. Fuji*   CHIBA

HAKONE   YOKOHAMA

SHIZUOKA   ATAMI

PACIFIC OCEAN

Oshima Is.

IZU ISLANDS

Miyake Is.

Hachijo Is.

1:6,000,000

0   100 km

Area: **377,384** square kilometers
          (**145,670** square miles)

Coastline: **29,751** kilometers
          (**18,475** miles)

THE ARLINGTON
BUSINESSMAN'S
GUIDE TO
JAPAN

THE ARLINGTON BUSINESSMAN'S GUIDE TO

JAPAN

Ian McNeil

Arlington Books
Clifford Street Mayfair
London

THE ARLINGTON BUSINESSMAN'S
GUIDE TO JAPAN
first published 1979 by
Arlington Books (Publishers) Ltd
3 Clifford Street Mayfair
London W1

© *Ian McNeil 1979*

Typeset by Inforum Ltd, Portsmouth
Printed and bound in England by
A. Wheaton and Company Ltd
London and Exeter

British Library Cataloguing in Publication Data

McNeil, Ian
The Arlington businessman's guide to Japan.
1. Japan — Economic conditions — 1945–
I. Title
330.9'52'04   HC462.9
ISBN 0–85140–292–5

I dedicate this book to all Japanese
badgers, especially those whose earth
is at Shiba Daimon. May they long
assume the shape of the autumn moon,
continue 'tanuki no hara tsuzumi'
and send their children to the noodle
shop for Suntory Imperial. Also to
S.S., my sensei, and 'samurai salesman'.

CONTENTS

THE ARLINGTON
BUSINESSMAN'S
GUIDE TO
JAPAN

INTRODUCTION

I started planning my first business trip to Japan several months before my departure date. As the weeks passed, my thirst for knowledge grew and I became the bane of public librarians as I badgered them for books about Japan. I took to combing the gloomier shelves of dusty second-hand bookshops in my quest for useful information. From the libraries I obtained some interesting tourist guidebooks and a handful of chatty volumes, mostly written by professional travel writers with elaborate descriptions of the ancient architecture of Nara and Kyoto, and sometimes of nightlife in Tokyo. The bookshops turned up little more than slim, yellowing offerings like *The Life of Admiral Togo*, published before the First World War, and essays on the problem of what to do with the Emperor after the Second. I amassed a fund of useful statistics on the number of pin-ball or 'pachinko' machines that had been in the country ten years earlier, and equally unprofitable figures on the number of taxi-cabs, ladies' beauty parlours, Shinto shrines, brothels and the mileage of canals in Tokyo. So far as giving me an insight into the Japanese mind and spirit and the introduction I sought into the business scene and its motivations, I might just as well have read the poems of Milton or the London telephone directory. I confess that I didn't always look in the right places and missed a number of useful reference sources, but that wasn't due to lack of effort but rather to ignorance and its misdirection.

It wasn't until the high speed lift plunged me into the lower basement shopping arcade of my hotel in Tokyo, and I found there the cramped, brightly lit, little stationers and bookshop, that I struck on anything really enlightening. Here were row upon row of translated Japanese novels in paperback, splendid photographic travel books and a whole section of hardbacks devoted to Japanese trade, industry and business. Without exception, these were all published and printed either in Japan or the United States. Here was a whole storehouse of all the knowledge I'd been looking for at home. Only two problems now faced me. First, the cost of the books was astronomical and second, I wasn't going to have much time for reading now that I was caught up in the whirlpool of activity that constitutes the world of business in Japan. I compromised, bought all I could afford and put them aside to be studied later when I got back home to England.

I can still clearly remember the sort of information I was looking for in those early days. More than anything it concerned people in Japan, how they think and what motivates them. I had tried to get a basic understanding of the language and was fairly convinced that, in spite of the surface similarities between our two nations, this was no more than a veneer beneath which our thought processes were contrasting and widely divergent, an opinion which I hold even more strongly today. It was confirmed during a lengthy airborne conversation on a following visit to Japan. The passenger sitting next to me was a vigorous youngster approaching sixty. We fell to talking about Japan, which he obviously knew well, and a point was reached where he wanted to refer to some papers in his case. He extracted a fat file containing the thinnest sheets of typed paper which he explained was the catalogue of his library on Japan which he took with him to avoid buying duplicates. I asked how many books he had about Japan and was stunned when he replied, "Between five and six thousand!" I enquired his name which he gave as Fosco, and then the light dawned on me. By the greatest of good fortune, I was travelling with Dr Fosco Maraini, author, scholar, mountaineer and photographer, who was then Professor of Japanese History and Literature at the University of Florence and who had lived and taught in Japan for some years. I had read his *Meeting with Japan* and should have noticed the finger missing from his left hand. In that biographic work he had described his internment near Kyoto during the war. When his countrymen had capitulated, the Japanese police captain in charge of the civilian Italian internees had shouted indignantly that Italians were traitors and liars. Dr Maraini was in the kitchen at the time and quoted an extract from his wife's diary. "Fosco took up a meat cleaver, chopped off his little finger and threw it at the Japanese captain" to which the author appended a modest footnote, "Actually I handed it to him". This act of self-immolation quite reversed the captain's attitude, akin as it was to a minor form of suicide. The whole incident indicated to me that I was in the presence of, not just a major scholar, but a European who really understood the mind of the Japanese, the very soul of Japan. Neither of us got much sleep on that plane but I learnt more about the Japanese on the flight than I could have gained from devouring a whole library of books. Even more important was the enthusiasm that Dr Maraini conveyed which kindled an interest in me that has never waned to this day.

Personally I make no claims to scholarship about Japan, though in that fascinating country I am often pleased to be honoured with the appelation, 'sensei' rather that mere 'san'. This means teacher or scholar and came about from the fact that I was the author of some books on the subject of the type of engineering products I had gone there to sell. However, that is another matter but I mention it to stress that, should other exporters have combined their business lives with authorship, this can have a profound and advantageous effect on the Japanese, with their deep respect for scholarship and their love of knowledge. Britain has her quota of recognised and respected Japan scholars, as well as trade officials and businessmen whose success has far exceeded mine and whose knowledge of the country, the people, the culture and the language I can never hope to emulate. However, few of them seem to have set themselves to putting their expertise on paper as so many Americans have. I suspect, too, that if they did, many of them would produce texts too erudite for the average beginner in business in Japan. As stars in the intellectual and commercial firmaments their outlook may be too remote from the simple world of the business tyro, reflecting a quotation that Dr Maraini made to me, "Only the sun never sees a shadow." In any case prognosticating on what might flow from their pens in a purely academic exercise. They haven't put themselves out in the main towards filling the need that I hope this book will satisfy.

While my manuscript was in its quite early stages, a young university undergraduate of my acquaintance announced that he was going out to Japan to work for some weeks in a bank there on a student exchange scheme. He asked for my general advice and I lent him two of the chapters which had passed through the typing stage. On returning them, he politely added a pinch of mild criticism. The small part of the book that he had read was, in his opinion, short on facts and contained material that he didn't consider relevant. I can appreciate his point of view for he hadn't the full text in which I have endeavoured to weave factual information into my main theme. However, I must point out that facts have not been my primary concern, since facts on Japan are freely available from a number of reliable sources if you only know where to look for them, and I have been at pains to list sources of such factual data both in the text and in the relevant appendix. My main concerns have been to try and interpret what makes the modern Japanese people tick and to give the reader a background of knowledge about the country and people such as I lacked on my early visits but have since found an invaluable help in understanding Japan.

I have included as many facts as possible but would point out that in a constantly changing world a large proportion of so-called facts have strong elements of impermanence. The latest trade statistics, for instance, have their relevance but are generally well out of date by the time they are published. In Chapter 13 I have gone further than pure facts and tried to identify trends of change, thus introducing a further field of uncertainty. What seems to me to be most significant is the identification of those factors that appear to have the greatest permanence, such as the influences of geography, climate, history, religion, language and culture on the thinking, attitudes, activities and methodology of the present day people of Japan and, to some extent, of the generations that will succeed them.

The British and the Japanese have many problems in common, but the ways in which they solve them are often very different. Housewives in both countries have at one time or another had to contend with a shortage of that essential element of civilisation, lavatory paper. In the UK we tend to adopt the typically British solution of an orderly queue for unofficially rationed supplies. Some time ago a report in the *Financial Times* quoted the number of millions of pounds worth of waste paper that Britain was importing as we seem to be too disorganised to collect and separate our own weekly rubbish efficiently. I was reminded of this one late summer Sunday afternoon while sitting in the artistic pocket handkerchief-sized garden of a friend in suburban Tokyo. An English-style afternoon tea had been put on for my benefit and, as we munched small cakes and sipped our cups of 'black' tea with a warm breeze rustling the leaves of the irises and with the water burbling gently over the worn stones of a tiny waterfall, the peace was suddenly shattered by the blaring voice of a mobile loudspeaker. It sounded like a political broadcast and I took it to be something to do with local election campaigning and said so. "No," said my host, whose wife was dutifully lugging a huge bundle of old newspapers towards the gate, "It's just the wastepaper contractor." This was apparently a one-man operation with an ancient truck licensed by the local authority to deal in this scrap commodity. Minutes later Mrs Nishizawa joined us again, her face beaming with pride as she showed us the three rolls of toilet paper that she'd obtained in exchange for that wad of the family's old newspapers. Back at home my wife was still having to queue at the local supermarket for this essential material!

I mention this incident, not as having any deep Confician, Shinto or Buddhist origin or significance, but as an example of the practical way in which the Japanese tend to set about current problems, and to stress that behind their apparent contemporary Westernism other influences are at work. I hope to analyse some of these, to trace their sources, and to suggest how they are changing and may affect Japan as a potential export market in the future.

Many years ago when I was selling engineering products in the UK I destroyed all hope of obtaining a substantial order from the National Coal Board at lunch one day. As the sellers, we were entertaining a group of their senior executives. The Chief Buyer had relatively recently been appointed and spent most of the meal expounding his concept of the ultimate role of the computer in the 'buying situation' as the cliché goes. His thesis was that, if he had his way, the N.C.B.'s computer, fully cognisant of stocks, consumption and future demand, would automatically place orders with our computer (if we'd had one!) without the need for human intervention. Foolishly but, I think, relevantly, I pointed out that if this were to be the case, there would no longer be any need for my colleagues and me to push the boat out to stand him further lunches with all the alcoholic trimmings. Our computer would just have to stand his computer a lunch every now and then and that would be the end of the need for our beautiful friendship.

That experience isn't directly related to the Japanese market but it emphasises a point of particular significance there. We may be faced in the end with an era in which the computer takes over the great majority of our normal day-to-day decisions at work but, at present, business is, in the main, a matter of people talking to people. When those people are of different nations and different cultures such as ourselves and the Japanese, the matter of personal relationships and communication becomes all the more significant. It is, in fact, the keystone of the arch that bridges the gap between us. An understanding of this and a belief in it is vital to success in Japan and is the principal motivation behind the writing of this book.

In the historical chapters which follow I have used the conventional arrangement of Japanese names, ie a sequence in which the family name precedes the given name. Due to the impossibility of deciding where history ends and current affairs begin, I have kept to the same sequence throughout the whole of the book. This may result in your reading in the newspapers of the recent Ambassador of Japan to Britain as Mr Tadeo Kato, whereas I would refer to him as Kato Tadeo-san or Mr Kato Tadeo. I hope that this style of nomenclature, true to the Japanese, will not inconvenience the reader.

I am indebted to all the authors of books that I have listed in the Bibliography in Appendix H and hope that I have omitted none whose works have helped me. I also hope that I have dropped no major bricks but, if I have done so, at least I have the comfort of being in good company. Seasoned globe-trotters, professional travel-writers such as Laurens van der Post and Georges Mikes can slip up when faced with the anomalies of Japan. One, writing of the difficulties of the language, related that 'hashi de tabemasu' could mean either I eat with chopsticks or I eat on the bridge. He then added that 'hashi' means I eat. On the contrary 'hashi' means either chopsticks or a bridge. 'Tabemasu' means I eat! The other expert wrote of 'asa-gohan' as evening rice. I find this difficult to believe as 'asa' is one of the Japanese words for morning. It just shows that even the best of writers can get mixed up in Japan.

Lastly, a word for the benefit of any of my Japanese friends or acquaintances who may come across this book. It is, I hope, not without its moments of laughter, an essential element of communication to my mind. Where humour does intrude, I hope that they will believe my sincerity in saying that I am laughing with the Japanese and not at them.

Georges Mikes calls it the "Land of the Rising Yen"; James Kirkup, "A land flowing with silk and tunny." Whichever it is, let's get on with the business of trying to understand it.

CHAPTER ONE

Armchair Exporter

You don't have to be in the furniture business to read this chapter. The chapter title is only intended to suggest what you can do either to prepare for a business trip to Japan or, in some cases, how to sell to the Japanese without even leaving the United Kingdom. This chapter is intended to summarise for the would-be British exporter primarily the sources of help, advice and information that can be of use to him while he remains within the shores of Britain, and which will help him when he arrives in Japan.

There is a host of useful people and organisations, both British and Japanese, in London whose purpose in life is to help, to encourage and to inform. When I was planning my own first visit, I knew of only one, now known as the British Overseas Trade Board. They offer tremendous and invaluable assistance but I would have achieved more with a lot less effort, if I had known of and approached some of the other organisations whose existence and activities I have since discovered. All were open to me, happy, even eager to assist, but in spite of concentrated effort in planning my first assault on the Japanese market, ignorance of their existence denied me access to much useful help. "In the country of the blind, the one-eyed man is king," as the 16th century proverb puts it. In eight years of visiting Japan I have at least acquired a degree of cyclopean vision which I hope to pass on!

London and Tokyo are some 6700 miles apart via Moscow — or 8000 miles if you take the Polar route. As they are capitals of nations of totally different cultures no right-minded businessman would expect that they would hold equal opportunities for the aspiring exporter to Japan. They certainly don't but it is true that there is a small but real potential, depending very much on the product, for selling to Japan without leaving London. In my repeated mention of London I mean no disrespect to those in the provinces. I am merely stating the fact that many Japanese organisations do have a base in London where business negotiations can be started, and some idea of Japanese reaction to product and price can be obtained with a view to assessing the value of a visit to Japan. In a few cases of consumer goods and some consumer durables, direct sales to Japan may be negotiated through a buying office in London such as those discussed below. For most of us, however, the chances of doing business this way are extremely remote and we would do better to adopt the slogan that I am told Sir Jack Cohen of Tesco has initialled on his gold tie clip. It bears the letters YCDBSOYA, the latter half of which I regret does not refer to the bean that makes the sauce that makes practically every Japanese meal! The message is appropriate to anyone who wants to sell in Japan: "You can't do business sitting on your arse!" You have to shift it, for a start some 7000 miles!

Since I first had dealings with them around 1970-1, the government offices concerned with Japan, helpful then, have been greatly strengthened and are funded, I believe, more heavily than their colleagues dealing with other potential export markets. In 1976, a special 'Task Force' of experts, headed by Mr J.T. McGhie, previously principal trade adviser in the British Embassy in Toyko and a noted authority on trade with Japan, was set up. Mr John Field is now Special Adviser on the Japanese Market to this 'Exports to Japan Unit'. One of its main objectives is to help and advise those smaller companies who want to tackle the Japanese market but probably lack both the skills and the resources to do it on their own. As with other countries the B.O.T.B. Booklet *Hints to Businessmen* is an invaluable starting point containing basic information and a useful bibliography.

Another useful and knowledgeable organisation is The Anglo-Japanese Economic Institute in Trafalgar Square who publish the Anglo-Japanese Trade Directory, some 180 pages of useful addresses and contacts which is revised as occasion demands. The same address houses the Japan Society whose cultural and social activities can be worth the attention of those whose interest in Japan extends beyond the purely business horizon. The Trade Directory, by the way, not unnaturally has a bias towards the inclusion of companies and organisations to a greater or lesser extent motivated by a desire to trade with

Britain. It also includes the names and home addresses of many Japanese Trade Associations, who can be helpful in making useful contacts in Japan in the specific industries they represent.

Business protocol in Japan is such that formal introductions to companies you want to visit are more or less obligatory. No matter how grand a Company or Group you may work for, a casual call is unlikely to get you in touch with anyone of importance and is likely to be a waste of time. One of the functions of the London offices of Japanese organisations is to screen potential visitors and make a preliminary assessment of their companies and products. This is practical commonsense from the viewpoints of both parties, and a potential saving of the visitors' valuable time in Japan. If they believe that there is a possibility of business, they will arrange the necessary introduction to the most appropriate Japanese Company. A word of caution is advisable though. In a later chapter we will have more to say about a typically Japanese characteristic — the desire never to say "no". The Japanese will go to great lengths to avoid disappointing you and hence will always try to give you the answer they think you want. Hence too much faith shouldn't be placed in an apparently enthusiastic reception of some proposal for cooperation. It is wise to be cautious, even sceptical, and to make similar approaches to other Japanese organisations even if they are competitors.

A very real source of help and advice is the Japan External Trade Organisation. Originally set up to assist Japanese companies to export, JETRO has for long been equally active in helping would-be exporters to Japan in the realisation that trading is a two-way affair. Envious of Japan's export success, there are those who malign her with often unfounded accusations of price-cutting and 'dumping'. I wouldn't say that this never happens but I believe it is far less frequent than those less efficient than their Japanese competitors would like to believe. It is significant that Japanese companies are generally content to operate on much smaller profit margins than their Western counterparts and are able to counter the upward valuation of the yen only by maintaining a bouyant home market. It might be mentioned, for the benefit of those who would accuse the Japanese of flooding the markets of the world with their products, that Japan's exports constitute only some 12% of their Gross National Product, compared with nearer 20% for the United Kingdom and West Germany. There is a tendency to ignore the vast importation of oil, coal, metalliferous ores and other raw materials which are essential for Japan to convert them into cars, motorcycles, ships, zips, cameras, watches, radios and television sets, and a thousand other manufactured industrial and consumer durable products. JETRO exists to help the two-way process of export and import. The need to obtain a better balance in Japan's external trade has been so much in the news recently that it does not need stressing here.

In case any trader has failed to do his homework and has only bought this book in the Departure Lounge at London Airport, I would add that JETRO have cooperated with Japan Air Lines (JAL) and have set up an Executive Lounge at the Imperial Hotel in Tokyo, where free advice is available to the visiting businessman, and introductions to suitable prospective partners can be arranged. He may have left it rather late but help is at hand!

Never forget the British Embassy in Tokyo, contacted direct possibly if you are going on a Government sponsored trade mission or a Joint Venture — trade association stand at an Exhibition in Japan, but better through the B.O.T.B. There was a time when the "Posts" abroad, as they call them, had a very obvious diplomatic slant and the Commercial Staff were looked down on as inferior citizens. Today the picture has changed and these devoted but once denigrated members of our foreign service are considered every bit as important as their purely diplomatic brethren. Whether British or indigenous, the Commercial Staff at our Embassies and legations are highly attuned to the nuances of local affairs and have the barrister's capacity to assimilate new subjects, facts and situations in the minimum of time, combined with a Holmesian talent and enthusiasm for investigation. As Japan is the only country where H.M. Government has pushed the boat out to the extent of building and running a British Export Marketing Centre, it is natural that this should be backed by an Embassy Commercial Staff of outstanding ability and acumen. Apart from the advisory services of the Embassy, the Centre is available for trade association or individual company exhibitions and has rooms available for presentations, functions or what you will. Specialised exhibitions are mounted periodically by the B.O.T.B. 'Export to Japan Unit' in consultation with the Embassy in Tokyo.

Much information is available in the booklets put out by the B.O.T.B. on various aspects of trading with Japan, these being compiled by British Embassy Staffs in Tokyo. Unfortunately, the series, which starts with the admirably concise and succinct *An Introduction to Doing Business in Japan*, seems never to have been completed. B.O.T.B. have also published a number of market surveys for specific products and industries, though constantly up-dated information is important in such a changing market.

We shall be dealing in more detail later with the Japanese trading companies but mention of them must be made here. There are basically two types whose attitudes and functions are very different. First, there are the major general trading companies, all of whom have London offices and are typified by the giants such as Mitsui and Mitsubishi. Most of them have their roots well in the past (Mitsui, for instance, dating from 1637 and said to be the world's largest big business today though Mitsubishi may now exceed it) and grew enormously in size and importance in the early years of the modernisation of Japan in the mid-nineteenth century (see Chapter 3). Typically these giants have interests in manufacture, banking, trading, shipping and other activities and, though they were chopped up into smaller individual units during the post-war MacArthur Administration, they have largely regrouped into conglomerates with complex inter-company shareholdings so that they are now, in effect, little different from their original form. The London offices are concerned with both import and export and, handling, as they do, literally thousands of different products, are organised into separate divisions and departments. Main divisions such as food, chemicals, transport, energy and machinery are subdivided into specialist departments while a 'general' division usually deals with products that do not conveniently fall into any main category. These giant trading companies, or 'sogo shosa' as they are called, have a strong interest in promoting international cooperation in major turnkey projects in third world countries, such as steelworks and petrochemical plants. They deal not only with the purchase of all manner of merchandise, but also handle finance, shipping, insurance and subsequent distribution in Japan. However, due to their vast size and huge turnover, it is in their nature to be interested principally in products that will sell in appreciable volume or are of high capital value per unit.

The motivation of these trading companies is nearly always sincere and genuine and the decision to act for a British or other foreign company, which will be taken back in Japan, should be followed by results. It should be appreciated, however, that it is not uncommon for a Japanese company to take on the marketing of competitive products from different suppliers and hence sales effort may become diluted to the point of ineffectiveness. It is advisable to do one's best to check that any prospective Japanese agent or distributor is not already handling products that compete with your own before making any commitment. B.O.T.B. or companies such as Dodwells (see below) are sources of help in doing this. In common with large groups in other countries, too, it is not unknown for the big Japanese organisations to accept agencies mainly to prevent them going to their competitors, though this is not a common attitude among them.

Apart from the giant 'sogo shosa' there are some 6000 smaller trading companies specialising in narrower fields of activity from fancy goods to farm equipment, sports gear to sweets and confectionery. Naturally only a small proportion of them are represented in London but some are listed in the Trade Directory of the Anglo-Japanese Economic Institute with their Japanese addresses or their London representatives. This Directory, by the way, also lists British companies with special connections with Japan and British importers and exporters trading regularly with Japan. Prominent among these is Dodwell & Co. probably the biggest British company in the field with a staff of over 1000 in Japan, their connection with the country dating from soon after the company's establishment in Hong Kong in 1858. Dodwell's market research department is highly enough regarded to have been used by B.O.T.B. for a number of specialised industry surveys and they are active in many fields as agents for UK companies.

Japanese department stores or 'departos' who collectively handle some 13% of all retail trade, (while chain stores account for another 10.5%) such as Mitsukoshi, Isetan, Matsuzakaya and Takashimaya, are noted for their special promotions of imported goods in the major Japanese cities — and 40% of the population live in the 1% of the land areas represented by the conurbations of Tokyo, Osaka and Nagoya. They handle both consumable and consumer durable goods. Though only Mitsukoshi, who have had a store in Paris for some years and have recently opened another in Lower Regent Street, appears to have its own London buying office, most of the major departos, some of which are also associated with the supermarket chains in Japan, have British associates who act as purchasing agents for them. It is, of course, the job of these companies to be on the look-out for British products with good potential sales in the stores they represent and they are hence very approachable. Acceptable products are usually of high quality and therefore not in the cheaper price bracket and display originality in design, novelty or a strong element of snob appeal. If an article is the best of its kind, the Japanese are likely to want it. As a member of an affluent nation, the Japanese consumer today is looking for excellence in most of what he or she buys, though many articles from simple chopsticks upwards are considered disposable, so price is not a major consideration. A high price may even be desirable as an indication of quality!

For selling to the departos it is more or less obligatory for the British Exporter to channel his negotiations from the start through their London buying offices. A direct approach to Japan will normally result in its referral to London. In dealing with the departos' purchasing offices, instant reaction should not be expected. Details of your products, if they show the necessary characteristics and sales potential, will be sent to Japan for consideration, probably with samples, and much correspondence may go on for some months— particularly about your company's reliability both financially and with regard to its ability to keep delivery promises. This is of special importance with seasonal goods. Unfortunately some of the big stores have been let down in the past too often, receiving consignments of spring merchandise just in time to put them in their autumn sales! They are thus understandably sensitive on this point, and you may expect exhaustive enquiries into your production capacity and commitments. The main time to expect action is in January and February when large delegations of specialist buyers arrive from Japan to make final selections, place their annual orders and work out delivery schedules. By this time their budgets have been agreed and they can and do make instant decisions involving many millions of pounds. The only exception to short-circuiting the London buying offices— and not many would want to do so— is where a British exporter already has an agent in Japan. As a general rule it is essential to have an agent there, even when dealing with department stores, as many of them take goods on a consignment basis.

All the major Japanese banks are to be found in the City of London, some like Mitsubishi, Mitsui and Sumitomo revealing at once their association with the big industrial and trading conglomerates. Others, though not disclosing their connections so conspicuously, can be equally helpful with market advice and can often help with introductions to suitable Japanese business partners. A notable characteristic of Japanese industry is its heavy reliance on the banks for investment, and hence the banks have great knowledge of and connections with industry. There are, of course, also non-Japanese banks such as Barclays International and the Chartered Bank who have special interests in Japanese affairs. Many of the Japanese Securities Companies also have London branch offices.

Successful selling in Japan for many products depends on good sales literature in Japanese. The number of companies who can do competent translations is on the increase and some can also undertake production and printing in Japanese. Where technical products are involved, it is, of course, important to ensure that your translators combine linguistic talent with adequate technical knowledge, not always an easy matter. Hence, if you are planning to participate in a trade exhibition in Japan, it is advisable to have the matter of sales literature in hand early so that a draft, at least, can be submitted to the scrutiny of an expert in Japan before going to press. Incidentally, I have found that if your product is susceptible to data sheet presentation, ie with technical drawings and performance figures, most Japanese technologists of the level you are likely to meet are perfectly capable of understanding the English language version of the data sheet. (Though they are a metric nation, however, S.I. units are not always understood as I found some years ago when I had used the unit 'bar' for pressure on some exhibition stand captions.) English language data sheets combined with an introductory leaflet stating the merits and advantages of the product factually in Japanese provide an acceptable and intelligible means of technical communication, at least in Engineering. Typesetting and printing in Japanese in the UK is naturally not cheap and cost may be cut by having the work done in Japan (or Hong Kong, though they are more attuned to Chinese there). It adds, however, to the complication of the matter and increases the chance of error. While there are laughable examples of poor Japanese translations into English, the provision of your own literature translated into good and appropriate Japanese will be well appreciated and gain kudos for your company which will well offset the extra cost.

There are other sources of information on advertising in

Japan, but to my knowledge only one major Japanese agency has a London branch. Dentsu Advertising Ltd. is the biggest Agency in Japan, and probably the third in the world, and is knowledgeable in all the media. The Dentsu Advertising office in London is geared up mainly to advising British exporters about the media in Japan rather than to going all out for business— and this advice is free! Other international agencies such as J. Walter Thompson, of course, have their own offices in Japan employing local staff versed in the local mind and media.

In Appendix A I have listed, not only the organisations mentioned above, but others which may help to give you some of the flavour of Japan before you leave Britain. There are Japanese food shops and gift shops (in case you forget to bring back that kimono you promised your wife!). Japanese books and magazines can be obtained here, though mostly only on order if they are in the English language. Japanese Art is on sale, as is equipment for the martial arts, and you can even visit an extensive Japanese garden. Combined with a short course in reading Japanese books in English and books about Japan, I believe that some use of these sources may help to give the first-time visitor a better understanding of the country and its people, possibly a slightly enhanced stature when he gets there, and increase his enjoyment of his visit.

I have considered the matter of learning the Japanese language (Nihongo) in Chapter 4. Apart from the phrase book or 'Teach Yourself' approach, I must mention that language laboratory courses are available here. The well-known Berlitz School of Languages will cater for the more exacting needs, while on a more modest level, The Polytechnic of the South Bank have a very reasonably priced preliminary course. Neither the course nor the cost can alter the fact that Nihongo is a very difficult language for Western people to learn, nor lessen the appreciation that I have found the Japanese give to one's efforts.

I have mentioned JETRO and the British Embassy in Tokyo but not the Japanese Embassy over here. Naturally it carries out the normal range of diplomatic and commercial functions but its Information Centre (housed in a separate building) is an open-cast mine of information. The Japanese are masters at the collection and collation of statistical information, and the *Annual Statistical Handbook of Japan* prepared by the Business of Statistics Offices of the Prime Minister and available from the Embassy Information Centre is worth a visit in itself. Obviously

JETRO are tuned to come up with more detailed and specific information on particular problems, but the Information Centre has a lot to offer. In calling on either it is, of course, advisable to define one's queries as precisely as possible and to have a typed copy to leave behind if the matter is of any complexity. Japan Air Lines (JAL) and the Japan National Tourist Organisation, conveniently near one another, are other useful sources of help and information when you reach the detailed planning stage of a visit.

The importance of introductions in doing business in Japan cannot be over-emphasised. It can happen that you can sometimes make your own introductions by meeting Japanese businessmen and industrialists when they are in the UK, or possibly in Europe. The Japanese are well-known for their study groups, and friendly contact with these can be invaluable. Often these coincide with major trade fairs, such as the Hannovermesse and/or other specialised exhibitions, at which Japanese companies often exhibit too. In my own case, my first contact with the Japanese was at a technical exhibition in London where we were both exhibiting. After attending a meeting of our respective associations, I was invited to a reception given by the Japanese body at which I was well looked after by two of their party, whom I subsequently invited to dinner. Two years later came my first opportunity to exhibit my products in Tokyo, and I wrote advising my two contacts of my arrival. My small gesture of hospitality in London has been repaid many times by their friendship and welcome during repeated visits to Japan. I have always believed that if you cast your bread upon the waters, if it returns at all, it will be soggy and inedible. In this case it came back as a hundred bowls of delightful nourishing rice and, of my two new friends, one became a director of the company who became my firm's agents in Japan while the other already was a director of a small company who became our first customers. I have searched without success for a Zen Sutra that is applicable to this experience but the moral seems clear!

Assuming that you are not one of those fortunate few whose products are eagerly seized upon by a Japanese buying office in London, how should you plan a first visit to sell in Japan? B.O.T.B. and JETRO are the first people to help you with advice, and may no doubt guide you to other London offices that I have mentioned. Exhibition joint venture stands and outward missions promoted by Trade Associations and sponsored and subsidised by B.O.T.B., are undoubtedly the cheapest way of getting staff, products and sales literature into Japan. The London and the Birmingham and other Chambers of Commerce also work with B.O.T.B. on similar schemes and are worth contacting. It is worth mentioning that the sponsoring bodies have to get a minimum number of participants to obtain government sup-' port and are sometimes more than willing to accept a fellow-traveller from outside their ranks to make up their numbers. Usually these come from some allied or inter-related industry, if it is a trade association that is sponsoring the exhibition stand or outward sales mission.

If a foreign visitor merely needs to get himself to Japan and back, he need go no further than the airlines, but if he needs to plan an intinerary within the country he may require a different type of travel service. JAL and the Japan National Tourist Organisation can cope, but some other specialists are listed in Appendix A. I should add that most internal travel services in Japan, at least in and between the main industrial and commercial centres, are highly efficient and do not present major problems to the foreigner. Except in really out-of-the-way places, there is usually someone who can speak English especially at airports and, on railway stations, signs are usually written up in Roman script as well as in Japanese. In London the Miki Travel Agency and Nippon Express Ltd are specialists in the Japanese travel scene. More will be said of internal travel in Japan in Chapter 10.

What advice can one give on climate, clothing and suchlike to the new visitor? I would sum it up as "get the B.O.T.B. booklet *Hints to Businessmen Visiting Japan*," where all the essentials are listed. The climate varies with the seasons as ours does, only to greater extremes: more torrential downpours in the rainy season when typhoons touch Japan; deeper and more prolonged snow, particularly if you go to the northern island of Hokkaido; hotter sun in midsummer and much higher humidity, especially in the capital, from mid-July to early September. Light-weight clothing is needed, particularly at this time of the year, and it is worth noting that not all Japanese offices are air-conditioned! A pack-away plastic raincoat is advisable — or a folding umbrella if you want to look Japanese — and you will need to take presents for people you meet in business. These need not be expensive but should, if possible, be characteristically British, tasteful and the best of their kind. (You can take in three bottles of Whisky duty free but you will be advised to take Black Label or Chivas Regal, both much respected and highly priced in Japan. The difference in price at London Airport is minimal compared with the price difference in Japan.) Presents shouldn't be handed over in brown paper bags, for the wrapping is important to the aesthetic eye of the Japanese. In spite of the ugly jumble of buildings and factories that make up so much of the urban scene, the majority of Japanese are a deeply artistic people.

Most Western-style Japanese hotels are efficient and well equipped to provide for every need the visitor may have, though with the steady decline of the pound against the yen, room service, purchases at the hotel shop (some even incorporate a supermarket) and laundry are expensive. If you are likely to be moving about Japan, travel light as the Japanese do.

A final hint before you depart, a point which we will deal with in more detail in Chapter 9. Do your homework thoroughly and make sure that you are as fact-filled as possible on every aspect of the organisation you represent. The Japanese will want to know more than just the characteristics, price, delivery and performance of your product. They are likely to ask about your company's history and that of any group to which it may belong; its capital and equity; sales turnover and profits; the number of staff and employees; factory space and facilities; organisational structure; what other countries you export to; your other overseas agents and licencees, spares and service facilities and back-up; applications of the product if it is technical; production methods; your capacity for expansion, both in area and turnover, and your existing and previous customers (a reference list of these is invaluable, especially with industrial products — take plenty of copies— they'll want to keep them) .... the list is inexhaustible, as is the curiosity of the Japanese. The degree of your ability to satisfy the insatiable Japanese desire for facts will greatly influence your chances of success in business in Japan. You just can't know too much about your own business, to say nothing of such broader issues as the British and European, even the world, economic and industrial climate, and the political, technical and ecological issues of the day.

You should also have a basic knowledge and understanding of the people and the country you are visiting. This is one of the purposes of this book and I hope that studying it (and perhaps some of the sources listed in the bibliography in Appendix H) will provide you with the sort of background knowledge that I have found useful in understanding Japanese life, business and industry today.

One last essential point is the question of your business cards. Whether all the people you'll meet in Japan can read in English is irrelevant. Common sense and courtesy call for cards printed on one side in English and the other in Japanese. If you travel by British Airways or Japan Air Lines, they will arrange for your cards to be printed for a small charge and ready to be collected at their city office when you arrive. They'll need a couple of copies of your card and at least a couple of weeks. Order plenty. You'll have no problem in getting rid of twenty or thirty a day, for everyone you meet will give you his and not to reciprocate can be considered impolite, even implying that you don't want to know someone. Make sure that your card gives your job title or position in the organisation you represent. Don't expect mock-modest miniatures or egocentric extravaganzas. All business cards in Japan are a standard size, about 90mm x 55mm which makes them easier to handle and to file. We'll have more to say about cards or 'meishi' in a later chapter, but it is important for you to arrange for them before you leave unless you already have contacts in Japan who can get the job done quickly when you're there.

CHAPTER TWO

Land, People and the Past

People who do not care for history and don't believe that it is relevant to the problems of today are fond of quoting Henry Ford as saying that "History is bunk." In fact, in cutting off his words at that point, it becomes a misquotation for his remark in full was, "History is bunk as it is taught in our schools," which puts a very different complexion on Mr Ford's opinion.

The value of history is more truly reflected in one of the analects of K'ung-fu-tzu, better known as Confucius: "Study the past if you would divine the future." A more recent and directly relevant comment comes from David Wilson, a noted specialist in selling technical products to Japan. In one of the excellent little booklets on *Business in Japan*, put out by Japan Air Lines, Mr Wilson is quoted as follows: "Before sending a man to Tokyo be sure he is interested enough in the country and its people to learn about Japanese history and culture." The crux of the matter, as Mr Wilson puts it, follows: "In so many ways, the modern Japanese are motivated by the same things which motivated the Japanese a thousand years ago."

As a nation, we are what our history and the geography of our country have made us, and the same applies to the Japanese. Certainly, in trying to understand us, they do not neglect to study our history. One weekend I was entertaining three Japanese business friends in England and drove them out to Windsor. As we approached those lush hill-ringed meadows by the banks of the Thames, I searched my memory for long-forgotten historical facts and said, "This place is called Runnymede." Without a moment's hesitation, one of my passengers said "Magna Carta" while another chimed in with "1215." I would add that these three gentlemen of Japan had been doing business with the United States, with France and with Germany long before Britain came into the orbit of their interest, and they were equally conversant with the histories of those countries as they were with that of the British Isles. Yet, when I first visited Japan, I confess that, so far as I was concerned, its history began with Pearl Harbor! I have since found that the correction of my ignorance has not only been an interesting personal experience but that, on further visits to Japan, I got far more pleasure in those few moments when there was a little time off to see the sights, while my hosts were clearly appreciative of the increased interest I showed in their history and culture. Perhaps most important was the fact that my studies gave me a greater insight into their national character and enabled me to understand several aspects of the business world that had puzzled me previously.

I hope I have by now made my case in favour of the British businessman having some knowledge, however slight, of Japanese history. In the space I have available, I can do no more than give the briefest outline, while laying some stress on certain factors and events that appear to have particular significance. In any case, those who wish to, are perfectly entitled to ignore this and the following chapter.

It appears self-evident that the basis of any nation's history and character lies in the geographic and climatic conditions that prevail, and have prevailed for the last few thousand years. Demographically, there has been greater change, but past and present population changes are clearly of importance in all types of business activity. In view of this — as well as commonsense arguments that would suggest that the same factors are of considerable influence in current business affairs for the aspiring exporter — it seems reasonable to start with a brief geographical summary.

At the front of this book is a map of Japan. (For a larger and more detailed map, the Japan Information Centre in London or the Japan National Tourist Organisation will be pleased to help you). As the map shows, Japan is an island country (and hence has characteristics in common with Britain) made up of four principal islands, from North to South, Hokkaido, Honshu, Shikoku and Kyushu, together with over 3000 smaller islands, the largest of which, right in the south, is Okinawa, noted since the last war as a point of contention for the American military base which remained there long after the end of the Occupation in 1952.

The main and largest island of Honshu (some 60% of the total

Table 1. COMPARATIVE LAND AREAS AND POPULATIONS OF JAPAN AND THE UNITED KINGDOM

JAPAN	Area (sq. m.)	Area (sq. km)	Population (million)
Honshu	89,149	230,897	89.0
Hokkaido	32,244	83,513	5.4
Kynshu	16,249	42,084	12.4
Shikoku	7,257	18,795	4.0
Okinawa	867	2,246	1.0
Total	145,766	377,535	112

Population per sq. km: 297 (1975)
Total land area: 1.55 × UK

UNITED KINGDOM	Area (sq. m.)	Area (sq. km)	Population (million)
England	50,332	130,360	46.0
Scotland	29,812	77,213	5.2
Wales	8,016	20,761	2.8
N. Ireland	5,241	13,574	1.5
Isle of Man & Channel Islands	592	1,533	0.5
Total	93,993	243,441	56

Population per sq. km: 230 (1974)
Total land area: 0.64 × Japan

area of the country) includes most of the major cities: Tokyo, the capital, Yokohama, Nagoya, Kyoto, Kobe, Osaka and Hiroshima. The land areas and populations of the islands are shown in Table 1 with equivalent figures for the UK to put them into perspective, while Table 2 gives the populations of Japan's major cities. From the administrative point of view Japan is divided into 47 prefectures, roughly equivalent to the counties of Britain.

Also shown in Table 1 are the relative densities of population for Japan and the UK overall, ie 297 people per sq. km in Japan compared with 230 for the UK. No great difference you might say but the figures are misleading. The mountainous nature of the Japanese islands is such that only 17% of the land area can be used for purposes other than forestry and tourism. Thus the real population density is closer to 890 people per sq. km. Whilst the population of the UK is by no means evenly distributed (England and Wales have some 323 people per sq. km) the situation is far less drastic than in Japan where land shortage results in not only high prices but extensive reclamation by building out into the sea. Table 3 shows the comparative rates of population growth from which it is apparent that Japan's population has been growing far faster than Britain's (approximately 19 births per 1000 against 13 per 1000 in the UK in 1974), although this growth has now stabilised.

Apart from having very little land on which to grow food (cultivated land is 15.9% and grassland 1.5% of the total, 2.9% being classed as residential land), which makes the Japanese the world's biggest consumers of fish, existing land is poorly

Table 2.   Populations of Major Japanese Cities

Tokyo (metropolitan area)	8,643,000
Osaka	2,779,000
Yokohama	2,622,000
Nagoya	2,080,000
Kyoto	1,461,000
Kobe	1,361,000
Sapporo	1,241,000
Kitakyushu	1,058,000
Kawasaki	1,015,000
Fukuoka	1,002,000
Hiroshima	853,000

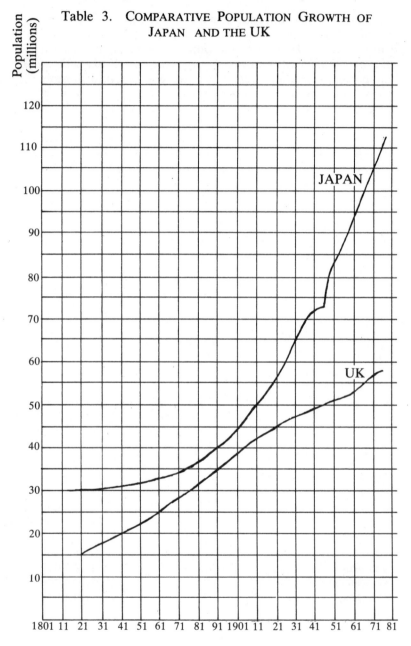

Table 3. COMPARATIVE POPULATION GROWTH OF JAPAN AND THE UK

YEAR

endowed with natural resources. Development of hydro-electric power supplies has reached its maximum and now 77% of Japan's energy requirements come from imported fuels. The same applies to mineral ores and most other raw materials so that Japan's 114 million population is dependent for many of its basic needs on imports (this does not include food since they are 100% self-sufficient in rice and 75% in cereal). Hence the Japanese are forced to be a nation of 'converters' to survive, importing raw materials and exporting sophisticated finished goods and products.

The intervening processes of manufacture combined with intensive agriculture and the day-to-day living of a large population, densely concentrated, leads to a further problem today — pollution, an 'in-word' in most industrialised countries but nowhere more necessarily so than in Japan. The persistent smog of Tokyo against which many people cover their mouths and noses with little white masks is characteristic (though the Japanese are so polite and considerate that many of these masked faces are those of people with colds who don't want to spread their germs around).

An interesting pollutionary story is the case of the Dancing Cats of Minamata Bay. The use of mercury in industry (in P.V.C. and paper making) and as an agricultural seed-dressing is as widespread in Japan as elsewhere. In the late 1960's fishermen in Minamata Bay, which lies sheltered and enclosed to the west of the island of Kyushu, were found to be showing the same symptoms of those of the proverbial mad hatters who used mercury in their trade — the fumes causing brain damage which could lead to madness. The toxicity of quicksilver is multiplied severalfold if it is converted bacterially to methyl mercury as had happened in the effluent from a P.V.C. factory near Minamata.

Doctors attending the affected fishermen were at a loss until the behaviour of the local feline population was brought to their notice. It seems that the cats who had been indulging in free meals of the offal of fish and crustaceans caught in the bay were ingesting mercury to the extent that, in mad mood, they were seen to be dancing and falling about.

The inclusion of this cautionary tale is not irrelevant, for the sequel illustrates one of the most remarkable and significant characteristics of the Japanese today — their collective ability to act with great speed and purpose once a decision has been reached, a characteristic to which we will have later to revert in detail. In this case fishing in Minamata Bay was instantly banned, the source of pollution traced and rapidly dealt with. The Japanese may sometimes show themselves as being over-reactive to unfavourable situations. The Nixon 10% Import Surcharge is a case in point where one major manufacturer of electrical and electronic products in Japan cut production overnight not by 30% but to 30% of what it had been, though it was soon stepped up again. One may cite what the Japanese refer to rather charmingly as 'Oil Shock'. In Britain it was, I believe, over twelve months after the first OPEC price increases that the government passed lukewarm legislation to restrict such trivia as shop-window lighting. In contrast, it was only a matter of days in Japan before in a land of neon-signed city advertisements, massive displays which dominated the night sky, few neo lights were to be seen and two out of every three street-lamps were extinguished. The Japanese may sometimes over-react but at least they act!

If I seem to be digressing from history, let me quote — in the hope of illustrating my quotation from David Wilson — from the Tokugawa Military Code of the early 17th century where it was written, "The arts of peace and war ... should be pursued single-mindedly." Never was there such a single-minded people as the Japanese, whether at work or at play. In both, total commitment and concentration are the order of the day — or the night, if you are going out for an evening's drinking! As Georges Mikes put it in his book, *The Land of the Rising Yen*, "If they are told that a sense of humour is a desirable proclivity, they will form serious study groups to discover how to acquire a really robust sense of humour." Mikes is a little unkind in his cutting wit for I have found few Japanese whose sense of humour was not robust, but he does drive the point of their single-mindedness home.

Before launching into the apparently impossible task of condensing over 2600 years of Japanese history into a few thousand words, I would like to put forward a personal opinion which attempts to reconcile the conflicting behaviour of the Japanese in the last World War and my own observations on their ways today. (I apologise to my Japanese friends for raising this issue but, even more than 30 years after the end of the War, I know many people in the West who are still troubled by it. I do not wish to raise contention but rather to suppress it.) I have never found a nation, a whole people, more friendly, kind and considerate than the Japanese. If my judgement is correct, how, I have been asked, could the Japanese have possibly committed the atrocities attributed to them in the War?

An elaborate defense could be prepared but this is not a Court of Law. I believe, however, that there are three factors of significance which, as fundamental characteristics of Japanese life and character, should be mentioned. Their importance in other aspects of modern Japanese life will become apparent later. My three points are: (1) That the historically hierarchical nature of Japanese life has resulted in a nation in which the 'group', of whatever type or nature it may be, is more important than the members who compose it. Simplifying this to the extreme, everyone knows his place in whatever class and type of society he lives in. He keeps his place and only exceptionally does he not do what he is told.

(2) That the Japanese take a very different view of the value of life from our conventional Western viewpoint. Students, even schoolchildren, on failing their exams, not infrequently commit suicide. Rather than disrupt production by a strike, I have known of cases where a couple of workers would make their colleagues' point by the same drastic measure — suicide.

(3) Though instinctively considerate, peaceful and kindly, the average Japanese will subjugate his own impulses and emotions to those in command to such an extent that there will be nothing half-hearted about actions he takes that may be quite contrary to his natural instincts.

I would comment further on point (2) that the value of both life and property are viewed differently by the Japanese for historical and geographical reasons. The Islands of Japan are as prone to the occurrence of natural disasters as any place on earth. Earthquakes, volcanic activity, tidal waves and typhoons, and the resultant loss of life and property, have become so frequent as to be accepted as an integral feature of life — and death. The nightmare inhumanity of the Hiroshima bomb, for example, killed some 70,000 people but, in comparison, in the last great Tokyo earthquake of 1923, more than twice as many lives were lost and more than two-thirds of the buildings in the city destroyed. A nation whose gods have treated them thus for centuries is bound to view life with different perspectives from ours. This is not to say that the Japanese do not value life. They value it highly and take great delight in it, but I do not believe that they feel quite so deeply the sense of shock that their counterparts in the West do when it is suddenly taken away by accident, disaster or self-destruction. They have lived with these for centuries so that the cutting edge of sudden death is a little blunted. At the same time, the Japanese have a deep sense of obligation, and failure in meeting it may lead to taking the only honourable way out by taking their own lives. In the last War one of the greatest dishonours was failure in duty to the Emperor by falling into the hands of the enemy, with the result that very few prisoners of war were taken. Most servicemen preferred to take their own lives rather than face the disgrace of capture. Their attitude was to view allied prisoners of war that they took in the same light and hence to give them little consideration.

The value that is placed on honour and obligation is suggested by a man who is now a restaurateur in the United States and is said to be the unhappiest Japanese in the world. He is the only 'kamikaze' suicide pilot who went into action but failed in his duty to the Emperor and did not die in the attempt to destroy himself and the warship that was his target. After the war he could not face the disgrace of returning to Japan and remained in America.

"Japan's ancient history is covered with the mist of mythology." These are the introductory words of the *Statistical Handbook of Japan, 1976*. In fact it is only since 1946 that it has been permissible for Japanese scholars to research the nebulous borderline between history and mythology seriously. It was in that year that the Emperor formally renounced any claim to divine status such as he and his forebears were purported to have been blessed with since long before the days of written history. To question one iota of the legend of the Emperor's descent, at least from Jimmu Tenno who founded the Empire in 660 BC, was sacrilege for which a teacher or university lecturer could lose his job, and the mythology contended that Jimmu was the great-great-grandson of the Amaterasu, the Sun Goddess. Her story is too long to tell here but it may be mentioned that legend relates that she was tempted out of hiding in a cave by a jewelled necklace and a mirror hung in a tree and these are part of the Imperial regalia of the Emperor today, perhaps regrettably now kept in the inner sanctum of a Shinto shrine, the sacred shrine of Ise where even the Emperor cannot obtain access to them! Hirohito, Emperor or 'Tenno' since 1926, is the 123rd in line of descent from Jimmu — the term Mikado (literally 'Noble Gate') having apparently fallen somewhat out of use, perhaps since Gilbert and Sullivan adopted it. In spite of this, I have heard

"Tit-willow" played as background music in the kimono department of Mitsukoshi 'departo' store in Tokyo's Ginza district! In
fact Papinot's Historical and Geographical Dictionary of Japan
of 1910 says: "This title is especially in use among foreigners: the
Japanese use Tenshi and Tenno etc." (Tenno meaning Lord of
Heaven; Tenshi, Son of Heaven.)

In passing, and with the Sun Goddess in mind, it is of interest to
note that the word 'Japan' is a Westernised distortion of Nippon
or Nihon, Ni meaning the sun (or a day) and Hon, a root or
source. Hence, the Land of the Rising Sun.

It would be an oversimplification to say that little happened
from Jimmu Tenno's foundation of the Japanese Empire for the
next thousand years but, in fact, the next major historical event
did not occur until the 4th century AD when the Empress of
Japan organised and, so it is said, led a military expedition to
nearby Korea, not entirely to the immediate joy of the Koreans.
However, the Empress, whose name was Jingo (but, in spite of
her efforts, regrettably not to be credited with originating our
word 'Jingoism') did open up a line of communication with the
mainland which was to have most beneficial results for Japan. In
the years that followed there was a constant flow of Koreans —
and, from farther away, Chinese — who contributed much to the
advancement of Japan with such skills as metalworking, ideographic writing and finally with the introduction of the Buddhist
religion and all that went with it. Until then the religion of Japan
had been Shinto — "the way of the Gods" — a curious fragmen-
tation of the Great Creator into an infinity of lesser spirits
associated with animate and natural objects and places and even
with a number of artefacts. Buddhism undoubtedly enriched the
life and culture of Japan in many ways and continues to do so, but
even today the two religions coexist without conflict, both
embraced, even if somewhat informally, by the modern population. Shintoism is much concerned with the reverence, if not
worship, of one's ancestors and, should you have the chance to
visit a Japanese home, you are almost certain to find the 'Kami-
dana' or 'God-shelf' at which respect is paid in various ways to
these elders. A miniature Buddhist altar may also be present.

Such resistance to Buddhism as existed, was finally reduced to
nothing by its approval by the remarkable Crown Prince Shotoku
towards the end of the 6th century. Shotoku was an enlightened
and cultivated man who died in 621 (AD). He is reputed, in 604,
to have promulgated the "Constitution of 17 Articles", part of

which is worth quoting, as the words of this Sinophile Japanese ruler are still so relevant to almost every aspect of life in Japan today. The initial, timeless, and so significant words of the Constitution are:

"Harmony is to be valued, and an avoidance of wanton opposition to be honoured. All men are influenced by class-feelings ... But when those above are harmonious and those below are friendly, and there is concord in the discussion of business, right views of things spontaneously gain acceptance. Then what is there which cannot be accomplished?" These words could have been written by almost any 20th century Japanese.

Harmony is such a profoundly essential element in Japanese life today — including business activity — that it is vital for the foreign businessman to understand its importance. We will have more to say later about this in modern Japan, but the realisation that its concept was being propagated by Royal decree over 1300 years ago should indicate how strongly ingrained in the Japanese character is this desire for harmony in all things.

It should be mentioned here that written Japanese history originated some 200 years earlier, about 405 AD, when Japan made one of her first 'borrowings' from abroad. This was the importation and adoption of the Chinese script which we will discuss in more detail in Chapter 12.

It was in these early centuries that powerful clans emerged and contended with each other for power, while the Emperors became, more and more, mere figureheads, more gods than men concerned with day to day affairs. Notable among these clans were the Soga who might even have usurped the throne but for their defeat by the great Fujiwara Kamatari whose enthusiasm for things Chinese led to a new and complex form of government which attempted to regulate even the minutest details of everyday life. For nearly 400 years— until about 1045 – the Fujiwara were the power behind the throne. The influence of the Chinese T'ang culture resulted in the building of the capital at Nara about 715 and subsequently of the even more splendid Heian-Kyo in 794, later to become Kyoto. The Heian period, as it is known, with its formal, ceremonial, elegant and artistic culture, lasted until 1185 when the Minamoto family became all-powerful, supplanting the Fujiwara who had governed as regents (sessho) and later as civil dictators (kampaku). Opposed to the Minamoto was the Taira clan from the East of Japan.

The final overthrow of the Taira by Minamoto Yoritomo in the sea battle of Shimonoseki Straits in 1185, resulted in the move of the seat of Government to Kamakura on the coast some 60 Km from modern Tokyo. At the same time the title of 'Sei-i tai-shogun', or 'barbarian-subduing great general', was awarded on a permanent basis by the young Emperor to Minamoto whose 'bakufu' or 'tent-office' government produced a most effective administration and lasted for about 150 years — the Kamakura period as it is called — though its power passed into the hands of the Hojo clan who acted, in turn, as regents for the Shogun. The Kamakura period is noted for its religious and artistic activity, including the founding of the great Nichiren and Zen sects of Buddhism. It also includes the time of the first invasions of Japan — by Kublai Khan in 1274 and 1281. The typhoon which wiped out the Mongol Emperor's fleet in 1281 is the origin of the term 'kamikaze' or 'divine wind', later to be adopted by the suicide pilots of the last war, and now jocularly applied to the taxi-drivers of Tokyo!

The defeat of Kublai Khan is significant in two respects. First, it was the only attempt made to invade Japan — until the Pacific war of 1941-1945. In earlier centuries the Japanese had wel-comed the arrival and settlement of Chinese and Koreans who were in a minority but, by now, totally integrated into the native population. Thus it is that today, apart from the remaining few Ainu of Caucasian origin, the 'hairy people' of Hokkaido, the Japanese are probably the purest and most homogeneous people in the world. This is a factor which, combined with the strict regimen of the Tokugawa Shogunate later, is considered by some authorities to have contributed substantially to the success of recent Japan through collective thought and action. The second significance of Kublai Khan's defeat was that it was a victory for Japan.

From the 1330's to 1573 there were numerous changes of power with consequent chaos, violence and civil war which included the temporary deposition of the Emperor. From 1339, when the new Ashikaga Shogunate moved the capital once more back to Kyoto, there was almost a total breakdown of law and order, this period being known as the Muromachi period from the district of Kyoto where the so-called government had its seat. The Shogunate, living in great luxury and elegance, were more interested in the art of graceful living than in governing, while at one time the poverty of the Imperial Court was such that one Emperor was forced to go out into the streets of Kyoto to sell samples of his calligraphy!

One effect of the failure of government in the Muromachi era was that, freed from previous restraints, trade with the outside world flourished in both directions, the Japanese taking to the sea, while the first foreigners set foot in Japan and established themselves, at least temporarily. Portuguese traders and Spanish Jesuits, notably Francis Xavier in the mid-16th century, introduced not only Christianity but firearms to Japan, the latter having some beneficial effect in helping three Daimyo or great lords to subdue the disorderly elements and restore peace after a century of disruption and strife. These three are mong the most famous names of Japanese history — Oda Nobunaga, Toyotomi Hideyoshi and Tokugawa Ieyasu, the last being the founder of the Tokugawa Shogunate which was to rule from 1603 until 1868, the year of the restoration of Imperial rule under Meiji Tenno and the beginning of the modernisation of Japan. It was the Tokugawa who once more uprooted the seat of government, settling it this time at Edo or Yedo (now known as Tokyo, or Eastern Capital) where it has remained ever since.

When Nobunaga, Hideyoshi and Ieyasu successively accepted the leadership of their country (the last being made Shogun in 1603), they inherited these first contacts with the West and the possibility of expanding them, a course upon which Hideyoshi certainly was intent but which came to nothing due to his death in 1598. Had this been achieved, how much of the course of world history might have been changed! Instead, mainly due to the schism between the European settlers and visitors, based largely on religious differences between the Christian countries of origin of the four nations concerned — Portugal, Spain, Holland and England — entirely the reverse policy was put into effect. In 1639 Hidetada, son of Ieyasu (who died in 1616), after the Christian defence of the castle of Hara on Shimabara peninsula, banished all foreigners, except for a small Dutch trading post on the island of Deshima, and decreed that no Japanese should leave the country under penalty of death which same fate would await any Japanese who had left the country and decided tosreturn. Missionaries and merchants from the West were massacred and for the next two and a quarter centuries the ordinary people of Japan remained totally isolated and insulated from the outside world. The consequences of this policy were enormous and long-lasting. Some of its effects were of the greatest significance to later generations.

A small English trading post had been started in Japan in 1613 but was closed ten years later as, in contrast to its other European competitors, it was not running at a profit. A prophetic augury of the 20th century?

It would be regrettable to omit mention here of Will Adams, supposedly the first Englishman to set foot in Japan. Adams, from Gillingham in Kent, was the pilot of a Dutch ship that reached Japan with only 24 of its original 100 crew alive. In 1600 he was summoned to the presence of Tokugawa Ieyasu who took to him, largely from his ability to satisfy Ieyasu's typically Japanese thirst for knowledge about Europe, navigation, mathematics ... the construction of ships. Ieyasu conferred a substantial estate on Adams while employing him in diplomatic negotiations with other European traders. The man who was soon to become Shogun would not allow Adams to go back to England and he married a Japanese wife and settled comfortably in Japan. His outspoken opinions on the Catholics from Iberia may have strongly influenced their later treatment and expulsion.

(Will Adams' story forms the core of a remarkable novel *Shogun* by James Clavell (Hodder & Stoughton, 1975). This lengthy work (1240 pages) gives a most vivid picture of early 17th century Japan and is a splendid read.)

Previous Shogunates had laid the foundations but it was the Tokugawa who built upon them the strictly hierarchical structure of society which is still fundamental to modern Japan. Order, respect, obedience, knowing one's place, loyalty, diligence, duty and obligation, privilege and responsibility were all elements which became inculcated into the very soul of Japan during these 250 years that terminated with the forcible intrusion of the West upon the Japanese in the shape of the American Commodore Perry and his 'Black Ships' in 1853 and 1854.

Space does not allow more than the briefest treatment of what must be one of the most remarkable episodes in human history— a nation living not only in isolation but in almost total peace for such a period of years. The elegantly contrived class barriers between the 'Daimyo' and the 'Samurai', their warrior servants, the farmer-peasant population, the merchants and the 'eta' or untouchables, such as tanners and similar artisans who handled dead animals, were carefully preserved but could be circumvented (a financially embarrassed Samurai might marry his son into the family of a wealthy merchant to the benefit of all concerned). Other aspects of what amounted to perhaps the world's first 'police state' were inescapably rigid but were established with the best of motivations — the maintenance of peace. An example is the ingenious arrangements which required the Daimyo to spend several months of the year in his own domain while his wife and family stayed in the capital, Edo, virtually standing hostage for his good and peaceful behaviour. Should any of these great war-lords appear to the Shogunate to be amassing unreasonable wealth which might lead him to equip excessive forces of his own, he would be invited to contribute to some desirable cause of the Shogun's such as the extension of Edo Castle or the preservation of some costly Tokugawa shrine. Improvements or even repairs to the Daimyo's own castle were controlled by the Shogun, as were the marriages of his children.

Such an introspective and rigidly controlled society throughout the nation was ultimately bound to lead to a decay of one sort or another. It could not last forever, and the increasing replacement of copper coinage instead of rice as the staple form of exchange of wealth was probably a major factor in the weakening of the Shogunate style of government. It was so much more moveable, so much less cumbersome and ultimately more negotiable. It led to the decline of the Samurai and the rise of the lowly merchant class, the attitude of the former being to scorn the learning of arithmetic as being the "instrument of merchants". But it was the much scorned merchants who could do their sums who became money-lenders, brokers and ultimately bankers. In addition, there was the problem of the fluctuating value of rice according to the quality of the harvest. Even the Samurai were paid by the Daimyo in rice, their income thus depending on the market situation, and consequently many became unable to keep up the show and trappings of their station in life.

Additional to this development was the Shogunate's desire to improve the education of the warrior Samurai — partly as a means of keeping them occupied, and hence not troublesome — throughout these peaceful years. It was young Samurai scholars who in intellectual earnest questioned the direction of loyalty which had been taught to them and ingrained in their forebears. It was they who first seriously questioned the relative positions of Shogun and Emperor and asked to which of the two they owed the greater loyalty. Between 1603 and 1868 there were 15 Tokugawa Shoguns in virtually direct line of descent, accompanied by a steady decline in administrative ability, intellectual capacity and even in personality. Circumstances were combining to lead to the overthrow of the Shogunate and the restoration of the Emperor. A slight impulse from outside was all that was needed to set the process in motion, and this was bound to come.

The check-points at the staging posts on the Tokaido road, Japan's main thoroughfare between the Court of Kyoto and the government at Edo, still symbolised the Tokogawa police state but its power was waning. In the West the Industrial Revolution had come and gone, leaving developed nations which wanted no trammels to their trading throughout the world. The ships of many countries, in need of supplies, had been given short shift at the ports of Japan. To the rest of the world, the seclusion of the Japanese Islands was unnatural. What's more, to them it was downright inconvenient!

The first to set out for Japan with a trading treaty were the Russians, but they were pipped at the post by the Americans. In 1853 the autocratic Commodore Matthew Perry with his four black ships (two steam-driven) delivered a letter from the President, asking for a treaty of trade and addressed to the Emperor. At Uraga, at the mouth of Edo Bay, an official of sufficient rank was eventually found to receive it with due ceremony and Perry departed, making clear that, when he returned for an answer in a year's time, it would be with a larger force. The sight of the great warships belching forth smoke, their decks bristling with huge guns, had a startling effect on the Japanese, who could hardly believe their eyes.

The declining power of the Shogunate, together with the increasing movement towards the restoration of the Emperor to real power, gave the former a real headache when faced with the dual threats from both America and Russia. The latter, under Admiral Putyatin, returned to Nagasaki early in 1854, as Commodore Perry did to Edo, by which time the Shogunate had decided that Japan must give way to the demands of the foreigners for, having no navy, she had no means of protecting her shores, her fishing fleet, nor ships bringing essential food imports for her 30 million or so population. At the same time Japan would take such steps as she could to arm herself against the powers of the West. After as much procrastination as Perry would accept, an American-Japanese treaty was signed at Yokhama on 31 March 1854. Treaties were shortly signed, too, with the Russians and the Dutch and later with the British and French until, in all, 18 foreign countries had gained concessions from Japan, and in 1856, with little welcome from the Japanese,

Townsend Harris arrived at Shimoda, a village on the tip of Izu Peninsula, to take up residence as the first United States diplomatic representative. Though only some 200 Km from Edo, it was eighteen months before his perseverance resulted in an audience with the Shogun but this achievement finally proved that the doors of Japan were at last open to the world, and to Western trade and influence. The modern era was about to begin, although, until 1868, the country was to be riven again by strife, this time between the supporters of the Emperor and those of the Shogunate. Attacks upon foreigners and foreign legations were common. Foreign gun-boats engaged the fortresses of the Satsuma and Chosu clans who had tried to close the straits of Shimonoseki, the north-west entrance to the Inland Sea. Even after Shogun Tokugawa Keiki had surrendered his powers to the Emperor, the strife continued, ending in the 3-day battle of Toba-Fushimi, the Imperial supporters of Satsuma, Chosu and others marching on to take Edo, the capital. Emperor Komei died in 1867 and in April 1868 the new Tenno, taking the name Meiji ('Enlightened Rule') at the age of fourteen, took the 'Charter Oath', or the 'Five Articles Oath', initiating the end of feudalism and the beginning of the modernisation of Japan.

CHAPTER THREE

From Meiji Modernisation to Militarism

The flexibility and adaptability of the Japanese, and their ability to change course or policy at the dictates of circumstance, is well known today. The forcible intrusion of the West on the isolated island nation was to call upon these qualities and release a flood of energy and ingenuity that has changed world history in a way that would have amazed Commodore Perry had he lived to see it. But the man who unlocked the door to Japan died in 1858.

Having to accept the treaty terms laid down by the United States, Russia, France, Great Britain, Holland and a further 13 nations, was a moral defeat for the Japanese which involved a loss of face. The primary concern for her leaders was the preservation of her independence, which involved both military and economic considerations. Though no direct military threat ever materialised, the treaty terms imposed were unequal and harsh on the impoverished feudal agrarian state. It was under these conditions, with her independence threatened, that the nationalistic tendency of the Japanese came to transcend all lesser internal feelings, factions and issues, accompanied by an increase in the spirit of loyalty to the restored Emperor.

The Japanese had foreign trade forced upon them, with tariffs placed under international control and at levels which made the handmade products of Japan totally uncompetitive with those of Western capital and technology. They had seen other Asian countries go through the process of ruined local handicrafts, financial instability, followed by foreign political encroachment. It is to the credit of the Meiji government that at practically no time in their struggle to modernise their country and to put it on a level footing with the West, did they depend on foreign capital investment with its implied threat of future foreign control. Their achievement is all the more remarkable for this.

When, today, one reads frequent reports in the newspapers of many countries' complaints against unfair competition from the Japanese, it is ironic to reflect on the words of Matsukata Masayoshi (b.1840), one of the most remarkable politicians of the Meiji era who occupied several ministerial positions and was president of the Council of Ministers. In 1875 Matsukata said, "If we henceforth make every effort to increase production and reduce imports, we may confidently expect such growth of industrial production that after a decade financial stability will be achieved as a matter of course. If we fail to do this, and continue to buy imported goods with specie, our government and people may give the appearance of making progress but the reality will be quite different." This was at a time when the government was investing heavily in industrial projects — railways, roads, communications, shipyards, and plant for manufacture of cement, glass, bricks and textiles. Only by making her own industry more efficient than that of the West, could Japan prevent the eventual bankruptcy that faced any country that continued to import more than she could export. This simple economic lesson was learnt early by Japan, while it is only now that we seem to be divisively and half-heartedly facing up to the same problem.

Emperor Meiji's Charter oath of 1868 promised assemblies so that matters could be decided by 'public discussion', the uniting of all classes to carry out the affairs of state, the right of all common people to pursue their own calling "so that there may be no discontent", and the replacement of the Shogunate control by "the just laws of Nature." It ended with the significant clause, "Knowledge shall be sought throughout the world so as to strengthen the foundations of Imperial Rule." A few notable men had already visited the West but now a series of missions travelled constantly to study industry, banking and commerce, science, law, politics, culture and naval and military matters among those powerful countries who had forced themselves on Japan. The insatiable curiosity and desire for knowledge that characterises the Japanese was at last to be satisfied and put to good use. Perhaps the most notable was the Iwakura mission of 48 members and 54 students who set out in 1871 and spent two years in the United States and Europe. Thus started the flow of energetic 'study teams' to be found worldwide today.

The achievement of the small band of men who were to abolish the feudal caste system, introduce social mobility and to revitalise, industrialise and modernise Japan totally in the next quarter of a century is all the more remarkable in that few of them had any experience of government, politics or statesmen. They mostly came from the younger members of lower Samurai families, able men who could adopt and adapt new ideas with incredible speed and whose Samurai background gave them the courage to execute the most radical and widespread reforms, never turning back on their course once it was set.

Initially, a Council of State was formed with six ministries (including an Office of Shinto Worship). Edo became the seat of both emperor and government and was renamed Tokyo, the 'Eastern Capital'. The leading Daimyo voluntarily surrendered their lands and powers to the Emperor and others followed their example until, in 1871, all lands were surrendered by edict and the country divided into 75 administrative prefectures, governed by appointees from the capital. Samurai were deprived of their rights and given pensions, resenting the introduction of universal conscription in 1873 as much as the banning of their swords in 1876. Of the 34 million population in 1871, one and three quarters were Samurai, many of whom suffered in having to accept work much below their previous status. (Over half the workers of the Tomioka silk mill in 1872 were of Samurai rank, but some attained management status.) There were small Samurai uprisings but these were effectively suppressed by the new army, based on the 9000-strong Imperial guard and modelled on the French Army. We will return to the Samurai shortly.

Elsewhere the new government was busy in every sphere of activity. Much stress was placed on education, it being made compulsory in 1872 with a plan for 54,000 elementary schools, one for every 600 of the population. Political development took the shape of the formation of the first cabinet in 1885, mostly Samurai aged from 31 to 45; a new civil code of law in 1888 and in 1890 the opening of the Diet (parliament), a new Constitution having been promulgated by Emperor Meiji the year before.

Tokyo Imperial University was founded in 1879 followed shortly by Kyoto University and others. Weights and measures were standardised in 1873 to replace local standards. A mint was set up in 1871 in Osaka to unify the new coinage, and bank note printing started in Takinogawa in 1883. The first national postage system opened in 1871, followed by a telegraph system and in 1899 telephones in Tokyo and Osaka. In the early 1870s newspapers were established and distributed, even free to villages who could not afford them, the government introducing the ingenious innovation of allowing free postage of contributions to assist the flow of news and opinion. Four national banks were established in 1872. The Tokyo Stock Exchange was opened in 1878. In 1872 the first railway started to run between Tokyo and Yokohama. Gas lighting, which started in Tokyo's Ginza in 1874, was followed by the first electric lights in 1887 and electric trams in 1895. (London's first electric lighting appeared in 1878.) In agriculture, the government fostered 'seed-exchange meetings' from the 1870s, experiments in cross-pollination and the widespread use of fish fertiliser to improve rice crops in particular and, by 1885, instructors were employed to tour the country advising on the new methods. An agricultural management institute was founded in 1882, its first but vital job being the improvement of the primitive ploughshares in use.

Socially, Western dress was encouraged from the Court downwards — it became obligatory for government officials in 1876 — and Western social activities, such as evening dress balls where waltzes and quadrilles were danced, were introduced. Hairstyles went Western: haikara (or high-collar) became the word for fashionable, sebiru, (or Savile Row) the word for a good business suit. The demand for Western books kept translators squatting at their writting desks for long hours, for until then only a few Dutch works had come in through the little trading post at Deshima and been put into Japanese. Everyone sought "the light of Western civilisation". The Emperor set an example by eating beef, contrary to the Buddhist religion, the only previous consumer of such meat having been the American Consul, Townsend Harris. (The local butchers erected a monument in 1936 to commemorate Harris's deed!) The motivation behind all this social Westernisation was the desire to be accepted by the leading nations of the world, for Japan to take her right place among them — and ultimately for the revision of the unequal treaties and unfair tariff rates. An observer in Japan today may note that, in spite of the drastic changes in the relative positions of Japan and the West on the economic front, many Japanese are still motivated by similar impulses, a desire for equality, for acceptance, both personally and as a nation even though the need may be imaginary.

But what of industry? The government tried constantly to preserve Yamato Tamashii — "the spirit of old Japan" and the old cry of Sonno Joi — "Revere the emperor: Expel the barbarians" was now replaced by "Fukoku-Kyohei" meaning "Rich country— strong Army". Such aspirations depended not only on a strong economy but on the establishment of modern industry. Initially for an economic base, the government had to depend almost entirely on the Land Tax which replaced the earlier harvest tax and came largely from a predominantly agricultural population. (In 1880 about 75% of the population were employed in farming, and over 72% of the tax revenue came from them. At the end of the Meiji era, 1912, land tax contributed less than 20%.) Apart from railways, roads and communications, the government concentrated its resources on industries which were necessary for the establishment and supply of the army and navy, the latter being formed round the nucleus of the fleets of the old Shogunate and the Satsuma and Choshu Daimyo and modelled on the British Navy initially. The Yokosuka shipyard completed the first really Japanese-built warship, the 'Soryu-Maru', in 1872.

A major problem was to induce the merchant class and the wealthier Samurai to invest their savings in industry, for they knew nothing of it. Accordingly, the government initiated a policy of establishing various enterprises — mines, steelworks, shipyards, textile mills and the like — and operating them themselves, although often at a loss due to the shortage of trained management. These assorted plants became models, showpieces, through which the basic technologies were introduced into Japan often with the help of foreign technicians. In 1879 for instance, the Bureau of Mines were employing 34 and the Ministry of Industry 130 foreign experts. Knowledge was being "sought throughout the world".

It was by no means the government's policy to create a system of nationalised industries— and even today government participation in industry and services is minimal compared with that in the UK — and, as soon as possible after these plants had been proved, they were sold off, usually very cheaply when a suitable buyer could be found. There was a strong entrepreneurial spirit among the merchants and Samurai, who were willing to lay out their capital against the government's very advantageous terms once they had seen that what they were buying was a practical going concern. In a few cases, it was the prefectures who took over, as with Hiroshima which accepted the management of the cotton mills, with up-to-date English machines, in 1882. Glassworks, spinning mills, cement factories and even railways were disposed of by the government, often at only a tenth of the price it had paid to build them. In the marine field even further extremes were reached, such as in the case of Iwasaki Yataro, a Samurai of the Tosa clan, founder of Mitsubishi, who obtained 13 ships used for military transport in the 1874 Taiwan (Formosan) Expedition at no cost at all. Iwasaki went on to form his own shipping line, the Nippon Yusen Kaisha (or Japanese Mail Line), and successfully took over much of the work previously handled by the P & O Steamship line. In this and other instances the Government even threw in an annual subsidy to help the new owner-operator! It was intent upon building up a strong mercantile marine fleet and by 1899 Japan had 1221 steamships totalling over half a million tons of shipping, some contrast to the sighting of Perry's Black Ships in 1853!

The Mitsui organisation of today is nearly as big as Mitsubishi and goes back to a small family concern in Tokugawa times who diversified from saké brewing into the sale of dry goods and then into banking when it was little more than money-lending. In the mid-19th century, its manager, Minamoru Rizaemon introduced modern banking methods and set about diversification. Mitsui acquired the Tomioka silk mill, a government project, for a modest price, and was one of the first firms to engage in heavy industry and started up its chain of Mitsukoshi department stores as a separate concern. The Daiichi or First National Bank was founded by Shibusawe Eiichi, son of a peasant, who at one time was director of over 200 companies. He had been employed by Iwasaki as an accountant and had the good fortune to be sent to the Paris Exhibition of 1867 and eagerly absorbed all aspects there — and in the Bank of England — of Western banking and finance. To him must be credited the introduction of the joint-stock company in Japan.

There are endless examples of these characteristics of entrepreneurial activity in the period 1860 to 1900. They display not only the adaptability of the Japanese, and the fact that a socially classless society had been created but two features of Japanese business that are inherent to this day. The big companies originating in this period, the 'Zaibatsu', or financial clique are still very closely interlinked with government policy and institutions, the two being mutually supporting and reliant. Secondly, they show a close interdependence between industry and the banks, the two in many cases being in fact only two faces of the same organisation. This interlocking of government, banking, commerce and manufacture is like a jig-saw that is difficult for the foreign businessman to piece together totally, but the existence of which he must be aware. We shall revert to it in later chapters. The Vice-president of a Japanese company once showed me his balance sheet and his list of principal shareholders. "You see," he said with obvious pride, "we are not like most Japanese companies who work for the bank!" This was certainly true but I could not help wondering if the substantial shareholdings of some major insurance companies didn't amount to much the same thing. A study of the Japan Company Handbook (see Appendix A) shows that the banks have substantial shareholdings in the non-life insurance companies as do the securities companies which again are largely owned by the banks. The complications are endless! The Mitsubishi Bank owns 66,688 shares (8%) of the Mitsubishi Corporation, while the latter owns 29,000 shares (2.2%) of the Bank. Mitsubishi Heavy Industries owns 49,415 shares (3.7%) of the Bank, but Mitsubishi Bank also owns 122,368 shares (5.7%) of Mitsubishi Heavy Industries, and the Mitsubishi Corporation owns 55,205 shares (2.6%). This excludes the other 15 major Mitsubishi Companies — the Mitsubishi Chemicals, Electric, Estate, Gas chemical, Kakoki, Metal, Mining & Cement, Oil, Paper Mills, Petrochemical, Plastics Industries, Rayon, Steel Manufacturing, Trust & Banking, and Warehouse & Transportation Companies!

Casting a permanent cloud over the political, economic, social and industrial progress of Japan was still the feeling of resentment about the unequal treaties with the West, and this was the major bone of political contention. While, by ingenuity and persistence, the Japanese had largely overcome the economic handicap that the West had imposed on them, the fact that the treaties had not been revised in spite of continual negotiations suggested to the Japanese that they were still regarded as a second-class nation, not rated as highly as the vast people of China under their then soporific and decadent government. Internal and external pressures were combining to force Japan out into the arena of international politics. She was no longer the puny, feudal, agricultural state of 50 years ago, but a modern industrial and economic force with her own armed forces. The first miracle had been achieved and she was ready to flex her muscles, if need be, in battle.

Apart from Empress Jingo's expedition in the 4th and Toyotomi Hideyoshi's 12 month campaign in the 16th century, Japan's only extra-terratorial belligerence had been the two very minor sorties into Taiwan and Korea in the early 1870s. Since then Japan had asked for and obtained concessions from the latter, rather on a 'Perry' basis while China claimed, as she always had, that Korea was hers. In 1894 Chinese troops came to the aid of the King of Korea to suppress a revolt and Japan declared war on China. Victorious after nine months, she signed the Treaty of Shimonoseki, gaining substantial prizes, not least Formosa (Taiwan) and the independence of Korea. Another gain, the Liaotung Peninsula with Port Arthur in South Manchuria, was returned after quite unwarranted intervention by Russia, Germany, and France. That these three countries within the next five years should move into this and neighbouring territory must have appeared as no less than the meanest treachery to the Japanese — particularly the Russians' obtaining control of the Liaotung Peninsula. Russia's encroachment eastwards was no less than a positive threat to Japan. (For non-geographers, I might point out that today Vladivostok is only some 450 miles from Tsuruga, while north of Hokkaido only some 30 km separates Japan from the Russian occupied island of Sakhalin with the La Perouse or Soya straits.)

An event that did much to raise Japanese morale in the face of the menace of Russia was the signing in 1902 of the Anglo-Japanese Alliance. By this agreement the Japanese not only gained a degree of prestige in the eyes of the world but additional security. While the British gained an ally in their rivalry with Russia and Germany, they offered military assistance in the event of any other power joining with Russia in conflict with Japan, though not if Russia was the sole aggressor. This was the first equal-basis treaty signed with a major Western power and is still remembered today by older Japanese.

Negotiation failed to halt the threat from Russia which had secured the right to build a railway across Manchuria, a shorter route to connect Vladivostok with the trans-Siberian railway than could be obtained in purely Russian territory. Tsar Nicholas II continued sending troops eastwards while the negotiators talked on until, in 1904, the Japanese acted. The war on land, ending in the Battle of Mukden, was short and the Japanese Admiral Togo put paid to 32 out of the 35 ships of the Russian fleet in the Tsushima Straits in May 1905. At Portsmouth, New Hampshire, under Theodore Roosevelt, a treaty was signed, much to the advantage of the Japanese who, to the amazement of the world, had challenged and beaten the great Russian bear. As a world power, Japan had come of age.

Emperor Meiji, revered, loved and respected, died in 1912 leaving a nation practically unrecognisable from the one he ruled over at his accession 44 years before — in short, a world power. When the 1914-18 war broke out, Japan immediately joined the Allies and attacked Germany's Pacific interests as well as her assets in Shantung. In spite of some rather dubious 'politicking' with China, Japan ended the war with economic and political gains and enhanced prestige as a major power.

The 1920s were years of liberalisation in the domestic sphere, with political power being spread over a much wider field, the growth of labour unions, and the achievement of universal male adult suffrage in 1925. Many social reforms were carried out to the benefit of the poorer classes. The disastrous earthquake of 1923, which destroyed half of Tokyo and Yokohama, became the opportunity to rebuild on modern lines, and the subsequent importation of modern social trends and fashions from the West, such as films, jazz, golf and skiing. Western classical music, too, became a vogue. Everything seemed to be improving, yet some viewed the changes as decadent and to the detriment of the "spirit of old Japan", including its nationalistic tendencies and loyalty to the Emperor.

This is a simplistic view of the conditions which led to the resurgence of militarism, aided by the depression of 1929-32 which was blamed on the Zaibatsu. A young military clique began to expand, propagating the concept of Japan's economic ills being cured by Imperial expansion in Asia — in the name of the Emperor, of course!

The first sparks were struck by Japanese officers in Manchuria who engineered an excuse to attack the Chinese forces after the explosion of a bomb on the railway north of Mukden in 1931. They expanded northwards against weak opposition, in no way supported by their government in Tokyo, until they controlled and were able to make a puppet state of the whole of Manchukuo. The Chinese appealed to the League of Nations who condemned the unwarranted Japanese aggression and conquest. Japan left the League but there were no reprisals or sanctions and the Japanese military extremists, dissuading any civilian development in the area, now had a vast training ground where they could build up strength in total seclusion. They turned Manchuria into their own police state and set about its industrial development based on the South Manchuria Railway. At home, army and civilian extremists assassinated a number of political and Zaibatsu figures, including Premier Inuki in 1932.

According to the Meiji Constitution, the Emperor was the head of the Armed Forces and the service ministers were not only serving officers but automatically held seats in the Cabinet. These posts then became subject to the approval of the majority of officer opinion below them while they, in turn, could block the formation of a cabinet or specific cabinet decisions and policies, all of which they did when it suited them, but always invoking the name of the Emperor to whom they were so loyal. In 1936 a group of young extremist army officers used open force in revolt in the capital, assassinating a number of cabinet ministers and members of the Ministry of the Imperial Household, and occupying the Diet Building and the Army Ministry. The Navy did not support them. The coup was eventually crushed and thirteen of the leaders executed. In 1937, the army again decided on further incursion into China, reaching Peking that July as well as taking Shanghai. However, although already having to cope with the Chinese Communists, the forces of Chiang Kai-shek were not going to give in without a struggle this time. In spite of stepping up their campaign with heavy reinforcements, the Japanese army, though now supported by their government, never succeeded in conquering the Chinese.

The motivation behind the Chinese exercise in the minds of those Japanese who supported it, was the possible threat that Russia had posed ever since her defeat in the Russo-Japanese War of 1904-5. In an effort to break the stalemate in China, Japan signed a Tripartite Pact with Germany and Italy in September 1940 and the following April a neutrality agreement with Russia, the two conflicting when Hitler attacked Russia, giving no prior notice to Japan. In 1940 the United States banned the export to Japan of iron, steel and oil. In dire need of fuel, Japan decided on an attack on South East Asia, resulting in the freezing of her assets by the USA.

The moderate Japanese politicians, who favoured negotiation, were overruled and, in October 1941, General Tojo became premier. Meanwhile America was demanding the withdrawal of Japan from China and Indo-China. In December Japan's Imperial Council declared war on America.

A description of events between the Japanese navy attack on Pearl Harbour on 7th December 1941 to the dropping of the first atom bomb on Hiroshima, Southern Army HQ on 6th August

1945 has no place here, being of too recent and painful memory. It is a salutary lesson in man's inhumanity to man. Thirty years later, Hiroshima is a thriving modern city, where a largely new generation lives and works and where cherry trees blossom in the once charred soil. A visit to the Peace Memorial Museum in the park between the Rivers Ota and Motoyasu will make clear the Japanese willingness to sign Article 9 of the 1946 Constitution, "The right of belligerency of the state will not be recognised."

Not far from Peace Memorial park where careworn old Hiroshima women clad in baggy dungarees, aprons, and wide brimmed straw hats crouch over the flower beds as they fork up weeds, stands a solitary building. The Atom Bomb Dome, as it is called, is the only surviving building of pre-atomic Hiroshima. Its scarred brick and concrete, topped by the twisted skeleton of a once steel and glass dome, is preserved as a permanent reminder of the evils of the past. To stand before it is a moving experience, regrettably enjoyed by all too few Western people, which gives an insight into many deeply rooted Japanese attitudes today.

CHAPTER FOUR

The Labyrinthine Language

To my mind most foreign writers on Japan make too little or too light of the problem of language. They brush it aside as they would a fly off a slice of sashimi for, as politicians, travel writers or peripatetic journalists, it is of little more interest than a pair of stone lanterns at the entrance to a Shinto shrine that they are intent upon visiting. In writing of the Japanese language, I am not as yet referring to the vexed question of whether one should try to learn it. What I believe is more important and what I am at present concerned with is whether one should make an attempt to get any understanding of it at all. In most of my travels in Japan I have had the benefit of being accompanied by business friends who have ensured that I have had few practical problems in the matter of communication, but I believe there is a far more fundamental reason for taking a close interest in the speech and the writing of Japan.

From my own experience it is not enough to sit back in the comfort of having friends to interpret and translate for me. I am firmly convinced that, without some concept of the peculiar (at least to us) structure of the Japanese language, the visiting businessman will be hampered in his affairs by a self-imposed barrier of ignorance, not just of the language but of the people with whom he is dealing. He will miss the vital clue that would perhaps not reveal to him how the Japanese think but which would at least convince him of one of the deepest and essential truths: that the way they think bears little or no relationship to the thought processes of Western nations. They may wear the same clothes, consume the same consumer goods and build ships, cars, cameras, watches and electronic equipment better, cheaper and faster than we can ourselves, but the system of mental operation that they employ in these activities is quite different from that of the West.

If you think about it, abstract thought is virtually impossible, except perhaps for such rare breeds as mathematicians and musicians whose basic working materials are something other than words. For the rest of us common folk, words are the media of our thinking as are the means by which we string these words together to make them into connected patterns of thought. Our mental processes are conditioned not only by the range of our own personal vocabularies but also by the grammar and the syntax of our native language, the language in which our thoughts are inevitably framed. Similar constraints, naturally, are likewise imposed on the Japanese as on speakers and writers of European languages. From the cradle our minds are forced to think in the word forms that we copy from our parents and, later, from our teachers. Our whole intelligence derives from these verbal origins.

In an amateur way I have dabbled in the shallows of a number of European tongues and have found that, with the exception of the curious German habit of saving the keyword, the verb, as a surprise until the end of the sentence, the structure of most Western languages is substantially the same. I discount here the irritating propensity of some Continentals to give genders to inanimate objects such as tables, chairs and houses and am glad to be able to report that this is one useless complexity that the Japanese have avoided. A nodding acquaintance with the Middle East, too, suggests that their language structures are not too different from our own. But the matter is very different when one comes to look at Nihongo, or Japanese. I write, please note, as a simple exporter rather than as a professional linguist, so please do not take me to task for such vague generalisations. I believe that my main contention is true: that the Japanese speak differently from us because they think differently, while conversely they think differently because they speak differently — and how differently!

The difference between our language and thought processes is characterised by an observation of Lafcadio Hearn. Hearn went to Japan in 1890, in the early days of modernisation if not of the Meiji restoration, with a commission to write a series of newspaper articles. He never wrote them nor did he leave Japan again. He taught English, worked on a Kobe newspaper, married a Japanese, became lecturer in English at Japan's top university, Tokyo Imperial University, changed his name to Kuizumi

Yakomo and died in Japan in 1904. In spite of writing a number of books, now rare classics though somewhat out of date, that are among the best interpretations of the Japanese nation and character, Hearn never learnt the language. As he put it, "Could you learn all the words in a Japanese dictionary you would not make yourself understood in speaking unless you learned to think like a Japanese — that is to say, to think backwards, to think upside-down, and inside out!"

A few examples will show how Japanese sentences are constructed.

Two of the most gifted teachers of the language are Mr Oreste Vaccari and his wife, whose output of textbooks, phrasebooks and dictionaries is truly prodigious. The first example come from their 757-page *Japanese Conversation-Grammar*. It has a curiously abrupt ring of denial that I feel sure no Japanese would use, but this does not detract from its value. The sentence is: "In a word I don't approve of your plan." The literal translation of the Japanese for this is: "One mouth if in said your plan to approval make fact impossible is." Backwards, upside-down, inside-out!

This is a simple sentence but the Japanese have a love of complexity and, when a number of connected sentences involving dependent clauses is involved, the end product borders on nightmare.

Another early classic in the list of foreign books endeavouring to explain Japan to the Western world is Basil Hall Chamberlain's *Japanese Things*. Professor Chamberlain's book was originally published in the late 19th century but has now been reprinted in paperback. Under the heading of "Language" he gives this example, the English being as follows: "At the present day, Buddhism has sunk into the belief of the lower classes only. Few persons in the middle and upper classes understand its 'raison d'être', most of them fancying that religion is a thing that comes into play at funeral services."

Professor Chamberlain gives the direct translation of the Japanese for this as: "This period at having arrived, Buddhism that (they) say thing as for merely low-class-people's believing place that having-become, middle-class thence-upwards in as-for, its reason discerning-are people being few, religion that if-one-says, funeral-rite's time only in employ thing's manner in (they) think."

A final example to show the unfathomable gap between our languages and hence our thought processes, this time from Vaccari again. It is part of a newspaper report of the inauguration ceremony for Japan's new Constitution in October 1946. For a change I'll give the direct translation of the Japanese first. If you can put it into anything like comprehensible English, perhaps you are well on the way towards understanding the Japanese mind if not the language. This is the direct translation:

"Commemorative folk song 'Our Japan' of the chorus flowing Constitution Minister of Kanamori Minister of State of closing ceremony of the address at the end to be when suddenly National Anthem being played rain by the august presence cancelled that been the Emperor His Majesty all at once his presence made. By himself the umbrella held when platform on to stand when hurrah hurrah of the voice spontaneously gushing forth Yoshida Premier of cheers the formality renewing to be tried again enthusiasm while it was continuing. His Majesty eleven o'clock sharp return made."

Well, how did you make out? Mr Vaccari gives the proper translation as follows: "While the strains of the folk song 'Our Japan' sung by a chorus were flowing and when the State Minister Kanamori, nicknamed the Minister of the Constitution, was at the end of his address at the close of the ceremony, the National Anthem was played and His Majesty the Emperor, whose august presence had been cancelled on account of the rain, suddenly appeared. Holding an umbrella himself, and when he stood on the dias, shouts of 'Banzai!, Banzai!' spontaneously gushed from the crowd, and so excited were they that Premier Yoshida had to give the start to new formal cheers. His Majesty left sharp at eleven o'clock."

Apart from showing the different construction of the two languages, these pieces are useful in pointing out the difficulty if not almost impossibility of simultaneous translation. An interpreter cannot begin to interpret until he has heard the whole of a sentence, an important point to remember in business or social discussions.

Spoken Japanese has other complications. Though some simplification has taken place in recent years, it is still a 'respect' language with different modes of address being appropriate for different grades of people. Charles V of the Holy Roman Empire is quoted as having said, "I speak Spanish to God, Italian to women, French to my wife, and German to my horse." The variety of speech forms that the ordinary Japanese must cope with today is almost as extensive. Apart from extremes, such as meeting the Emperor, and nobody ever does, in daily life a Japanese will use different modes of speaking for his superiors, his equals and his inferiors or juniors. Even this is overlaid by other intricacies. I was once out with a party of businessmen in a Tokyo beer-hall and we were joined by the daughter of one of them and her recently married husband. He was a young Englishman who had been working in Japan for about a year and he translated much of the conversation for me and joined in quite frequently. At the end of the evening I commented on his excellent command of Japanese. "Not at all!" replied his father-in-law, "He speaks it very badly for he has been learning from his wife. He speaks it like a woman!"

Only once has His Majesty, Emperor Hirohito, spoken to all his people. On 15th August 1945 he made his only broadcast to the nation. One earwitness recorded the following account, "The words and expressions were very ancient and difficult ... but I could understand the meaning quite well; we had lost the War ..." It is interesting to note that Chairman Mao also once broadcast to the people of China but never repeated the act. Far from speaking in courtly, regal expressions like the Tenno of Japan, Mao spoke with such a strong provincial accent that practically none of his listeners understood a word of what he said. It is some slight comfort that the Japanese language is almost devoid of dialectal variations, at least within the business orbit.

One major difficulty of the language is the use of particles — suffixes which indicate whether a word is the subject or the object of a sentence and which merge imperceptibly into a range of prepositions. In 'Watashi-wa sashimi wo tabe masu', (I eat raw fish), the '-wa' shows that 'watashi' (I) is the subject, while '-wo' or '-o' makes it clear that the raw fish is the object. The suffix '-no' can be peculiarly confusing to European speakers for it takes the place of our 'of' but is closer to "'s" as the word order is reversed in Japanese. Thus, 'watashi-no hon' is 'I's' book' or my book. As one might expect, of course, there is a wide range of words for 'I', to use when speaking to superiors or inferiors, and by women, children and men. In spite of the variety available — and the same applies to 'you' — personal pronouns are rarely used except when confusion could result from their omission.

The complexity of the Japanese language, particularly in compound sentences, brings with it a degree of imprecision of speech that one might think would be deprecated as forming a hindrance to the communication of ideas. Not at all! It is part of the

Japanese way of life and a feature very much to be admired. "In the Japanese language exactness of expression is purposely avoided," as one Japanese author puts it, while, to quote another, "To give in so many articulate words one's innermost thoughts and feelings is taken among us as an unmistakable sign that they are neither profound nor very sincere." There is a Japanese saying, "Isogaba maware" which can be translated as, "When in a hurry, go round." Circumlocution is at its peak when a Japanese is faced with the problem of saying 'No' to someone. Listening to Japanese conversation the different use of and attitudes to 'yes' and 'no' become immediately apparent. 'Hai' or yes is heard frequently. The word is barked out repeatedly with a staccato enthusiasm and vigorous nods of the speaker's head. I cannot describe how 'Iie', or no, is intoned. It is a word in my Japanese dictionary but used on so few occasions that it is difficult to recall its sound!

I quoted Vaccari's "In a word, I don't approve of your plan". Writing of a typical 'cultivated Japanese friend', Lafcadio Hearn said, "As a private adviser he will not even directly criticize a plan of which he disapproved but is apt to suggest a new one in some such guarded language as 'Perhaps it might be more to your immediate interest do thus and so ...'." In a more recent and light-hearted work, Don Maloney describes a visit to a shop which is a typical example of the Japanese urge to avoid the possibility of giving pain or offence by saying 'no'. It is very characteristic of many Japanese conversations carried on in English and similar exchanges take place frequently in the business world. Maloney's tale runs as follows:

"In the stores in Japan, the sales-girls never say 'No'. They make you say it. Here's what I mean:

"First I'll give away the whole plot of my example story. Unless you know the ending ahead of time, you really won't understand the story as it unfolds.

The plot is that you've decided that you want to buy a few pads of simple blue-lined paper. And, the store you have decided to buy it in doesn't have blue-lined paper. They never did have blue-lined paper.

O.K. That's the plot. Now, the dialog:

You walk in and ask, 'Do you have blue-lined paper pads?'
The girl asks, 'Blue-lined pads?'
You: 'Yes, blue-lined pads.'
She: How many?'

You: 'Oh, three or four.'

She: 'Three or four?'

You: 'Yes, three or four.'

She: 'What size?'

You: 'Regular size, legal size. I don't really care.'

She: 'How many sheets to the pad?'

You: 'Makes no difference, really. Thirty or 40 or 50 — any number is O.K.'

She: 'You want them now? Today?'

And on and on it can go. I'll spare you the rest. But the point is, she's not going to say she doesn't have blue-lined paper. You are. Because after about 45 minutes of conversation like this ... the light will finally dawn on you and you'll say to her,

'You mean you don't have blue-lined paper?'

And then she'll smile broadly and, with a sigh of relief, say,

'Yes', meaning, of course, 'Yes, we don't have blue-lined paper.'"

Mr Maloney, I should add, is an American businessman who has lived and worked in Japan for a number of years. His book, *Japan: It's Not All Raw Fish*, is a reprinted series of articles from the *Japan Times* and is packed with wisdom behind the humour.

This use of the English word 'Yes' is one that must be understood if the visitor is not going to get into trouble. The Japanese use of the word 'Yes' is really short for, 'Yes, I understand you' or 'Yes, I agree with what you have just said'. Whereas we would answer 'No' or 'No, thank you' to the question, 'You don't want another beer, do you?', the Japanese would reply 'Yes', meaning 'Yes, your supposition is correct. I don't want another beer'. It pays to get a good grasp of this apparently topsy-turvey logic. Otherwise you may find your company overstocked when you think you're going to get a big order that you aren't going to get!

One reflection of the linguistic vagueness of Japanese is seen in the omission in many expressions of what to Western people would be the most important part of the sentence. For example, the equivalent of our 'Pleased to meet you' on being introduced is 'Hajimete o me ni kakarimasu'. The literal translation of this is 'In the beginning (or, for the first time) in my eye takes'. The sentiment of pleasure is left unexpressed. Again, when giving a person a present, and present-giving and receiving is a most important part of Japanese life, which will be discussed in Chapter 10, the giver will say, "Kore-wa sukoshi desu keredomo", which literally means 'This is only a little but ...' The most important part of the communication, 'it is for you' is assumed. In this the language resembles Sumi-e, or Japanese ink-painting, where in contrast to the precision of the wood-block prints of Ukiyo-e, or the 'Floating World' (see Chapter 12) the outlines of parts of the painting are indefinite and large areas are left completely blank. Some experts say that the blank areas are the most important parts of the picture.

Together with the spoken language go expression and intonation, the interpretation of which can be as important as understanding the words. When something is being explained to a Japanese, he will often reply with the words 'Ah so!', meaning much the same as they do in English. As the explanation proceeds, the 'Ah so's' are repeated at more and more frequent intervals, the whole growing into a sort of lilting chant which ends, 'Ah, so ... Ah, soooo ... Ah, so desu! Ah, so desu ka?', the final phrase meaning, 'Ah! Is that really so?' Whether the message has really got home or not depends very much on the expression given to those last four words and practice is needed in interpreting this! The final 'ka', by the way, indicates a question. A statement and a question are identical in Japanese except for the intonation and the addition of the 'ka', a sort of spoken question mark.

Verbal expression is accompanied by facial expression, the interpretation of which may be even more of a problem, especially for the foreigner. The Japanese of today are the most polite, thoughtful and kindly people it has been my pleasure to know. They are impelled by an inner desire to please and not to disappoint, combined with an instinctive wish to be liked. Hence it is that so many Japanese are seen to be smiling so much of the time. Lafcadio Hearn wrote of the smile: "But the smile is to be used on all pleasant occasions, when speaking to a superior or an equal, or even upon occasions which are not pleasant; it is part of deportment. The most agreeable face is the smiling face; and to present always the most agreeable face ... is a rule of life. And furthermore, it is a rule of life to turn constantly to the outer world a mien of happiness, to convey to others, as far as possible, a pleasant impression ... On the other hand, to look serious or unhappy is rude, because this may cause anxiety or pain to those who love us; it is likewise foolish, since it may excite unkindly curiosity on the part of those who love us not." The double entendre should not be missed. It is characteristic of the duality of so many aspects of Japanese life.

When considering Japanese language and Japanese thought, there is allied to them a fundamental truth that needs to be grasped— the relative rather than the absolute nature of truth to the Japanese. While, in the West, we may say that there are two sides to every question and that circumstances vary with the point of view taken, we generally hold that truth is absolute and that from one point of view— no doubt one that is inaccessible to all those concerned — the truth would always be apparent. The Japanese, on the other hand, are more inclined towards the view that, if absolute truth is generally unattainable to Man, for practical purposes it can be considered to be non-existent. Therefore to them the apparent or relative truth is something nearer to the reality of this imperfect world. I am not for a moment suggesting that the Japanese are untruthful. Far from it: I have never come across a deliberate untruth among them. But it does no harm to realise that they and we may not always have exactly the same concept of what truth is, and who is to say which of us is right?

Should some disagreement or dispute unfortunately occur in dealings with the Japanese, the wise negotiator would do well to reflect on the possible influence of this fundamental difference in attitude of mind before acting or speaking precipitately.

In spite of their fierce national pride, the Japanese do not see anything wrong with borrowing and, if necessary, adapting concepts and ideas from abroad. While the French and the Iranians have set up special bodies of learned men to purify their respective languages of foreign taint, the Japanese are content with the borrowed elements — mostly Chinese — in theirs. The most noticeable manifestation of this is the curious dual system of numerals in everyday use. The true Japanese numerals, from one to ten, run, 'hitotsu, futatsu, mittsu, yottsu, itsutsu, muttsu, nanatsu, yattsu, kokonotsu, to'. But you will hear just as frequently, if not more so, the Chinese series, 'ichi, ni, san, shi, go, roku, shichi, hachi, ku, ju'. In fact, the Japanese numerals are rarely used above the number 'ten', so that 'ju-ichi' is universally used for eleven, 'ju-ni' for 12 and so up to 'ni-ju' for 20 and so on. All this is logical but perhaps too simple for a Japanese system. Hence there is an added complication, the need for suffixes or numeral adjuncts, which differ according to the type of article being counted. Thus, '-mai' is added to the numeral when counting flat things like sheets of paper, '-hon' or '-pon' for long cylinders such as trees or pencils, '-hiki' for animals, (like our pack of wolves), '-kumi' for sets or pairs of things, and '-hai', equivalent to our -ful as in spoonful or bucketful. People are counted as people or '-nin'. The list of adjunct is, if not endless, too long for us here. It is enough to point out that even the adjuncts modify according to the numeral that precedes them!

Ten minutes with one of the Samurai films which appear nightly on Japanese television on one channel or another, like an endless saga of Japanese Robin Hood pictures, makes it almost impossible to believe another intriguing facet of the Japanese language. Rich though it is in vocabulary, it contains hardly any swear words or terms of abuse! In a moment of disaster when a monumental clanger has been dropped, one of the worst imprecations available for the release of whatever pent-up emotion a Japanese has at such times is 'Shimata!' This literally means 'Mistake has been made', the unspoken implication being that the speaker is the idiot who made it, ie 'I have made a mistake'. A sympathetic listener, and there is usually one around, will reply softly, 'Shikataganai', meaning 'It can't be helped', and attention is then turned to picking up the pieces. Whether this derives from Buddhism, Shinto or Confucian philosophy, all of which are inextricably interwoven into the Japanese character, I have yet to discover but I feel sure that it must account for a more unusual feature of personnel relations in the Matsushita Electric factories, which is related in Chapter 7.

So far we have only considered the spoken Japanese language. The written version raises a completely different set of problems, both for the foreigner and for the Japanese. The visitor will discover this as soon as he lands at Haneda Airport at Tokyo, if he hasn't done so before.

The Japanese have three forms of script, namely Kanji, Hiragana and Katakana. Kanji are ideogramatic pictures of what they represent, sometimes quite recognisably. These kanji characters were brought to Japan from China via Korea in the 5th century AD, the same characters still being used in China today, each one having just the same meaning but expressing a completely different word sound in the two tongues. Thus the Chinese and the Japanese can largely read each other's languages but are quite unable to converse with one another without learning the other's tongue.

No-one knows how many kanji ideograms there are in Japanese, not even the greatest academics and scholars. Some will tell you 5000, some 10,000 and I have even been given a figure of over 30,000! However, some years ago after the war, the Japanese government decided to regularise and simplify the matter for the future and decreed that from then on only some 2000 characters would be used in printed texts. This naturally eases the task of schoolchildren, lessening the time that must be spent on learning this tedious but vital part of their education but, at the same time, breeding future generations who will be quite unable to read the older texts such as those in which many of their classics of literature are written. In fact an eleven-year-old should know about 900 kanji out of a minimal 1900 now in general use in books, newspapers and magazines, ie, only some 47%. At the same time these 1900 characters do not include those used commonly in many names of both people and places, and there are many other special ideograms in ordinary use in periodicals, especially in the technical field so that, to be truly 'educated', a knowledge of 3000-4000 is still necessary.

From time to time there have been moves towards the complete abolition of the Chinese method of writing for in Japan there are two other forms of script in which the whole language could be written. These are the 'kana' or substitute letters. Hiragana are the flowing or informal signs used for writing Japanese words; Katakana, the formal or stiff characters used for foreign words (such as your and your company's name on your business cards.) These kana represent sounds rather than our simple letters of the Roman alphabet, all except 'n' combining a consonant and a vowel sound. Including 'n', there are some 48 basic sign/sounds which, modified, extend to another 80 'turbid' and compound turbid elements, a prodigious number to learn at school on top of the Kanji ideograms.

The practicability of the kana scripts for writing the whole of the Japanese language is shown in some of the earliest written classics. About the end of the 10th century AD and the beginning of the 11th, there was a great flowering of Japanese literature with the writing of such works as *The Tale of Genji* (1004 AD), *Lady Murasaki's Diary* and *The Pillow Book* of Sei Shonagon, all of which are available in English translations. These and other works flowed from the pens, or rather the writing brushes, of ladies of the Heian Court for at that period it was not customary for ladies to write in Kanji ideograms. They used the latter only when necessary, as in some names, and wrote in Hiragana, the flowing script. The same could be done today.

It could be argued that Japanese educational standards would be raised if the burden of all this learning by rote could be lifted.

On the other hand it is difficult to see that our own standards have improved since we gave up compulsory Latin and Greek, so beloved of our forefathers as mental exercise and excellent training to stretch young minds. Since we have more recently eased ourselves into decimalisation of our monetary system and now into the comfort of metrication, there seems to have been a positive decline in the educational standards of school leavers. On the other hand, the Japanese, who have the most complex spoken and written language imaginable and have had state education since the early years of the Meiji Restoration, are the most literate people in the world. Illiteracy is variously quoted as 'nil', 'negligible' and 'zero' and this in spite of every kanji having at least two readings. Chamberlain quotes an old Jesuit missionary on the writing of Japanese who 'declared it to be evidently the invention of a conciliabule of demons to harass the faithful'!

The various attempts to abolish kanji, and even kana, replacing it with a romanised (Romaji) script have all failed and not surprisingly. It is understandable that a nation— and particularly such a proud one as the Japanese — should not want to abolish and deny itself a great part of its cultural heritage. Perhaps even more significant is the fact that writing or calligraphy is considered in Japan to be a true and much appreciated art form. This is rightly so for there is a powerful spiritual expressionism and an infinite variety of form and beauty in fine Japanese brush writing that puts even the best of our formal italic hands to shame.

An important side effect of the kanji and kana scripts is to be seen in business houses. From the vast quantity of characters needed, it follows that a Japanese typewriter must be a complex and costly machine. It is in fact about the size of a desk, has some 1800 keys with their appropriate characters and another few hundred stowed away in drawers. It will be no surprise that such machines are probably more easily available to companies who can afford them than is a ready supply of suitably trained young ladies to operate them.

The consequences of all this are that a high proportion of all business correspondence and memoranda is hand-written and that Japan has a flourishing industry with some excellent designs in the manufacture of copying machines. We have commented on the vagaries and imprecision of spoken Japanese and here a further hindrance to exactness of communication is introduced. In spite of their admiration for the artistry of the calligrapher, with ink-block and brush, the pressures of the business day do not allow the Salaryman (see Chapter 5) to exercise much skill with his ball-point or fibre-tip. An error in handwriting, all too easily made in Kanji, becomes multiplied by the very power of the photocopying machine.

Should the visiting businessman try to learn Japanese and, if so, how? I think it depends largely on how seriously you view the potential of your business with Japan, what proportion of your turnover you think could be generated there, how frequently you will visit and how long you will spend there. If you reach the more distant goal of forming a joint venture with a company in Japan, it is likely that a resident British director will be wanted to go and stay out there, at least in the initial few years after its formation. It is obviously much easier to learn this very difficult language when living in the country and the need to do so increases with the opportunity. One is immersed in it daily and there are many more language schools and private tutors in Japan than there are over here. But all that is a different question.

Of one thing I am certain, and that is that any effort you may make to learn the language will be much appreciated by the Japanese. It may not reach the stage where it is really of any practical value to you but your hosts will admire you for trying and will take your efforts as a gesture of politeness and friendship, important qualities to the Japanese.

Excluding learning in Japan, what are the alternatives? Phrasebook language, learned parrotwise, is better than nothing and there are some excellent pocket volumes available, even in the UK, which will teach you the common greetings and courtesies and many useful day-to-day expressions. However, these books will do nothing to give you an appreciation of the structure of the language and hence the way the Japanese think. I have tried to give some idea of the importance of this but it will only really become apparent if you try it out for yourself. This can either be done by attending one of the limited number of language laboratories that provide a course in Japanese or by doing it from the book.

My own first faltering efforts were made with *Teach Yourself Japanese* by C.J. Dunn and S. Yanada (English Universities Press Ltd). If I had persevered and mastered the whole of this excellent volume, I believe I would have reached a higher standard than I have by changing horses or at least books in midstream. While in Osaka a friend bought me what seems to be an easier book, but the differences in teaching methods between the two books only tends towards confusion. I confess, too, that I have another trouble with this second book which is by Eiichi Kiyooka and is published by the Hokuseido Press in Tokyo. The trouble lies in the optimistic title of the book and my habit of studying it over and over again to the surprise and amusement of my family. When, for the sixth year running, my son sees me mugging up *Japanese in 30 Hours*, his only comment is, 'Long hours they have in Japan, Dad.'

I have mentioned the Vaccaris' *Japanese Conversation-Grammar* on which the brief language lab course that I did at the Polytechnic of the South Bank in London was based. It is a vast tome of nearly 800 large pages, costing some £10 a few years ago, and far too complex for the casual learner.

I have listed these books and some others with suitable notes in Appendix H. My only advice from experience is to concentrate on one book or course and, whichever you choose, stick to it.

I started this chapter by saying that abstract thought is a virtual impossibility for most of us, and later mentioned the moves that have been made from time to time to dispense with kanji ideograms. In fact, the have one outstanding advantage over any form of alphabetical script in involving a degree of abstract thought. Like road signs the world over and certain other symbols, once learnt, they are much more quickly read than alphabetical print or writing, for they are instantly recognisable as graphic representations of their meanings. This is an added reason for keeping kanji as the national script.

CHAPTER FIVE

The Sarariman Observed

According to T.F.M. Adams (1969) there are over 25 million white collar workers in Japan. This is hard to believe as the latest official statistics quote the total working population (1975) as 51.8 million employed and 990,000 unemployed (now nearly 1¼ million). However, whether one accepts this figure or not, the white collar worker clearly accounts for a sizeable slice of Japan's 114 million population and, with his wife and family, has considerable purchasing power and influence, at least in the consumer goods field, an important point for potential exporters in this category.

In Japanese the white collar worker is called the Salaryman or, due to the absence of the sound 'l' in the language, the 'Sarariman'. Apart from some dealings with company directors, bank managers and government officials, the visiting businessman is likely to be involved with sararimen more than anyone else, and so the more he can understand of what makes this class of the Japanese working population tick, the better. To give some insight into the motivations, the thoughts, actions and reactions of the sarariman, I have endeavoured in this chapter to put an average specimen under the microscope for your examination. I appreciate that there is no such person as the 'average' Japanese sarariman any more than there is an 'average' British businessman on the export band-wagon. However, I believe that a look into the life of my fictitious Nakamura Isamu will reveal many factors and influences that are characteristic of this important sector of Japanese business and society. Please note in passing that the Japanese family name comes first, followed by the given name, though, on the English side of his 'meishi', or business card, it will most probably be transposed into the Western sequence, the family name coming second.

Purists might argue that, since Nakamura is advancing up the executive ladder of his company, he is a manager rather than a sarariman. This is, of course, all a matter of degree as it is almost impossible to draw a strict line between the two. It is, as in a different field altogether, like hills and mountains as defined in the *Concise Oxford Dictionary* where you will find that a mountain is a large hill while a hill is a small mountain. The dividing line between them is blurred, if it exists at all.

Nakamura Isamu, whose family name literally means "inside the village", is a fictitious amalgam of statistical averages and characteristics of his type and class. Many Japanese names, by the way, are similar compounds, eg Kitagawa or north river, Kuroiishi or black-stone, Yamamoto— mountain source, Honda — source of rice fields, Mitsubishi— three stones. Breaking them into parts and meanings is often a great help in memorising them, which can be a problem to the visiting businessman. In case any of my Japanese friends should read this book, I must emphasise that Mr Nakamura bears no direct resemblance to any single Japanese of my acquaintance, though I hope he typifies the Japanese of his class and status.

Nakamura Isamu-san is aged 37 and is married to Nakamura Shizuko-san who is four years younger. They have been married for nine years (average marrying age is 28 for men and 24 for women). Note that the suffix -san can mean Mr or Mrs and that it is a minor honorific term so that one never applies it to oneself: "I am Smith"— never "I am Smith-san". Age expectancy for the Nakamuras is 67.2 years for the husband and 72.3 years for his wife. Unless fortune blesses him with promotion to the board of directors, he can expect to retire at 55 with the possibility of further employment at a reduced salary in an associated or subsidiary company. Since leaving Waseda University in Tokyo where he studied economics, he has worked continuously for the same company, medium-sized by Japanese standards, and employing some 3500 people.

Perhaps untypically, they do not live in the concrete jungle of company houses and flats (Danchi) that surround the factories but are buying their own house some 25 km from Tokyo where Isamu works in the head office of the Matsuda (or 'pine tree — rice field') Company. The house has four rooms and is currently valued at about £30,000, largely on account of the very high price of land. It measures some 9 metres square and stands in a walled garden little more than 12 metres by 20. Although it is faced with concrete, the house retains much of the character traditional to Japanese dwellings, like the sliding wood-and-paper doors that take up much of three walls of the single-storey building. The Nakamuras are fortunate for only 13% of dwellings in Japan are non-wooden, while, of the wooden structures, less than 30% have been fire-proofed. They are also lucky in that their family of four have a floor space of some 20 m² each, compared with the national average of 16 m². (Houses and rooms, by the way, are measured in floor area in 'tatami' or rice-straw mats which have been standardised to a size of about 180 cms x 90 cms for the last thousand years or so. Based on this standard of measurement, Japanese houses have literally been 'pre-fabricated' for the same period!)

When they were first married, they lived with young Mrs Nakamura's parents, the Itos. When Mr Ito died, they bought their present house with the help of a substantial loan at low interest from the Matsuda Company. Mrs Ito came to live with them and they were a bit crowded with their two children, a girl, Fusako, now aged 8, and Ichiro, the boy, now 6. They were glad of the space when she passed on. She lies buried in the crowded grounds of a nearby Buddhist temple while her photograph is revered in the tiny family 'Kami-dana' or god-shelf in the living room.

The street in which the Nakamuras live is just wide enough to take a lorry and is criss-crossed with electricity and telephone cables, the asphalt surface crumbling at the edges into a dusty gravel channel which churns into a muddy morass after rain. There is nothing logical about the plots and buildings that border the lane. They lie in a heterogeneous jumble as though, bored with his more orderly work, God had taken all the basic elements up to a great height and dropped them wherever they landed. Crowded against the cement block wall of the Nakamuras' garden is an old wooden building, a soba or noodle shop, flanked by a small patch where someone is growing vegetables spaced with military precision in the rich black soil, and then a fish shop, a tiny rice field and a small general store selling groceries, stationery and ironmongery. To the other side of the Nakamuras is a bicycle repair mechanic and then a jumble of older houses, mostly with blue glazed tiled roofs. A similar chaotic juxtaposition lines the opposite side of the road, but with more houses and the gateway and path leading up to a little Shinto shrine perched on the leafy hillside behind. The red paint on the torii or arch at the entrance is faded and peeling, for the shrine is not rich like some in the cities which receive large subsidies and donations from commercial concerns. For this the priest will advise the directors on auspicious days for the launching of major projects. The Japanese businessman may not be very religious but superstition is still a strong influence in his affairs.

A primary consideration in the family is the children's education, particularly that of their son. One might rightly say that this is not a matter specific to Japan but the structure of society there makes it a more vital concern than to parents in most other countries. It is no exaggeration to say that the future career of a young Japanese boy may well be decided by the primary school he manages to get into. The first step on the ladder is a most important one for, while there is equality of opportunity for all, it is at this stage that the choice of ladder may well be made. The right educational ladder should ultimately lead to the right prestigious university, and hence to a secure lifelong job with an equally prestigious company. It is a curious feature of Japanese education and employment that to have been to the right university appears to be more important than what the student learnt or achieved there. To have passed the entrance to Keio, Waseda or, at the peak, Tokyo (Imperial) University, gives the student an aura which will never disperse and will admit him to a 'group' membership that will sustain him all his life. It is said that at least 60% of holders of all senior civil service and government posts, 20% of all top corporation executives and 40% of major business leaders are all 'Todai', ie graduates of Tokyo (Imperial) University. Access to the 'gakubatsu', or school and university cliques, starts very early in life so the Nakamuras' first concern is that little Ichiro gets the best start and works hard to make the most of it.

The morning we meet Nakamura is an unusual one for he has a slight 'futsukayoi' — a hangover. He had spent the previous evening at a farewell party for a young graduate who, after a year's training at Head Office, was being sent to the Company's branch in Osaka, 553 kilometres away. There had been only a dozen of them but, by Western standards, it was an unusual evening, for the party included the vice-president of the company and another main board director. All ranks were present and enjoyed themselves. The evening was an example of Japanese 'democarasu' together with the paternal spirit of the company. The vice president paid and Nakamura, among others, rather overdid it. In fact, he has a few drinks most evenings and rarely gets home until half past nine or ten. His wife would probably worry if he consistently came home earlier for this would suggest that something was wrong. The company give him an expense allowance, mostly tax-free, of nearly £6500 a year and expect him to spend it, if not all on entertaining customers, at least in enjoying the company of his colleagues, for this goes towards the integration of the company into a team. Mind you, although his working day is supposed to end at five pm, it is rare for him to leave the office before six-thirty or seven pm, and his loyalty to the firm would stop him from complaining even if business meetings kept him till nine, ten or later. Nakamura's company and his work is his life. Though his motivation may originate in the support of his family and the maintenance of his home, he is more likely to use the word 'uchi' (home) in reference to the organisation for which he works.

The Nakamura family eat breakfast in their one living-room flanked by the tiny kitchen; all are seated on a low Western-style suite. He is firmly attached to the traditional Japanese-style breakfast — Samurai food as he jokingly calls it — while his family go in for cereals, fruit and boiled eggs. Nakamura's breakfast is laid out in the precise traditional manner, in exquisite lacquered bowls and dishes on a lacquered tray (all of which can now be bought cheaply in plastic!) As with so many other everyday items in Japanese life, the whole meal is a minor work of visual, as well as culinary, art: Miso soup thickened with bean paste with a few strips of seaweed and cubes of bean curd cake in it, a raw egg which he mixes with soya sauce, a dish of sliced vegetables such as lotus root and the pickled giant Japanese radish, called 'daikon', another of Sashimi or cold raw fish slices and several smaller bowls of rice. All this he washes down with cups of pale green tea. While they eat, the colour television is on with news, weather reports, children's entertainment and the inevitable consumer goods adverts. Superimposed on the picture are the ever-changing figures of a digital clock reminding them that, even in the Land of the Rising Sun, time passes irrevocably and irreplaceably.

The breakfast does Nakamura's hangover good. He takes off his yukata, a printed cotton kimono, and puts on the jacket of his dark suit over the white shirt that is almost a uniform in Japanese offices. Only in his brightly-patterned tie is there any hint of flamboyance. In the lapel is the company badge that he always wears. In a society where rank is so vital an element, not only is his personal status important but, perhaps more, the status of his company. Company badges are not just for recognition purposes but are objects of pride, wearers of ichi-ryu (1st rank) company badges considering themselves superior to those of ni-ryu and san-ryu (2nd and 3rd rank) company badges. At the door Nakamura waves goodbye to his wife and children, picks up his umbrella and exchanges his 'tangatsu' for his outdoor shoes. Noticing that it has been raining overnight, he slips a light-weight pair of plastic galoshes over his shoes for the lane will be muddy, and dirty shoes are not welcome at the office. Before leaving he checks that he has his various pills in his pocket. He is very fit for his age but has a typically Japanese health complex, amounting almost to hypochondria, and carries a veritable armoury of vitamins, tranquillisers and pep pills, as well as his indigestion tablets. He is likely to visit the Company clinic about once a month with some ache, stomach pain, an incipient cold, or just because he hasn't been sleeping too well at nights. The clinic is a well-attended department and caters for all types of illness including the psychosomatic.

In the train Nakamura reads the paper that has been delivered at his house for, like most Japanese, he is a keen newspaper reader, getting through at least two a day, taking particular interest in the economic columns as well as the sport. (The three main national newspapers (shinbun) all have circulations of over 5 million.) There are other specialised commercial and industrial dailies which he will glance through at the office. Nakamura is still young enough to be among the section of businessmen who study management magazines in the hope of self-improvement, although the present promotion-by-seniority system leaves little scope for applying or gaining advantage from what he reads in them and books of the same type. At the kiosk he buys a packet of Hi-lite filter cigarettes and will probably get through forty in the day, though like most Japanese, he'll stub them out after the first few puffs. On the train, after skimming through the paper, he slips off his shoes and goes to sleep — at least on those mornings when he can get a seat! Though they may complain of insomniac nights, most Japanese seem to have an inordinate capacity for achieving 'instant sleep', even in positions of extreme discomfort.

As a commuter, Nakamura has a long, hard slog to get to work by eight-thirty. In winter there is the muddy walk, the half-hour run to Tokyo's Ueno station and the sardine tin subway trip to Shimbashi. The office doesn't open till nine, but it is prudent to be early and Nakamura is a prudent man. Although he is now a Section Manager, he works in a big open office which houses in his 'block' of desks, not only his twenty or so subordinates, but also the commercial director of Matsuda Ltd. Between them, at another grey steel desk, sits Hashimoto Seiichi, manager of the company's import-export department. The hard-faced Hashimoto has a good commercial brain but speaks nothing but 'Nihongo' (Japanese language) and he didn't go to Nakamura's university. Nakamura often wonders how he got the job with no qualifications or any ability in foreign languages. In fact, it was just a convenience in the company's promotion system. Though Nakamura resents Hashimoto's appointment, he's grateful that at least he's next in line for the job, an important one with further prospects as the firm's overseas interests and activities increase. Too often in Japanese companies, a man who can speak a foreign language tends to become a general dogsbody to all departments who can employ his talent and is at everybody's beck and call.

As it is, Hashimoto has only a year or so before retirement and Nakamura is poised to step into his shoes. As department manager he is likely to be constantly in contact with the company's president, Matsuda-san himself, leading to hopes of further promotion. Matsuda doesn't speak English, yet he is becoming more and more concerned with overseas business. If Nakamura could become his personal assistant, his power and influence, apart from material benefits, would be greatly increased. It is not unknown for a president's PA to become his successor, one of the few channels through which ambition may find expression without disturbing executive harmony.

Nakamura has experience of most departments of Matsuda Ltd, for Japanese firms are, except in technical positions, keener on producing generalists rather than specialists. He works long hours but, in common with many of his colleagues, he doesn't work particularly hard nor does he bring much originality to his job. To do so might destroy the harmony of the group in which his life is centred. Conformity is preferable and leads to security and a slow but certain progress up the company ladder. It is all part of knowing one's place in society, in one's company, in one's group — and keeping it. Any excessive display of initiative by a member of the group is likely to be to the detriment of others and hence to the group as a whole, and the group in Japan is far more important than its separate members. Action is dependent on collective decision, and such decision is only achieved by the agreement of all concerned. Even a majority decision is rarely, acceptable as it would necessarily have to be forced upon a minority. Thus the individual must subjugate his will to that of the group, unless he feels so strongly about the matter in question that he is willing to disturb the group harmony. The trouble is that even within his company, one man in his time — and some-times at the same time — is likely to belong to at least two groups. Of necessity, there is the group in which he works and, in all probability there is a group to which he is inherently linked by ties formed during his school and university days.

I have mentioned that Nakamura's firm and his life within it is basically more important to him than his home and family life, and in this lies one of the great anomalies, if not a set of anomalies, of Japanese society. The whole basis of its hierarchical structure is the 'household', which means not just the family but all who live in a certain dwelling. Here everything is guided by strict protocol — even the baby strapped on its mother's back learning to bow to its father when the wife bows to her husband. Somehow, however, although family protocol remains a feature of Japanese life, the concept of the family and the home, 'uchi', 'my house', 'my home' has become transformed so that its greatest significance, its principal focus, has become the place of work of the leader of the household, the company for whom he works. This is largely a reflection of the paternalistic nature of the Japanese company. Once Nakamura, the young graduate, had joined Matsuda, he and his employers entered into an unwritten social contract akin to marriage. He became bound in loyalty to the firm while, in its turn, the company virtually accepted responsibility for him for life. Nakamura did not just join a company — he became a member of a new 'family' and all his allegiance is now owed to Matsuda to which he is totally committed.

Nakamura's father-in-law, old Ito Susume, had been employed by Matsuda and it was thus that Isamu met his future wife, Ito Shizuko, a clerk in one of its factories. Part of their later prosperity was based on the engagement allowance and the marriage dowry that Matsuda paid to Shizuko when she chose to marry another employee, such an event being believed to add to the cohesion of the company as a team. When they married, they could have made their home in one of the many apartment blocks (Danchi) that surround the Matsuda factories but they preferred to live with the Itos until they could start buying a place of their own. In passing, we may note that the cost of the Nakamura-Ito wedding, a Shinto ceremony held in the resplendent wedding hall of a good but by no means top-class hotel, was some 3 million Yen, (over £6000) which is equivalent to about a third of the groom's family annual income plus 50 per cent of that of the bride— about 3 times the equivalent cost in Britain. In spite of its being a 'miai kekkon' (an arranged marriage), as are still about a third of the marriages in Japan today), with a 'nakodo', or go-between, to make the introductions, the Nakamuras are very happily wed. Where this custom still prevails, the future husband has the right of veto if his partner does not please him, a choice rarely afforded to the prospective bride. Though resplendent in Western morning dress, Isamu was totally eclipsed by Shizuko in full gold-embroidered kimono, obi, geta etc, her putative 'horns of jealousy' hidden beneath a broad-brimmed white hat about her raven-black hair.

While on the subject of expense, I should mention that Isamu's salary is now some 280,000 Yen per month or, at present exchange rates, about £7500 per annum. In fact he earns more, and his savings (some 20% of the total income) come largely from the twice yearly bonuses, 'o-chugen' at mid-year, and 'o-seibo' at the end of the year, that he is paid. The bonus rate is partly dependent on the prosperity or otherwise of Matsuda Ltd but the two generally amount to 25 or 30% of his basic pay.

These are the times of the year when the giving of 'okurimono' or presents is the custom, the New Year being the more important. Department store sales soar and it is at bonus time that the successful exporter of luxuries or consumer durables has the biggest chance of a killing if he can persuade a 'departo' to cooperate in a special presentation of his products. In passing, I would mention that in Japan the wrapping of a present is almost as important as the contents. Japanese shops and departos raise the business of gift-wrapping to an unbelievable level of artistry, and this applies to business gifts as well as to those among friends and families. The visiting businessman should bear this in mind as I found once to my cost. I had carefully chosen a particularly appropriate gift for an important Japanese business friend but left home without having time to wrap it. Though the kindest and politest of men, the recipient barely acknowledged it! Black and white wrapping, by the way, is used for funeral gifts— use bright colours.

Though I have given figures above, it is difficult to give a true comparison between Nakamura's financial position and that of his British equivalent. The cost of his tiny house has already been mentioned, as well as some of his perks and his expense account. But 280,000 Yen per month may not be all that much when beef costs 4000 Yen per pound and Scotch is around £16 a bottle! I might add that, while the general opinion is that Japanese women are second class citizens, Isamu, while taking major decisions himself, leaves most of the household's budgetary affairs to Shizuko. The Japanese wife is very much the family's Chancellor of the Exchequer, and hence is the important buying influence in all but the most major capital purchases.

The vast office is quiet when Nakamura, having hurried the kilometre from the subway, shakes the rain from his umbrella and slips his galoshes under his desk but, even at this time, one of the young secretaries is there to offer him a cup of green tea or a soft drink. She is dressed in a pale blue blouse with a darker blue tunic over it, making her look like a senior schoolgirl. The company women's uniform is, of course, all made of practical man-made fibres and, with suitable changing rooms, is provided free. Soon the office begins to fill up with noisy chattering employees, mostly under the age of twenty-five. Nakamura gets up and bows when Hashimoto-san, his immediate boss, arrives just before nine.

Nakamura doesn't get on with Hashimoto, but partly for the general good of the office and partly because he hopes to inherit the other man's job when he retires in a year or so's time, he does all he can to preserve a harmonious relationship. Nakamura is an athletic, outdoor type, fond of long country walks on Sunday and despises Hashimoto for his poor physique. Unlike some companies, the working day at Matsuda doesn't start with a company song — more like a hymn or anthem — but it does kick off with five minutes of physical exercises led by the senior man present. Standing next to his puny senior, Nakamura puts the minimum of vigour into the procedure so as not to cause his boss to lose face. Much of the motivation of the sarariman, as well as those above and below him in industry and business, springs from the desire neither to lose face himself nor to make others do so, that is to preserve the 'wa' or harmony of the group.

Whereas we, in the West, if we think of it at all, feel that benefits inherited from the past are our just and due rights, the Japanese, who mostly do think about it, consider that they are born with an onus of debt to the past. From birth they are under an obligation to parents, seniors, ancestors — to history — and more obligations are contracted on the road of life. These obligations and duties take many forms and have many names in the Japanese language, 'on' and 'giri' being the most common. The concept of these multiple obligations to everyone who has helped you, from the Emperor down, is intimately linked with the thoroughly hierarchical nature of Japanese society, the seeds of which were sown in the nation's early history, to flower ultimately under the Tokugawa shogunate and to live on into the Meiji, Taisho and Showa eras. (Japanese dates since the end of Shogunate rule are related to the reign of each emperor who, on accession, chooses a name for his reign: Mutsuhito (who wrote 38,000 poems in his lifetime) chose Meiji (enlightened government); Yoshihito, Taisho (great righteousness); his grandson Hirohito in 1926 chose Showa, meaning 'enlightened peace', perhaps foreseeing the latter part of his period on the throne. Thus 1979 is the 54th year of the present era.) Under Shogunate rule, every detail of action, behaviour, allegiance, even dress, were prescribed for every class of society. The Meiji modernisation may have totally changed that society but, in restructuring it, it built upon the existing customs and habits of orderliness, the security of knowing one's place and the hierarchical establishment. This consciousness of rank and position still pervades Japanese life, particularly in the working environment of the sarariman and this is strongly interlinked with a deep sense of loyalty. It is at times when loyalties conflict, that the sarariman is at his unhappiest.

Within his company, Nakamura is likely to owe some degree of allegiance to more than one group. First, he has a common tie with all those of his 'year-class', ie all those who joined Matsuda the same year. Then he is also closely linked to all those who were at university with him and, more loosely, to others, particularly seniors, who also went to the same university. Lastly, but to a lesser extent, there is a bond between members of the department in which he is now working, though this is likely to be less significant than the other two, formed earlier. When these loyalties conflict, which is frequently, they lead to the build-up of those inner tensions and nervous stresses which seem to be a characteristic of Japanese businessmen and of the sarariman in particular.

This day in Nakamura's life is an unhappy and complex one.

The telephone seems to persecute him more than usual, and he is worried by a number of particularly burdensome problems in which he must make personal decisions. A group proposal has been put forward that Matsuda should add an Italian company to its list of agencies and the vast majority of those concerned have approved of it. Nakamura is satisfied with the prices and delivery terms, but is not so sure of the quality of the Italian product nor of its marketability. Above all, he is convinced that communication with the manufacturers in Milan will cause major problems. The written proposal is among the papers on his desk awaiting the application of his 'hanko' or personal seal to add his agreement to that of his colleagues. Nakamura cannot bring himself to make the decision on how he should place the hanko. If he places it the right way up, signifying approval, he will be preserving the group harmony but will be acting contrary to his own strong feelings. To stamp the seal upside down means his total disapproval, and virtually the rejection of the scheme that so many of his colleagues believe in. Placing the seal sideways would indicate his qualified approval, but a degree of indecision that would not reflect to his credit with the director of his division of Matsuda. As he vacillates, the problem merges in his mind with another, the covering up of a mistake made by old Sato, an elderly clerk in Nakamura's department, that has cost Matsuda dearly. Though such practice may sound dishonest, it is not out of the ordinary in Japan. The group to which Sato belongs will take collective responsibility for his error and protect the offender. It is all part of preserving the harmony but Nakamura has to work out how the cover-up is to be done.

Nakamura usually lunches in the Matsuda office canteen with friends, where heavily subsidised meals are another company perk, but today he decides to go to a nearby coffee shop to mull over his problems alone. He has a hamburger with rice and salad and, unusually, a large bottle of Kirin beer. Back in the office, it's warm as the air-conditioning hasn't been switched on yet. He regrets the beer, finding it difficult to keep awake, and Iwabe-san, his director, who sits at the head of the block of desks of the department, is watching him. (Only the President and Vice-President have their own offices, the other directors using one of the many interview rooms for private conversations.)

Nakamura happens to glance at the calendar and is reminded that the following week the representative of a British company, for which Matsuda are agents, will be visiting Tokyo. He must make appointments for him with customers. Nakamura enjoys having Smith-san with him, but knows he may be in for a difficult time for sales have been far short of expectations. While phoning around friendly, prospective buyers, Nakamura starts working out what excuses he can make to Smith-san for falling so short of the agreed sales target. Traditional politeness demands that he should not be disappointed, yet the results of the sales efforts have been disappointing! Belatedly, Nakamura starts working out plans for a future sales campaign. By six o'clock he has become quite excited by the prospects he has worked out, painting a glowing picture of the as yet unrealised potential and suggesting an ingenious redeployment of the salesmen involved and their contacts with Matsuda's many sub-agents. (Most of these know little of Smith-san's product range.) He feels quite elated by his plans. Surely Smith-san will be pleased? How could it be otherwise?

Nakamura grabs his umbrella and dashes down to look for his friends, Shochi and Shingu, on the floor below, who are both concerned with the sale of Smith-san's products. They will go to a bar and discuss the English company's future sales plans and agree how they will handle the Englishman's visit. As things turn out, both Shochi and Shingu are still at their desks as are two of their junior salesmen, Kuroiishi and Yamamoto. The two youngsters, both eager to learn and to be taken into the company and confidence of their superiors — and to share a small part of their expense accounts, which they do not yet have — are happy to be invited along. The five take a taxi to the Roppongi district to spend the evening at the Badger Club where both Nakamura and Shochi are members. The club, one of thousands, is in a basement and, but for the dim, shaded lighting, would be a gaudy place. Like most of Tokyo's clubs — and those in other major cities — its purpose is to cater for the needs of the near-neurotic sarariman and executive, to soothe him and repair the ravages that his working day have wrought to his nerves.

The two members each have their own bottles of Suntory Gold Whisky which a tall young hostess sets before them with glasses, ice, soda and bowls of nuts. While drinking and talking, they order several platters of food that they share with their hashi (chopsticks), sashimi, salami and pickled vegetables. The conversation is curiously emotional rather than logical or intellectual, and many sentences are cut short to be left hanging in mid-air. "That pig ..." starts Nakamura, referring to Hashimoto but not defining him. Everyone knows who he is talking about, even the Kohai, the juniors, and all are sympathetic to Nakamura. The hostesses top up the glasses frequently and stay to talk attentively and long enough to distract the exhausted businessmen from the worries of their day. Around ten o'clock Nakamura makes his way a little unsteadily to the lavatory and is surprised to find a bundle of papers in his pocket. He peers at them short-sightedly and realises that they are his hurriedly-composed master plan for the new sales campaign. He returns to the table and finishes his drink. "By the way, Smith-san will be coming from London next week and we will have to report on sales and why they have not been so good. I have some notes here on what we should do to improve the performance. I must go now to catch my train or I would tell you about my plan. We will discuss it tomorrow in the office." He collects his umbrella and hails a taxi for Ueno.

We will leave Nakamura-san making his way unsteadily homewards with the comforting thought that he has worked off his inner tensions and can attack his problems afresh on the morrow. It is worth while noting that in Japan there is none of the social stigma of having 'one too many' that pervades Western society. There is no disgrace in getting slightly 'pickled' and this state is not viewed with the disdain and Victorian prudery that we self-righteously adopt. I remember a most enjoyable night out with three VIP Japanese directors of a well-known newspaper group. In a perfectly respectable club two of them fell to arguing the relative merits of their two universities most vociferously, almost to the point of reinforcing their respective opinions with their fists. It was quite a scene by Western standards. Later, as my third friend and I climbed into a taxi in the Ginza-dori, the two previously potential pugilists were left amicably supporting themselves with their arms round the same lamp-post. The most intriguing aspect of the whole affair was that none of the other people in the well-filled club took the slightest notice of my friends' noisy alcoholic altercation.

I do not in any way imply that all Japanese businessmen are 'yopparai' or drunkards, but those who do drink, and there are many, don't hold back. As with all activities, whether at work or at play, the Japanese can throw themselves in with a wholehearted enthusiasm and abandon of a staggering intensity that makes Europe seem like a land of zombies. Every time I leave Japan, I am struck by our wishy-washy Western approach to life in comparison with Japanese emotional ardour and earnest ebullience. This characteristic is doubtless an important element in their success in becoming the second industrial nation in the free world, with strong prospects of overtaking the USA to become 'Dai-ichi' — Number One!

Not only does Nakamura work a long day but he also works a long week. In theory there has been a progressive reduction in the working week of Japanese employees over the past seven years or so, but in practice it often doesn't work out that way — at least not for the sarariman. The scheduled programme of Saturday holidays is likely to be disrupted by unscheduled company meetings in the morning and even these are likely to spill over into the afternoons. Until about 1970 everyone worked the whole of Saturday with the slight concession that factories closed at four pm. (Even then there was no mad rush for the works gate as it was not considered seemly to be the first away!) At first the sarariman was allowed every third Saturday as a holiday but he could not completely cast away the company's cares. The holiday was a 'thinking day' on which he was supposed to contemplate outstanding job problems and the general affairs of the company. In many cases a written report on his cogitations was expected, so although he may have gained a little free time, the company's gain was greater in making him work at home and thereby save on lighting, heating or air-conditioning! However, this was the thin end of the wedge, and by now most staff and workers only work every third Saturday — apart from those special meetings. The latest Ministry of Labour figures published, however, still give an overall weekly average of 'hours worked per worker' as being over forty.

To round off the sarariman picture, it may be useful to add a word or two about Mrs Nakamura's day, though changes in her habits as a consumer will be discussed in a later chapter. The Japanese housewife generally leads a somewhat solitary existence, for her social life revolves round that of her husband and that is based, as we have seen, on his associations at work. Local friendships of any depth are not common so that, apart from a nodding acquaintance with other ladies of the neighbourhood, when the children have been packed off to school, she has a lonely time with little more than her household chores to occupy her. Of course she has the television with a wide choice of channels. She has an extensive range of household appliances to lighten her labours — washing machine, vacuum cleaner and floor polisher, electric rice boiler (percentage ownership figures for these and other consumer durables are given in Chapter 13), a stainless steel sink, gas water heater and a refrigerator. An interesting point about this last item is that, in spite of its efficacy, it has made little change in Mrs Nakamura's shopping habits as we shall see. This has significant consequences for those interested in exporting foodstuffs to Japan.

The Nakamuras are among some 35% of Japanese who have a Western-style bed, although the children, like old Mrs Ito when she lived with them, still sleep on 'futon' — soft mattresses — laid on the floor and, after hanging out to air on dry days, they are packed into cupboards, thus maximising the small space in the house. Mrs Nakamura hangs out the futon and washes up the dishes — by hand, as dish-washers are one of the few home appliances that are still not too common in Japan. Much of the inside of the house is of wood or veneer panelling and the natural patterns of the grain, brilliantly polished by Mrs Nakamura are a source of much pleasure to all who see them. She settles down to some dress-making with her electric sewing machine.

Later in the day, Shizuko cycles into the shopping centre which is concentrated near the railway station. The bicycle has greatly increased in popularity as a means of getting about since the 'oil shock'. It has long been used by tradesmen, restaurateurs and shop-keepers for delivering goods, and a common sight in city streets is a youth peddling recklessly through the dense traffic with an ingenious spring-mounted tray suspended from a frame above the rear wheel. The tray remains level no matter what the angle or change of speed of the bike, so that hot meals can be transported to customers at high speed without even a drop of soup being spilled! Over ten million bicycles are made a year in Japan, the second largest output in the world after the USA.

The shopping centre contains a supermarket, small by Western standards, which has recently opened. It is still adorned by huge excrescences of plastic sprays of brilliantly gaudy flowers indicating a new enterprise or a change of management in an old one. Shizuko is tempted inside and buys a few non-perishable necessities such as soap and toothpaste, her choice being considerably influenced by the continuous barrage of advertising to which the family colour television subjects her daily. She doesn't have to buy toilet paper often, as she gets supplies free from the contractor whose lorry comes round the neighbourhood collecting carefully saved waste paper!

There were over 12,000 self-service stores in Japan in 1974 (the last published figures) with over 10% of the total retail trade and, though increasing in popularity, these have to compete with over 720,000 smaller food and drink shops, two-thirds of them run by only one or two people. In spite of changes in the Japanese diet (discussed in Chapter 13) and in spite of her refrigerator, Shizuko prefers to go to the smaller shops for perishable foods. There she can enjoy not only personal service and a friendly chat with the proprietor, but often a gossip with other wives from the neighbourhood. Most important of all, however, is the question of the freshness of the food she buys. Old habits die hard and it is the confirmed custom of the Japanese housewife to satisfy her family's needs by buying each day just what she needs for the next twenty-four hours in the way of fish, vegetables and meat. So strong is this tendency that one may well wonder why some 95% of households have a refrigerator — unless just to keep the canned beer and soda water cool. Like most of her kind, Mrs Nakamura not only wants the freshest food available but she also wants to see exactly what she's buying.

While we are with her at the little food shops, it may be worth noting that the average diet of the Japanese today is some 2200 calories a day with 80 grams of protein, and consists by weight of 5% eggs, 5% meat, 17.5% milk and milk products, 12% fish, 30% fruit and green vegetables and 30% rice. Thirty per cent of the family's living expenditure goes on food, 10% on housing, 4% on fuel and 10% on clothing. Food is expensive, but the family budget stretches well as the Nakamuras do little entertaining at home, that side of living costs being dealt with by Isamu from his generous expense account.

The small percentage of meat in the diet derives from history, and contrasts oddly with the wide range of superb and ostensibly traditional meat dishes to be found in restaurants. As it is today, Mrs Nakamura is a poor customer of the butcher but spends well at the fishmonger.

Before leaving the Nakamuras, it is as well to take a brief look at how they spend the few leisure hours that they have as a family. At home television occupies a good deal of the time and, with pressure on the children to do well at school, firm parental control is necessary. The children have desks in their own rooms and are given every encouragement to study. Of TV programmes, sport and the endless succession of Samurai blood-and-thunder films which seem to me like an infinity of the tales of

Robin Hood, are popular favourites. The Nakamuras watch the periodical Sumo wrestling tournaments avidly, supporting their favourite contestants among the giant fighters. Whenever they have the chance they go to a baseball game or to a bowling alley. Baseball with Coke and hamburgers are the three most important elements of culture imported from the United States during the 1945-1952 Occupation, or so a jocular Japanese friend told me. Certainly, they have had a far greater influence on Japanese life than American management methods!

The Nakamuras have long resisted the desire to buy a car, and Isamu has the use of a company vehicle at work and can usually borrow one for weekends or holidays if he wants to. The latest (1976) figures show that there are over thirteen million cars in Japan (or 0.11 cars per person), but few of these are privately owned. Some years ago a major car manufacturer estimated that only one car in five was family owned. If the Nakamuras did buy a car, their prime motivation would probably be to keep up with the Tanakas, which was what drove them to buy the colour TV and the room cooler.

Holidays are irregular and disjointed in the Nakamura household for Isamu rarely takes the full period allotted by the company. There are, in the calendar, twelve National holidays from New Year's Day and the Emperor's Birthday (29 April) to Physical Education Day (10 October), the Autumn Equinox (23 September) and Old People's Day (15 September). (The visiting businessman would be well advised to check on these public holidays, listed in Appendix D.) When the Nakamuras do take a few days or a week off, they usually spend them at one of the company's holiday homes. Matsuda have two guest houses, one at the seaside near Kamakura, the other in the hot spring resort of Atami. At both, the excellent facilities are subsidised and cheap. Matsuda also organise several company or section outings during the year — days out to Nikko or Lake Hakone, all of which tend to strengthen the image of the firm as a home and a family, in a quite open and acceptable way. There is nothing subversive about it. It is an inherent element in Japanese company life.

We have noted Nakamura's desire to get to the top of Matsuda, but that the system makes him suppress open ambition. He is more likely to get there by healthy living and conformity. In the following chapter, we'll take a look at 'Life at the Top' in the Japanese business world.

CHAPTER SIX

Taikun At The Top

Life at the top in Japanese business obviously varies according to the size of the company concerned, but generally it isn't quite so lonely as it can be in the Western world. The Board of Directors — the subject of this chapter, rather than just the Chairman and President— is usually larger so that the many burdens of responsibility can be shared. At the same time the Japanese collective decision-making process by concensus does much to alleviate the stresses that such responsibility can bring.

I was once told by the President of a Japanese Company that if he was responsible for making a wrong decision, the choice of three courses was open to him: to resign; to commit suicide (seppuku — hari-kiri is only the traditional "belly-cutting" method); or to resign and then commit suicide! He was, of course, joking, for the decision-making process that is extensively used reduces his own degree of responsibility in company policy. In fact, only in the case of financial disaster is it necessary to find a scapegoat and even then, he may not always be the man at the top.

The hierarchy of a Japanese company is as follows:

Kaicho	Chairman
Shacho or Daihyo Torishimaryaku	President
Fuku Shacho	Vice President
Senmu Torishimaryaku	Senior Managing Director
Jomu Torishimaryaku	Deputy Managing Director
Torishimaryaku	Director

Below these, the executives are:

Hon Bucho	Divisional Chief
Bucho	General Manager

Bucho Dairi	Deputy General Manager
Kacho	Manager or Section Chief
Kacho Dairi	Assistant Manager
Kakaricho	Chief

At the bottom are:

Banto	Clerk, Secretary
Hambainin	Salesman, etc.

The chairman may or may not be a figurehead, taking little part in the company's (Kaisha) day-to-day affairs. More often than not, rather than an outsider elected purely for reasons of prestige, he is an ex-president, a gentleman with years of experience relevant to the company's affairs. Thus, even if his position is more honorary than executive, he is likely to wield considerable power. He is known to everyone in the firm and is a respected figure. Hence he retains a strong influence, particularly on the senior executives who know him best. The retention of retired senior men in business has a parallel in politics where the 'genro', a class of elder statesmen, continue to advise behind the scenes, to assist and sometimes to cajole, long after they have surrendered office.

Some commentators have stated that the company president, the real top man, is not always the brightest of the upper heirarchy, having obtained the position merely through promotion by seniority, but I have seen little evidence of this. Due to the intense reliance of Japanese companies on inter-personal relationships and the avoidance of disruption of harmony, one of the major concerns of the president is to select and train his successor, and it is here that the promotion-by-seniority system may be totally disrupted and even discarded. A younger man, only recently promoted to director, may be selected quite early to be groomed for stardom if he has the necessary qualities of leadership and empathy. Above all, the president is concerned with people, and the processes of judging their potential and placing them in the right positions and lines of promotion is probably his primary function, that is, when the man, at the age of about forty, reaches the end of the promotion-by-seniority ladder. The system by which this is carried out, especially in very large firms, is intriguingly unique to Japan.

The process is based largely on the 'gakubatsu' — the school and university cliques — or the 'old-boy network' as we would call it. 'Oya' is the word for parent and 'ko' for child in Japanese, and an informal system of 'oyabun-kobun' relationships serves to keep the top management informed of the progress of the junior executives, each of whom, as 'Kobun', has a senior man, the 'oyabun', taking a special interest in him. The oyabun who, in a large company, may have from fifty to a hundred kobun to watch over, will be a senior man not likely to be expecting much promotion and one who is not a direct superior of his kobun. For the first ten years or so of the young man's life in the company his progress will be watched and his good and weak points noted. His oyabun will see him frequently and always be available to give him advice, to listen to his problems and his ambitions. The oyabun acts very much like a supervisor or tutor in the British university system. At the same time he will have informal meetings periodically with the top management to summarise the progress of the protegés to whom he is father confessor.

In the previous chapter, the paternalistic nature of Japanese companies was noted and it follows that the president becomes, as it were, the adopted father of all his employees. So far as is possible, depending on the size of the company, he will know them and their families, their weaknesses, woes and worries. His approval will be sought for their marriages, his blessing at the birth of their children. The president's principal preoccupation is people, and principally the people who work for him. His job is to gain and maintain their confidence, to lead them, and to ensure that, as they progress, their talents are chanelled to the company's best advantage.

The taikun* (or 'Great Prince' from which we derive our 'tycoon') must preside over the slow and complex, but very effective, process of 'Ringi-Seido' or 'decision-making by concensus'. Progressive ideas may originate at any level in the company and at some stage will be crystallised into a 'Ringi-sho' or 'written proposal' which will be passed upwards through the heirarchical channels to the top. If the idea receives management approval in principle it will then be passed down again through a number of divergent channels so that it is seen and studied by everyone whom it may affect or who might be involved in its realisation. The proposal, if that is what it amounts to, will be discussed at every level and in every department concerned. Factions may form for and against it and the major factions will try to convert the minor factions to their way of thinking.

*This word is not a business term in Japan. Its use is purely historical.

Approval and disapproval may be expressed, as we saw in the last chapter, with Nakamura-san contemplating the application of his 'hanko'. Ultimately, after what we in the West would consider an inordinate delay, the Ringi-sho will surface again at the top and it is then that things start to happen.

There are many advantages to this apparently cumbrous system compared with our methods in Western business where decisions tend to be taken at the top, resulting in orders which will be received by subordinates with various degrees of enthusiasm or antagonism. In Ringi-Seido, the management can assess at a glance the impact of the proposal and who is in favour of it and who against. In some cases the proposal may be rejected, in others it may be returned for further consideration. If, on the other hand, there is a majority consensus in favour, management are able to channel it for action to the best effect by using their knowledge of its protagonists and antagonists.

A characteristic of the Japanese is their ability to reverse earlier policies and ideas totally and rapidly. As Peter Drucker commented in 1968, "The Japanese do not seem to have any economic theory at all. They swing back and forth from ultra-conservative to ultra-radical, all the time using whatever seems to work whenever the situation calls for it." This is perhaps the outward aspect of their 'system', which is in reality a most practical one. One of the benefits of Ringi-Seido is that small eruptions of original thought, from any level of the company, may lead to intensive and introspective thought about activities and policies of far greater significance than the Ringi-sho that provoked it. In questioning a suggested new path or policy, the Japanese tend to go further and devote their energies to defining the problem rather than finding the answer. If it turns out, by the consensus process, that a problem exists, then the same process will lead eventually to the answer. As in so many other ways, Japanese thinking differs radically from ours but is certainly not less effective. The important thing is for the foreign businessman to appreciate that, particularly in the early stages of negotiations and where a major policy or project is concerned, a long period may elapse before any decision is made or any communication received. Equally important is an understanding that to press the Japanese before they are ready is likely to be fatal. They will probably drop the whole thing like a hot cake and you will have to start all over again with another company.

Compared with the company's normal executive staff with

their compulsory retirement at the age of 55, the position is quite different in the upper management bracket. Once the senior executive has broken 'the sound barrier' into the rarified atmosphere of the boardroom, the situation changes completely. Consequently it is not uncommon to find company presidents soldiering on well into their eighties and still working effectively, as their major activity is the maintenance of good personal relationships between the company staff.

As well as these introvert aspects of top management, there is a wide range of extrovert activities requiring time and involvement due to the complex inter-relationships between business and government in Japan, to inter-company ties and responsibilities and to their heavy reliance on bank investment for capital. Labour-management relations may lack some of the vitriol that characterises them in the UK, but they are a problem that must be dealt with — which we will discuss in Chapter 7. Let us look first at some of the various aspects of Japanese company financial management.

For a start there is the matter of the banks. I have mentioned a Japanese company whose directors proudly boasted that they worked for themselves and not for the bank! This is, however, the exception, since it is most usual to find a Japanese company whose capital is largely in the hands of banks, usually from 20% to 80% of it. Exceptions like Toyota and Matsushita do exist but this leads mostly to the curious situation that frequently debt interest exceeds profits — but then profits generally are not the major concern of Japanese companies to the extent that they are in the West. Growth is the god of the taikun rather than profit to a degree that would frighten most Western money men. The goal of growth, in turn, often leads to diversification to which many Japanese companies and groups become addicted. Diversification frequently leads to an acquisition complex which neatly complements the distaste that the more successful firms have for passing inordinate amounts of money to their government in tax. Acquisition of foreign companies has the added attraction of gaining footholds in foreign markets in the most effective way. All these progressive activities involved consultation and decision in cooperation with major shareholders, ie the banks and insurance companies. An added complication may arise when a bank or more than one bank have substantial equity in more than one company in a certain field of industry or commerce, this being not at all uncommon when the bank is one of the giants integrated into the great 'zaibatsu' conglomerates such as Mitsui, Sumitomo and Mitsubishi. Originally family concerns, and often lead at first by ex-Samurai, these were the pacemakers in the Meiji Restoration forming then the first layer of cement between Government and industry. The close relationship formed over a century ago still exists and is still very much based on personal relationships on both sides. Our 'taikun' is thus still very much involved in government policy and at the same time dependent on it (the Bank of Japan having the whip-hand in all major financial policies). The success of Japan since the Second World War has relied much on the guidance of the economy by Government into the technologies of the future at the expense of those in decline. This has been achieved by easing the availability of capital for approved 'advanced' industries while restricting it for those in which the competitiveness of Japan was non-existent, negligible or likely to decline.

The tycoons of Japanese industry have multifarious backgrounds, for the history of the country has encouraged the entrepreneurial spirit since the inception of the Meiji era. The huge 'zaibatsu' organisations established then were mostly split up during the MacArthur occupation but have largely reformed themselves into commercial groups or conglomerates little different from their dichotomised ancestors. But Japan is a land of opportunity where the hard-working small industrialist with products that match Japan's vision of the future can prosper. Perhaps indirectly, Mikimoto Koichi was one of the first in prising open the secrets of the oyster and creating the cultured-pearl industry in which the most labour-intensive activity is that of the oysters themselves! His tale, dramatically displayed at Mikimoto Pearl Island in Ago Bay, Mie Prefecture, is rather one of the last century, dating from before his patent of 1896, but there are many who have displayed similar originality and tenacity of purpose and prospered while becoming national, if not world famous, names in more recent years. The New Otani Hotel, with over 2000 bedrooms, a dozen bars and many restaurants, is well known to British visitors and is said to be the biggest in Asia. It is a small town in itself, established, built and run by Otani Yonetaro who started work as a labourer, spent some time as a Sumo wrestler, then moved into commerce as a saké-merchant. The hotel, set incongruously in its vast and beautiful Japanese garden was, however, just a diversification, for Mr Otani's real business was the Otani Ironworks.

Honda Soichiro started the Honda Motor Company from scratch in 1948, and took only ten years to become the biggest motor cycle manufacturer in the world before moving into cars and agricultural machinery. Motorbikes are only 32% of total sales now while an output of 700,000 cars was expected in 1977. Banks, Trusts and Insurance Companies own 23% of the stock.

Matsushita Konosuke's story is equally dramatic. He founded his first company as a comparatively uneducated mechanic in 1935. Now the group, Matsushita Electric Industries, comprises eight major companies. Matsushita Konosuke is the Chairman of only one today, Matsushita Electric Works, but owns 3.7% of the stock of Matsushita Electric Industrial, 3.4% of Matsushita Electric Industries, 7.1% of Matsushita Electric Works and 8.9% of Matsushita Seiko. To keep it in the family Matsushita Masahara is President of Matsushita Electric Industrial and Chairman of Matsushita Communication Industrial. This remarkable pioneer industrialist, now 83 years old, spends much of his time on the PHP Institute which he founded just over 30 years ago. PHP stands for Peace, Happiness and Prosperity and the Institute is dedicated to the promotion of human understanding and tolerance on a world-wide basis. Dreams, he says, keep him young but his dreams are of the future and not of the past.

There are many similar success stories, like Bridgestone Tire, eighth among the tyre makers in the world and founded in 1931. Ishibashi Kanichiro, the Chairman, owns 13.4% of the stock while another 8.6% is in the hands of other Ishibashis and the Ishibashi Foundation has 9%. ('Ishi' is the Japanese for stone, 'bashi' is a bridge). Mr Hattori of the Seiko watch firm is another self-made success story.

These entrepreneurs, as well as being involved in the management of the major manufacturing and trading groups, are also considerably involved in a number of employers' industrial and commercial organisations which have interfaces both with government and labour. The different Trade Associations, too, form an important element in their activities. Prominent among the former are the Keidanren, the equivalent to our C.B.I., the Nikkeiren or Japanese Federation of Employers Associations, and the Japan Committee for Economic Development. There are government committees, too, on which industry is represented by leading management figures, such as the Prime Minister's Economic Deliberation Council which has many satellite committees in different fields, and the Trade Council again

chaired by the Prime Minister. There is also the Nihon Shoko
Kaigisho, or Japan Chamber of Commerce and Industry.

A vital characteristic of the Japanese industrial scene, and one
that has contributed much to the country's post-war 'economic
miracle' is the close cooperation that exists between government
and industry. While business in the West tends to resent the
intrusion of the men from the Ministry, in Japan the attitude is in
the main quite the opposite. Whilst other Ministries are involved,
the Ministry of International Trade and Industry (MITI), is the
most relevant to manufacturing industry and keeps continuous
contact with top management in key sectors of industry. The
two-way flow of information thus established, as well as the
contribution of the powerful and well-organised trade associations, contributes greatly to the formulation of national policy
and planning, the beneficial results of which are apparent in
Japan's surging economy, and her success in evolving from a
feudal state to the second industrial nation in the world in only
some 120 years. The origins of this friendly cooperation and lack
of antagonism between government and industry can be traced
historically to the early Meiji period when it was the bureaucrats
who literally created Japan's embryo industry when none but the
most primitive existed before.

Once again, personal relationships become involved and close
links become forged between industrialists and civil servants
which in turn lead to closer association. The latter tend to retire
early, usually at 55, on not very favourable pensions. While there
are regulations governing their further employment in companies with which they have dealt in their official capacities,
respected civil servants on retirement are welcomed warmly into
industry and appointed to responsible senior positions where
their previous experience and contacts can be invaluable.

What are they like, these hard-headed businessmen and industrialists who have got to the top? Obviously all types of men are
to be found among them, but they tend to have attributes and
characteristics in common. They are mostly, at this stage in their
lives, cultured, thinking men with at heart an appreciation of
beauty in the broadest sense, but in the smallest things — for only
in the vast unusable non-populated areas of Japan is beauty to be
found on the grand scale. They live their working lives, as do
their subordinates, in the ugliest, noisiest and busiest environment that man has probably ever created and hence derive the
greatest pleasure from small slices, tiny vignettes, of natural or

man-made art and, of course, they can afford to do so. A company president I have met has a 150 year old miniature tree (bonsai) outside his secluded office window. It cost about £10,000 and is a masterpiece of the cooperation between man and nature. Opposite his desk stands a 3-foot rock of some sort of striated granite or marble, the centuries of natural weathering having been embellished by hours, days of human muscle-power, bring out the grain of the natural material. Mounted on its ebony plinth, this stone cost more than the bonsai tree. Japanese objets d'art, paintings, sculpture, pottery and calligraphic scrolls (which we will discuss in greater detail in Chapter 12), are eagerly collected and proudly displayed. Just as companies vie with each other in their prestigious office blocks, and even their contributions to 'charitable' causes (and these include the political field), their leaders compete in the display of 'art'. A study of the 'Saleroom' column in the *Financial Times* indicates the rapidly growing trend towards buying (investing in?) Western art, particularly the French Impressionist school. Just as Mrs Nakamura can now afford all the best in home gadgets and labour-saving devices, her husband's boss, Matsuda-san, doesn't have to stint himself for a Renoir, a Picasso or a Vlaminck for his home or office. In fact he has to have one, for his major competitor, Takashima Masako, has bought a Manet for the boardroom!

Matsuda-san, and those like him, can afford, too, not only to buy the best set of golf clubs and all the gear that goes with them but he can even lay out enough yen actually to play golf— and on the best courses in the country. A friend of mine was promoted to director of his main group board. He wasn't a golfer but business ethics necessitated his membership of a major snob Tokyo golf club, so that he could entertain there even if he didn't hit a ball about, tactfully letting his important customers win. The company paid for his privilege. I do not know what club he joined but in a country where there are less than 1000 courses for perhaps 5 million players, the initial membership fee is between 3 million Yen and, for the classiest courses, 40 million (an incredible £100,000 at today's rate of exchange!). On top of this there is a proportionate annual subscription, and fees per round approach £100. Little wonder that the plethora of driving ranges around all the major cities do excellent business, for a great majority of the Japanese who have all the expensive equipment necessary have little chance of ever getting on to a real golf course.

Executive toys for those in the upper brackets of Japanese

business range far ahead of those swinging stainless steel balls seen in managerial office suites in the West. For example, a few years ago, production of a peculiarly sophisticated, highly priced best seller started. This was a mechanically-operated, full-sized replica of a horse, covered with a whole real horse hide. The 'rider' merely had to mount this mechanical monstrosity and switch on to obtain a simulated ride along whatever is the Japanese equivalent of Rotten Row, Richmond Park or Epsom Downs without ever leaving the privacy of his home exercise room. The Japanese preoccupation with health no doubt contributes to the popularity of this artificial 'uma', for riding is reputedly a good stimulant to tone up the system.

I do not need to record these remarks in a derogatory tone. I am only suggesting that top men in Japanese business and industry receive top salaries which are not immediately 'clawed back', as the cliché goes, in tax. They work hard, carry a heavy burden of responsibility to their employees, their stockholders, to their parent-group boards if they have them and to society as a whole, for which they receive due reward that they can spend as they choose. The extravagance of the executive 'rocking-horse' does not imply that senior Japanese industrialists are children, though they have an engagingly boyish sense of humour. There is no doubt, though, that they are prone to fall for the latest and most expensive craze and are as desirous of keeping up with their competitors as the sararimen in a lower price bracket. Clothes, accessories, office gadgetry or leisure equipment — if it's exclusive, they'll buy it. Yet, while owning and using the best that money can buy, a great number of these 'taikuns' will still change into a cotton yukata and relax at home with simple traditional pleasures.

Japan is a land of anomalies and anachronisms, and the contradictory components in the daily lives of V.I.P. businessmen and industrialists can be as puzzling as any others to the gaijin, or foreigner. Although many of them live in comparatively grandiose houses mainly of Western style,their homes will rarely be without one or more traditionally Japanese rooms where they can get back to real values and restore in themselves the traditional spirit of Japan upon which their day-to-day leadership of their subordinates is dependent. It is the company presidents

* earlier it was the name for one of the provinces of Kinai whose principal town was Nara.

who must channel this inherent spirit— 'Yamato tamashii' as it is called, Yamato being the old name for Japan* — into the drive that will carry his company forward. An important aspect of this harnessing of people's energies is a matter of industrial relations which we will discuss in the following chapter.

I have described the Ringi-Seido process of decision making and mentioned its merits and disadvantages. As with many other aspects of Japanese life and business, there are slow moves towards changing both Ringi-Seido and the system of promotion-by-seniority, but the pace of change is almost imperceptible. Tradition dies hard in Japan but some companies have been taking steps to overcome the slowness of the orthodox means of arriving at major policy decision. The Ataka-Sumitomo-Itoh affair is a case in point.

Ataka, tenth in the major trading company league, was on the point of bankruptcy in 1975 when its main banking support, Sumitomo, asked its own trading company partner to decide if it could take over the failing firm. A decision was wanted in three days! Sumitomo Shoji declined to consider it, as more like six months was needed to reach such a major decision if everyone concerned was to be consulted. The bank next approached C. Itoh, then fourth in the charts. Itoh agreed to a takeover almost by return post. C. Itoh, a relatively new company compared with the Mitsubishis, the Mitsuis and others, already had a process of by-passing Ringi-Seido. Their 'strategic planning team' or Sejima Kikan, was named after deputy chairman, Mr Sejima Ryuzo, an ex-army staff officer who headed it. Sejima, whose wartime experience had developed in him the ability to make urgent decisions and take action quickly, adapted military techniques to industrial problems. Highly respected in his company, his 'shock-troop' decision making team was able to short-circuit the usual ponderous process without disrupting the harmony of the company. Having lost out on this one, Sumitomo Shoji, under a new president, soon built up its own commando 'think-tank' of senior executives with a similar brief and function. These cases are the exceptions and it may be a long time before other major companies relax their inflexibility and adopt this sort of approach. It is apparent, however, in many medium-sized firms, like our mythical Matsuda Ltd, where the average age around the boardroom table is likely to be nearer forty than seventy.

Before we go down onto the shop-floor and take a look at the work-force, I should mention that normally in a Japanese company all the executives up to Hon-Bucho (listed on pages 88-89) are almost certain to be trade union members. In some of the younger companies the carrying of union cards goes even higher — I know a vice-president of a firm with 5000 employees who is a union member. The union? Well, it's not the Boiler-makers, nor the Transport and General, nor even the Association of Scientific Microscope Watchers and Firemen. It's just the company union!

CHAPTER SEVEN

Showroom On The Shopfloor

No nation that I know of is so full of anomalies as the Japanese and, as soon as you get used to one, another crops up. It's odd to find a language that can be written either horizontally or vertically and books that are read from the back to the front, but the ambivalence and dichotomous nature of Japanese trades unions seems even more curious to me, particularly when compared with the state of the unions in the West.

Though recent statistics suggest that the number of strikes and of those involved in strikes in Japan, which rose sharply during years of high inflation, is not very different to those in the United Kingdom and their average duration tends to be similar, there are very few long strikes in Japan. Disruption is generally less for a number of possible reasons. For a start worker solidarity is far less developed in Japanese industry. As many unions are one-company unions, here at least inter-union strife and demarcation disputes cannot occur. Again, while profit-sharing in the full sense of the term is not general in Japan, extensive disruption of production or service is bound to affect the company's prosperity and this in turn will be reflected in the size of the workers' bonus payments. Thus a lengthy strike in support of higher wage rates, even if successful, may result in a fall in a man's total annual income. In any case the democratic atmosphere in most factories, added to the more generally widespread accessibility of management, tends to allow grievances to be aired and discussed before they become major issues.

In reading so much about the major names in Japanese industry, one might get the impression that Japan is a land of giant manufacturing companies. This is quite erroneous. In the jumbled miscellany of buildings crowding the back streets of any Japanese city, you will find tiny workshops crammed alongside houses, restaurants and stores. Much of the year the front will be open and in the cluttered interior, with perhaps a single lathe or power press, one man and his family or helpers will be toiling twelve or more hours a day turning out machine components for a sub-contractor to a supplier who deals with the manufacturer using the assemblies. In suburban Osaka I have come across little engineering companies building prototype machines for bigger companies, the standards of their workmanship being remarkable in such primitive surroundings. According to the latest available statistics (1972) the manufacturing industry consisted of 794,000 'establishments' employing 13,336,000 workers (30.3% of the total workforce), yet 407,000 of these firms or 51% of the total number consisted of only 1 to 4 persons. In fact 754,000, or nearly 95%, had under 50 people in them and only 5000, or 0.63%, had over 300 employees on their payrolls. The total number of employed workers at this time was 43,949,000 and the total number of 'enterprises' in the country was 5,309,000. In the same year Japan had 63,718 labour unions with a membership of 11,772,000 people, ie only 26.8% of the workforce carried union cards.

In contrast to the nearly 64,000 unions in Japan, in 1973 in Britain there were 495 with a membership of 11,507,000 out of a total working population of 25,578,000, and there are many who would say that we have too many separate unions! (In 1973 in Britain there were 90 unions with less than 100 members, while at the other end of the scale 23 large unions had over 100,000 members each with a combined total of over 7 million members.)

A factor that strongly inhibits aggressive employee attitude towards management is the promotion-by-seniority system. Knowing that, unless he sins almost to the point of something criminal, his wages will rise annually and promotion will come as the years pass by until the stage when he himself becomes "management", has a sobering tendency that damps down excessive belligerence. Who is going to risk spoiling a reasonably certain future in his job by excessive displays of antagonism? Not the average man who earns his daily bread (or rice) from the paternalistic company — only the full-time union executive! Which brings us back to the structure of the Japanese union system. The fact is that organised labour is not nearly so highly organised as in the West, though almost yearly the muscle of the unions is developing.

For a start the craft-type unions are very few, the powerful

Seaman's Union being incongruously balanced at the other end of the scale by the tiny association that looks after the interests and establishes the pay and conditions of the declining Geisha trade (see Chapter 10). The great majority of unions are the so-called Enterprise Unions, one union per company (or in some cases two, a white-collar and a blue-collar union). Each union is thus very much more closely involved in the day-to-day problems of the management as well as the weekly, monthly and yearly performance of the whole company. Thus, while labour and management may have their differences, their interests are so closely linked that only rarely will the company union cause any major or prolonged disruption. A brief show of force is usually sufficient to put their point. Japanese industry, in fact, epitomises the obverse of the British industrial relations coin. While here our inheritance from being the originators of the Industrial Revolution is perpetual strife, Japanese industry has no such legacy of 'bosses v. workers' to contend with, but instead a long social tradition of everyone knowing his place and keeping it, together with the widespread and deeply ingrained desire to preserve harmony at, almost, all costs. In Britain all we have that is comparable is the good old public school spirit of 'not letting the side down' and 'it isn't cricket', in which the inherent dogma of privilege being inevitably accompanied by responsibility was taught, but only to the small minority who had the benefit of this restricted channel of education

Another factor possibly inhibiting the 'effectiveness' of union power is the diffuseness of their organisation. Whereas in Britain, we have a single body, the T.U.C., to which the majority of unions are associated, in Japan there are no less than four major labour confederations: Sohyo, the General Council of Trade Unions representing 35% of organised labour in Japan; Domei, the Japanese Confederation of Labour (18.6%); Chirutsu Roren, the Federation of Independent Unions (11.2%) and the very tiny but influential Shinsanbitsu, or National Federation of Industrial Organisations. The objectives of these four bodies may be broadly similar but their power is clearly diluted by their being divided. Only Domei belongs to the International Confederation of Free Trade Unions and seems to be active in learning techniques from unions in other countries. However, this is not to say that the unions are not active. I once went to the Tokyo head office of a company to find a noisy group of thirty or forty demonstrators picketing the front door, equipped with banners, head and arm-bands. They were, I later learned, 'professionals' from one of the federations and not members of the company, the company union having no affiliation. In spite of their vociferous display of belligerence, I found them strangely thoughtful. When they barred my way through the door, I explained that I had to get in as I had business with the company and had come all the way from England for it. One of them spoke good English and, on hearing this, led me round to a back entrance, bowing me in with the politest of smiles. The logic behind this strange behaviour was that his group had no quarrel with me, so I could go in, but only by the back door, for, to let me in the front door, would be for them to lose face! While I was going through my part of the pantomime, an even better act continued at the front door where the demonstrators were sticking up posters on the glass doors of the prestigious office block which were promptly torn down by company officials, to be replaced by the demonstrators, to be again torn down ... and so on until someone tired, ran out of posters or it was time to go home!

The basis for the existence of the unions and the present labour laws originates in the post-war Constitution of Japan of 1952. The Labour Standard Law, Trade Union Law and Labour Relations Adjustment Law go far to produce a legal framework for wages, hours, holidays, disputes and negotiations, overtime rates, etc. not widely different from our own situation. The very different industrial climate and the success of Japan in terms of productivity and GNP per head originates from the combination of a number of factors.

Pride in one's company and in the nation and the country, and pride in one's work are foremost. I have been in Japanese factories where the pace, enthusiasm and total involvement of the workforce made even the hard-working Germans look like zombies. Except in heavy industry, a large number of women are employed, and not just for their manipulative skill at fine machinery and assembly. Their dedicated concentration on the work in hand wasn't due to the presence of a scowling foreman looking over their shoulders. They were working hard for the success of their groups and their company, this in turn depending on communication.

Japanese management are experts in motivation through communication. Not only production figures but sales and profits, etc. are passed on to the workforce. If the company is doing well, this encourages them; if it is doing badly, everyone is concerned with finding out why and putting the matter right, and everyone works harder to make up for bad performance. Production figures for the factory are posted up and discussed daily, as also for each department, so that everyone is aware of any fall off of efficiency. It is notable, too, that where a number of workers are employed on the same task, they freely accept that the norm should be that of the quickest and most productive, rather than that of the slowest and least efficient on the shop. These attitudes are partly rooted in national characteristics inherited from the past and partly spring from the leadership of management and the paternalistic and hierarchic nature of the company of their society. Japan never passed through a period of Industrial Revolution like Britain in which the divisive attitude of 'bosses' and 'workers' was framed. In Japan, the president may be the boss but he is also accepted as a worker. Everyone in the company is on the same side.

This is emphasised by the wearing of the company uniform, generally a grey, blue or dark-green battle-dress type of garment, at least for the men, in a practical man-made fibre, together with a peaked forage cap. At the factory even the president is usually to be seen in battle-dress, and this tends towards unification of employees and management, and the building up of the company spirit. The 'oneness' of management and labour is further stressed by having a common canteen for everybody — no executive dining suites and cocktail cabinets here! Everyone is working for the common cause and receives the same treatment.

Obviously Japanese industrial life is not a total paradise. Differences and disagreements must occur — apart from the so-called 'Spring Offensive' that we will come to shortly. An ingenious solution to the problem of the discontented employee was reported some time ago to have been adopted in the Matsushita factories. Here, if any worker felt that he had a grudge against a superior, the matter would naturally be reported and action taken if warranted. In the meantime, however, the disgruntled employee was allowed ten minutes or so off work and went away to a special room set aside and equipped for a process of 'regruntlement'. One or more straw effigies would be suspended from the ceiling and a good stock of bamboo poles supplied. For the next few minutes the agrieved employee worked off his aggression by beating the daylights out of the effigy. Matsushita, it is reported, have few industrial disputes and an excellent record of labour-management relations.

A noticeable feature of most Japanese factories of any size is the newness of the plant and machinery. One of the advantages of losing a major war seems to be that the enemy make a clean sweep of all your old factories and machinery for you and then help you to replace everything with the newest and best. Japan and Germany both benefited in this way and both, being down on their knees, made post-war recoveries that have been called economic miracles. The German miracle seems to have slowed down somewhat, if not to have ground to a halt. The Japanese continue to forge ahead and a contributing factor must surely be their continual policy of replacement of plant. Being a land where natural disasters— earthquake, typhoon and flood— have been battering their property for centuries, the Japanese generally have an ingrained sense of the transitoriness of physical things. In the cities no street ever seems to be the same as it was when you last saw it. Demolition and construction seem never to cease and buildings, only a few years old, are replaced with others which are bigger, better or more suited to their purpose. (There is even a centuries year old temple at Ise which is deliberately destroyed and exactly rebuilt every twenty years!). Similarly in the factory, few machine tools are more than five years old. If something better comes on the market, the old one will be scrapped and replaced. Much the same attitude pertains in the average household. Except for a few highly treasured possessions, many other things are temporary and expendable. The West didn't invent the 'Throw-away Age.' The Japanese have lived in it for years.

Thus investment in up-to-date capital plant and equipment is high, and hence productivity per worker is at a level to be envied. Recently published figures show that in Britain each worker in manufacturing industry is backed by some £7500 worth of assets. In comparison, the Germans invest about three times as much, or £23,000, while the Japanese quadruple our investment at £30,000 per employee. The moral is self-evident when one looks at the states of our three economies.

Unemployment in Japan is low by our standards, even after the OPEC oil price rises which increased the country's import bill for fuel by a factor of 3 to 4. The latest unemployment figure I have is about 1,250,000 or 2.37% of the labour force. Yet, in their search for efficiency and their confidence in the future, the Japanese have invested much money in the development of industrial robots of far greater sophistication than those found even in the USA. A national development policy has laid the main guidelines to include such features as sensory feed back so that a telechiric hand, automatically controlled, will know if it has grasped two blanks or components instead of one. Again, the incorporation of 'vision' via a television eye is among the projects receiving attention. The result is that, in many Japanese factories, repetitious jobs like component and material handling and spot-welding are done by these machines. It is significant that at the same time, the same companies who have initially guaranteed lifetime jobs to their 'permanent' employees, will, if forced to cut production, ask some employees to stay at home on reduced salaries rather than make them redundant. Such a policy is reciprocated with an intense loyalty from the employees.

Expenditure on research and development is equally significant. Starting from the ashes of the last war, the Japanese began in many fields of industry by buying know-how in the form of technical licensing agreements. M.I.T.I. dealt harshly with the few companies who would try to perpetuate the reputation of the Japanese for 'copying', and ensured that the knowledge acquired was paid for. Now, in innumerable fields, the Japanese, by their curiosity, ingenuity and hard-work, have surpassed their licensors and the flow of know-how is in the opposite direction. In my own field of industry this hasn't yet happened. Japanese licensees have taken time to absorb existing technology from the USA and Europe and to master the production techniques involved. Twenty-five years ago they had no oil-hydraulic industry at all. Three years ago they overtook Germany to become the second biggest producers in the world. As a Dutch professor who lectures at Osaka put it to me, "All this time they have been studying the 'know-how'; soon they will get interested in the 'know-why' and then we shall see something.' One of my own motives in efforts to get a slice of the Japanese market was not just patriotic export-mindedness, but a similar belief that, when ultimately the Japanese had mastered all we had to teach them, their research and development effort would begin to churn out designs in advance of our own. Having a foothold there, my company would be in a favourable position to acquire knowledge from those who had once been our pupils. It has happened in many industries, and prospective British exporters of technical products would do well to consider such a policy in their long-term planning. Research and development departments in Japan range from the vast, hygienic, glittering laboratories of the big companies to the little back-street workshops I've described. They have one thing in common — Japanese ingenuity and brains and a high level of technological training. It all goes back to the wisdom of the Meiji rulers in making a top priority of education, while launching the Japanese from their isolation into a policy of finding out everything the rest of the world knew about a subject — and then adapting it and improving it.

I have mentioned the development and use of robots in industry: what about computers? As the development of the microprocessor and the mini-computer proceeds at such a pace, it is difficult to give any precise figures. It is clear, however, that as in other advanced technologies, the Japanese, if not being world leaders in development at present, are at least well up in the user league in which they are second only to America.

Some of the benefits that the bigger Japanese companies, at least, provide for their employees have been described in Chapter 5 and shop-floor workers obtain similar advantages to those of the sarariman: company housing, sports facilities, pensions, insurance, medical attention and subsidised canteen meals are among these. Housing is probably the most important since, though they may not always look particularly attractive, the big blocks of company flats near many factories are often a great improvement on the primitive and overcrowded dwellings into which those less favoured are often compressed. Housing and sewerage are two amenities in which Japan is backward in marked contrast to her modern face in other fields. Both are the subject of much Ministerial attention but progress is slow overall.

In writing about the unions I have perhaps given a rather excessively Utopian picture. Certainly there is opposition to changes in production schedules that might call for greater output with no increase in reward. Unions have opposed and do oppose mergers, the introduction of merit-based rather than seniority-based wages and many other aspects of work and its environment, but they are far less militant than those in many Western countries. Naturally they fight hard against any infringement of the Labour Laws, but such infringement by management is uncommon in any case. The real testing time of union power comes once a year when the annual review of wages, bonuses and allowances is due. This is the so-called 'Spring-Offensive or 'Spring-Struggle', although if a satisfactory agreement is not reached, negotiations may well drag on into the autumn and, with them, a continuity of minor disruptions that can be far from beneficial to a company's commercial activities. These take such forms as banning overtime, holding union meetings during working hours, and the occasional appearance of groups of professional union demonstrators.

The Spring-Offensive is the one occasion on which major unions tend to coordinate their actions and to work effectively together. While many of the 'enterprise unions' carry on negotiations with their own management individually, other meetings are held between union leaders and management representatives of major industrial sectors, and the results obtained at this level tend to be reflected in settlements throughout each industry. The settlements reached are not entirely uniform and the distribution of increase is mainly left to individual company managements. The averages are very much reflections of the overall economy of the country and hence of industry, relating to such factors as inflation, taxation and budgeting policies, while individual agreements are greatly dependent on the fortunes of the separate companies concerned.

Some people are still of the opinion that the success of Japan as an exporting nation is based on low wages, but the concept that the Japanese are paid a "bowlful of rice a day", if ever true, is certainly not now. Following "oil-shock" in 1973, Japan entered a period of severe inflation, but it is significant that average wages have increased, due to the Spring-Offensives, faster than prices. For instance, in 1973 while the consumer price index rise was 11.7%, average wages increased 20.1% and in the following year the figures were 24.5% and a staggering 31.8%. The workers continue to become more prosperous, although both inflation and wage increases have now tailed off to a more acceptable level. An interesting comparison made in 1974 of hourly wages in different countries converted into US Dollars at then current rates of exchange, unfortunately excluded the UK, but showed that while the US worker received 4.4 per hour average, the Swede 4.22 and the Germans 3.62, French and Italian employees only rated 1.84. The Japanese had by then reached 2.82 — hardly a "bowlful of rice a day"!

Compared with the preference for generalists on the commercial and management sides, down at the factory great numbers of specialists are employed in the required technologies. Most of these are university qualified engineers and scientists who may expect to keep to their own specialties throughout their careers. It is, however, not uncommon for them to be sent on refresher courses from time to time to ensure their expertise, particularly in rapidly advancing technologies. They will also probably attend far more technical symposia and seminars than their Western, counterparts. Knowledge to the Japanese is the key to progress, and knowledge in technology, at least, is constantly changing and growing. On the shop-floor, too, continuous processes of education are available for self-improvement and personal development. A man employed as a milling machine operator may be valued for his skill but will be encouraged to take a course in welding, electronics or sheet metal work if he expresses an interest. Such vocational training is mostly given in in-house courses in the training schools of larger companies, and the machinist will show no surprise to find himself next to a director or even the president! The men at the top never lose their desire to know as much as possible about what goes on at the bottom. They may not wish to become machinists or sheet metal fabricators, but the more they know about these esoteric practicalities upon which their businesses rely, the more they will be able to understand the lives and problems of those whose jobs they are. It is all part of the image and the reality of the company as a family, just as most intelligent parents take an interest in their children's schoolwork.

I do not know if Japanese companies have a greater tendency to take their customers to see their manufacturing facilities, but they can usually take a pride in doing so. The medium and large Japanese factories are truly show places of order, cleanliness, efficiency, planning, organisation, teamwork and the company spirit. Even where land is at a premium, trim lawns and beds of shrubs are carefully laid out and tended so as to rival the efforts of the groundsmen at Lords or Wimbledon. Spacious and impressive entrance halls may lead to stark and uncompromising interview rooms but are staffed by smiling and bowing young females in trim uniforms, permanently poised to refresh the visitor with a welcome and thirst-quenching cup of green tea or an iced drink in summer. Photographs, models and samples of the company's products are proudly displayed as well as such desirable acquisitions as awards from the Industrial Safety Council. If much of this sounds to you just what you've seen in the Western industrial world, my descriptive powers must have failed me. To me, there is in the Japanese factory an indefinable difference at all levels — pride in the job and the worship of the success of success. And everywhere, behind it, but exerting a powerful and sensible influence, 'Yamato tamashii', the spirit of

Japan. The Japanese have an expression for a particularly hard worker — 'Shigoti no Oni' or work devil. They seem to be oblivious to the fact that the whole of their nation, or a very high percentage of it are Shigoti no Oni.

The picture that I have painted here of industrial life may seem excessively Utopian and based on a degree of stability that may not exist for ever. Some hold this to be so, and perhaps it is true. There is no doubt that a great many Japanese workers are toiling in dirty, urban sweatshops for long hours at low pay and in miserable conditions in spite of the labour laws that prevail. It is true, too, that, without trade union support and protection, this section of the population has very little say in its own welfare. In contrast to the showroom shopfloors of the large factories, there are smaller workshops, badly heated in winter and excessively hot in summer, where cigarette butts litter the oily, grit floors and sexy pin-ups decorate ageing machine tools and presses. No country, no industrial society is perfect, and Japan is no exception. On the other hand, when they do anything well, the Japanese do it superbly well and this, I believe, is the overall trend in Japanese industry.

There is no doubt either that trades unions in Japan are learning, if slowly, to adopt the forceful techniques of their brethren in the West. They are finding out, if I may use the cliché, how to apply their industrial muscle. It is self-evident that, when obstruction and violence is the order of the day, the Japanese can obey it as well as any nation. Student unrest and rioting have long been an intermittent feature of Japanese life, and cooperation between left-wing intellectual students with leaders of industrial unions is no more novel in Japan than it was in France some years ago. More recently, the physical extremes that were reached in preventing the opening of the new airport at Narita for over five years have become headline news throughout the world. Should the same elements of force, bitterness and violence move into the present placid world of industrial relations, a very different situation would arise from the harmonious picture I have presented. Whether it will do so or not, no-one can say, but I have been harried by gloom-and-doomwatchers exhorting me to avoid neglect of these possibilities. Certainly there are destructive forces existing in Japanese society which, if let loose, could totally alter the face of Japanese industry and radically change the country's economy and its prospects for the future.

I have mentioned the trade union organisations and, elsewhere, that unknown quantity in the Japanese future, the Soka Gakkai sect of Buddhism with its Komeito political party. To give a totally balanced picture of Japanese society, I should add a mention of the 'Yazuka'. Little heard of but as real as Mr Masayoshi Ohira, the present Prime Minister of Japan, these 'godfather' type gangsters are as well organised and as powerful as any of the Mafiosa of Sicily. They are the opposite side of the coin, and to omit mention of them would be dishonest. Although not at present, to my knowledge, active on the factory floor, the Yazuka are (or at least were, when a few years ago they were filmed by a team from Yorkshire Television headed by Antony Thomas) in total control of the five thousand or so casual labourers who queue daily at the labour exchange in Kamagasaki, a suburb of Osaka. Their influence is said to extend into the field of politics; their wealth is prodigious. Oddly enough, one of the most powerful of the 'godfathers' of Japan, Mr Takei Keizo, is also a Buddhist Grand Monk, a commanding figure in his scarlet and purple robes! It was estimated at the time that he and his colleagues command a potential army of over 200,000 thugs. I do not know the influence of the Mafiosa on Italian politics and industrial relations and, in any case, the different leanings towards Communism in Italy and Japan are so different as to make such a comparison irrelevant but, should the Yazuka make a bid to control any of the trade union organisations, I, for one, would be delighted that I am not a Japanese industrialist. Perhaps in introducing such ominous organisations into my text, I am bordering on the edges of fantasy but, like sanity and madness, the distinguishing line between reality and fantasy is a nebulous and slender one. If life is both black and white, its true reflection must contain both.

What other potential problems and possible disasters face Japan today? While I am digging for gloom, we may as well look for them now. First, there is clearly the matter of the resurgence of competition from other nations in the East. For over a century Japan has been the spearhead of industrial development in Asia. Recently covetous eyes from countries like Taiwan and Korea have been watching the progress of the Japanese people towards the leadership of the industrialised nations of the free world, and behind these eyes have been intelligent minds studying the methodology of the Japanese. Whereas there was a time when labour in Japan was cheap and the Japanese were happy to look for even cheaper labour elsewhere, this is no longer so. The

Japanese invested in plant and factories in other Asian countries with lower labour costs, but now these countries have in many industries learnt how to go it alone, not only in shoes and shirts and suchlike but also in shipbuilding, steel and even in car production. Look at the Hyundai company in Seoul! The time may come when these countries are faced with steeply rising labour costs, but until then they are likely to present an increasing challenge to Japan (and to the rest of the world).

Japan is faced, too, by the problems of success at the present time. The strength of the yen against the dollar and other world currencies exaggerates the problems of export from Japan, for the Japanese economy depends on export-led growth. It cannot be denied that there is much unemployment at the moment (though less than half the British figure), or that bankruptcies are at an all time high level. There are companies in which middle and junior management are getting restive about the restraints imposed on their progress by the promotion-by-seniority system. Viewed pessimistically, as some do, there are probably very few aspects of Japanese society, industry or commerce today that do not have their faults. One could predict a total collapse of the whole structure. I cannot do so, myself, for I believe that the quick reactions, the team spirit, the national pride and the adaptability of the Japanese will pull them through any future problems far better and more quickly than any other nation in the world.

CHAPTER EIGHT

The Sinuous Sales Web

In Chapter 1 we took some notice of the nature and role of
Japanese trading companies, large and small. For any would-be
exporter to Japan there is one undeniable and significant fact:
that some 70% of goods and materials imported into Japan are
handled by these trading companies. (They are also responsible
for about 70% of Japanese exports.) If this is so, you might ask,
why look anywhere else?

For a start one must distinguish between the 'sogo shosha', the
top ten or twelve general trading companies mostly originating
from the Meiji era and handling about 60% of all imports, and
the 5900 or so smaller trading companies that specialise in different product fields. If the latter between them are only handling 10 or 12% of the goods imported, it is clear that we are talking
about two entirely different types of organisation. At the same
time if you consider that the value of goods imported by the
smallest of the sogo shosha is around £5000 million a year, it is
equally obvious that neither they nor their bigger brothers are
going to be very keen on taking on a product that might sell £50
or £100,000 worth each year. Unless you're in the First Division
of the British industry league these are not the people for you. If,
on the other hand, you are Export Director of British Shipbuil-
ders, British Aerospace, British Petroleum, British Steel Corporation, I.C.I., G.K.N. or whatever, the total capabilities of the
sogo shosha, including their huge financial resources, are what
you should be looking for.

The smaller trading companies are mainly specialists — in
food, textiles, electronics, machinery and a hundred other product ranges. Therefore they are experts in the markets they serve
and their special requirements, the competition and the trends in
demand. Obviously they vary in size and capability and the

quality of specialists, sales staff and distributor networks that they employ. Their financial resources are again variable and should be carefully checked as they will be useless as partners unless they are able to maintain stocks of goods and spares commensurate with the market demand. Some of these smaller specialist companies are partly or wholly owned by the sogo shosha and so, while operating as separate units, have the financial backing of the big groups behind them. They thus have the best of both worlds.

Obviously any budding exporter will be advised to find out whether the type of agent or distributor that he is thinking of using already deals in competitive products. The practice of doing so is much commoner in Japan than in Europe and it is not uncommon to find separate staffs in a single company handling the products of two direct competitors. This may or may not be acceptable to the British exporter who must at least assure himself that, if his products are added to the range handled by an agent or distributor who also sells for a competitor, his will get fair and equal treatment. Such assurances may be given in all sincerity, but I would be hesitant to accept them. The directors of the agents giving them may have the best of intentions, but those who have to put them into practice may not be so enthusiastic unless the matter has been fully aired in the Ringi-Seido process (see Chapter 6).

It should be mentioned here that while sole agency contracts are permissible and common in Japan, they do not hold the same validity in law that one might expect. While the principle was originally upheld, subsequent legal precedent now indicates that if your products are purchased from you by another British (or non-Japanese) firm and are subsequently exported by them or any third party to Japan through an importer other than your sole agent, no law has been infringed in Japan. Mind you, you will be selling your products, they will be getting on to the Japanese market and your agent will know it's not illegal, so maybe you've nothing to complain about, but it does seem an odd way of doing things.

As mentioned in Chapter 1, the sogo shosha have London branch offices and, if your product is likely to sell in sufficient quantity to come within the ambit of these giants, the first approach should be made to them. If interest is expressed back in Japan — and this may take many months — the London office will probably suggest a visit there and will make all the arrangements for your reception and introduction to the right people. If you have a product with a relatively small potential turnover, it may still be worth approaching a sogo shosha company, but a rejection of your offer of an agency will take at least as long as its acceptance, so you may just be losing valuable time in preventing you approaching one of the smaller specialist import traders. Many of these belong to trade associations which can be helpful in telling their members about your interest in selling in Japan and putting you in touch with any firms that express interest in your range.

Apart from the 'departo' and supermarket chains, discussed in Chapter 1, and the trading companies, a proportion of international trade is also handled directly by manufacturing companies in Japan, mostly medium-sized firms of perhaps 500 to 5000 employees. In fact some 30% of imports and a slightly lower value of exports are done directly by such companies. Especially in the field of technical products, there is an increasing tendency for such companies to diversify their product ranges and hence an interest in looking overseas for new lines and new technologies compatible with their existing production and sales facilities. Again, their respective trade associations can prove the necessary link between the potential exporters and importers.

Undoubtedly advice should be sought from the B.O.T.B. Japan Desk, who will communicate with the Commercial Department of our Embassy in Tokyo, from JETRO in Baker Street, and if needed from the Anglo-Japanese Economic Institute. These are the people who can produce market information and the necessary introductions to the right Japanese firms, but always remember it will take time and you've got to do the majority of the work yourself.

Trade Exhibitions sponsored by B.O.T.B. and Outward Sales Missions to Japan are excellent methods of obtaining cheap access to the country and, in the former, exposure of your products to Japanese eyes. Two types of exhibition exist. First, trade and technical shows organised by the Japanese, many sponsored by publishers of relevant journals, and second, entirely British exhibitions put on by B.O.T.B. as joint ventures either with British trade associations or British Chambers of Commerce, particularly those of London and Birmingham. The most popular venue for the former is the Harumi Exhibition complex across the Sumida River in Tokyo's dockland, though some exhibitions are held in the industrial city of Osaka. Wholly British shows are usually held at the British Export Marketing Centre near Aoyama-Itchome subway station. The B.O.T.B. Exports to Japan Unit can provide details of their future programme. Individual companies can rent exhibition or conference facilities for their own promotions there also.

Several years ago my company took a part of a B.O.T.B. trade association Joint Venture Stand at a technical exhibition at Harumi. We took the minimum of products, a well-prepared but brief summary of our range in Japanese, and filled the gaps on our over-large stand with potted palms. On the back wall the B.O.T.B. provided a small notice in Japanese saying "Agent or Licencee Wanted". Within three days we had a list of ten possibles, all but one companies of known repute and then the fun began. I narrowed the list down to four companies whom I stayed on to visit, and rejected two. Negotiations started with the two remaining firms. It was a long process — Ringi-Seido taking its toll of time. In fact nearly two years were to pass before we signed an agreement with the firm of our ultimate choice.

I had been advised — and I pass on this essential advice — that, apart from promptly answering the many queries that are likely to arrive in the post, it is imprudent, if not fatal, to put one's spoke in while the Japanese are going through the painfully slow decision-making process. They cannot be hurried and, if you start pushing, they may become suspicious of what to them is indecent haste, and shelve the whole project. Many a foreign company has come a cropper through impatience during the negotiating stage. I would add that while our own affairs were under consideration, I visited Tokyo twice and tactfully informed our Japanese correspondents where and when I would be and that I would always be available if they wanted me. They did, and had me over to their head office for several more grilling sessions, questioning and probing into every aspect of the company and its products. I carried out this costly exercise but never pushed them for an answer, which was all the more welcome when it came and proved favourable. My visits were valuable also in that, during them, I found out a lot more about the Japanese company who were to be our agents and associates and got to know the directors and staff.

The companies I met at this exhibition were mainly manufacturers with a stake already in the industry with which I was involved, but wishing to diversify or to extend their product range. Whilst the trading companies deal with the lion's share, about 30% of imports are handled by manufacturing industry. Knowing something of the business you are in or those allied to it, such companies can provide ideal partners, already having existing distribution and sales networks with at least a basis of knowledge on which you can build.

The selling of technical products in Japan is very different from that of consumer goods but the process and the sales force structure can be equally complex, tortuous and difficult to understand. There is often a reluctance on the part of the Japanese to give you a defined organisational structure chart for their sales force. If they are in any way involved in a diversity of products, different personnel may be involved and different sub-agents and distributors for different product ranges but even then there may be built-in anomalies. Once, on a subsequent visit to help our chosen agents, I heard that they had received a promising and substantial enquiry from a firm just on the outskirts of Tokyo, less than 15 km from their head office. Much to my surprise I found that the sales manager who was in charge of our affairs hadn't visited the customer. I asked why, and was told that that district was in the area of one of their main distributors and it wasn't politic to poach on his preserves. But what did he know of our products, only recently added to the company's range? Nothing! This wasn't a matter for Ringi-Seido so I pressed hard. The sales manager arranged for us to see the customer and we got the order, but if I hadn't been there, I doubt if we'd have had a chance.

Again, the departmentalisation of a Japanese sales force can produce some dangerous anomalies. Sitting one day in the luxury waiting hall at head office, a salesman I knew but who didn't handle our products came over to talk to me. He was full of himself, having just obtained a big order, and told me the details. Had he mentioned our products? No, he didn't think of it, and anyway they were handled by another salesman in that area. My product was compatible with, even complementary to, what this man sold and we'd had considerable success in Europe in selling to the type of customer he'd just come from. Nobody had thought of telling him. In subsequent technical sales lectures to the Japanese company, I always made a point of trying to get at least one representative of each other sales division or department to attend. Our products were in the power transmission field, not specifically marine, but used in some marine applications. The agent's marine sales manager was supposed to be selling other products to ship owners and ship builders but became one of our most enthusiastic supporters when he found that some of our range was applicable to his customers and that we had some experience of the field!

Only persistence and tactful insistence will help to overcome these flaws in Japanese sales organisations in the technical field, but one's efforts are usually appreciated and rewarded. As things developed, I would find all sorts of remote sub-agents attending my talks and usually expressing great interest. Being technical people, their natural Japanese curiosity in a field foreign to them was easily aroused and maintained.

Whatever type of contract or agreement you may wish to reach with a Japanese partner, agency, distributorship, licence or joint venture company (we will come to these last two shortly), it is important to appreciate one aspect of the Japanese approach. In the West we have a habit of going to excesses in the legal phraseology of our contracts, no doubt due to reasonable prudence and caution. The Japanese, however, faced with an excessively detailed and lengthy document, are apt to become somewhat confused. For a start few British people can easily understand a contract drawn up by the British legal mind in British legal language, so how are the Japanese likely to be able to do so? Obviously reasonable legal safeguards must be taken to protect your firm's interests— though I often have doubts as to what they would amount to if you fell out with your Japanese partner and were faced with an international lawsuit on a multi-lingual basis! Do your best to restrain your legal advisers from being over-expansive. Contracts should be as short as possible and it is sensible to accompany them with a short summary expressed in clear, everyday English rather than legal jargon. You may be reluctant to give this to the Japanese in writing. If so, at least prepare it, take it with you when you visit them for negotiations and explain the legal contract in these simple terms. This will do much to facilitate the Japanese understanding of what is intended and speed up the final signature of your contract.

The Japanese are, in fact, much more interested in the spirit of your proposed cooperation than in the letter of the law. Apart from exhaustive technical and commercial evaluation, their judgement on whether they wish to go ahead and work with your company will take little account of a load of legal claptrap, but will rest more upon their estimation of you as the representative of your company. Later they may visit you, see your plant and meet your staff and directors, but for the majority of the Japanese you are the man on the spot and the only visible, tangible evidence upon which they can form an estimate of the organisation behind you. What is most important for them is mutual trust, a willing commitment to cooperate and understand each other's problems, and this will largely be based on friendship and personality. It is the spirit of the contract, not the contract itself, that matters to them.

One cannot over-stress the importance of the ties of friendship and confidence that can and should be built up in the early days of negotiation. Continuing business relationships to the Japanese are based more on personal contact and friendship than on the motivation of pure profit. It is hence advisable to ensure that the man who goes out and pioneers your venture into the Japanese market is senior and respected in your company, but not so senior that he might retire before further friendships have been established between the Japanese and his successors and subordinates. I know of one case where the two senior directors of a British company, the only two who had visited Japan, were replaced. The Japanese interest in the company and its product range cooled appreciably and will take a long time to recover its previous enthusiasm, if it ever does.

The system of distribution of consumer goods in Japan is quite different from that of technical products, but is equally fraught with problems for the foreign exporter. Direct contact between personalities is equally important at the top, but lower down the difficulties are different and there is little the British exporter can do about them. We have noted in Chapter 5 the huge number of small retail outlets in Japan, and it is because of their great number that the present complicated distribution system has grown up. Once again we are faced with the influence of history. It has been stated often that this distribution system, in which multitudinous layers of middlemen may be involved, is detrimental to the prospects of goods being imported into Japan as, each middleman having to live, takes his cut and the price of goods retailed to the company becomes inordinately high. The argument is, of course, fallacious as indigenous products pass through the same system and hence suffer the same mark-up, but unsuccessful exporters will persist in it. It is difficult to generalise about freight costs and duty but commonly retail prices of imported goods are between three and four times F.O.B. prices. The level of import tariffs, though constantly being reviewed and reduced, does penalise the exporter and one can only hope that external political pressure will force the Japanese government into making further cuts in duty. It would also be fair to say that there are cases where Japanese importers sell foreign goods as luxury 'products and therefore charge high prices for them. This may sometimes have a deleterious effect on sales, but not generally or there would be no point in the Japanese taking on such products. However, it is a point that the British exporter should watch out for.

The complexity of the distribution system, with all its levels with which the British exporter is never likely to make contact, makes it all the more important that his choice of main agent or distributor is the right one. Knowledge of competitive products handled is not so important as in the industrial field, and in some cases an agent's or distributor's reputation may even be enhanced by the handling of similar lines with other known brand names. The number of intermediate stockists and wholesalers involved before the retail outlets varies with the type of product, the chain being longest— probably three stages— in foods, soaps and detergents. However, this need not concern the exporter, whose ability to understand and cope with the different mark-ups and the varying ranges of credit and risk capital involved is unlikely to match that of a capable and efficient importer. In any case the system involves loading an indigenous product with the same mark ups, customs duty being the only difference.

The greatest opportunities for imported consumer goods undoubtedly arise in luxury and semi-luxury products, for which the appropriate retail outlets are the department stores and supermarket chains and, in the big cities, a number of speciality boutiques. 'Departos' in the main and some of the chain stores have buying offices or agents in London (see Chapter 1) who should be approached initially. Some of the boutiques send buyers abroad while others deal through speciality trading companies. The experienced exporter will not need to be reminded that successful selling overseas entails a close study of local tastes and requirements among his other market research activities. Once the relevant information has been collected he must then assess whether his product conforms to the needs of the market as it is and, if not, can it be suitably and viably modified. If this is impossible, does the market warrant design and production of a completely new product or should the idea of entering the particular market be scrapped altogether? These considerations apply both to industrial products and consumer goods and are in no way specific to Japan. On the other hand, they are vital to any hope of success in that country.

I have mentioned both taste and requirements as separate factors but the dividing line between them is nebulous. An additional factor is 'custom', an example of which is the use of colour in fashion. You may have the most exquisite fabrics, and fashion-wear made from them, but they are unlikely to sell in Japan if they are purple. This is an Imperial colour and hence little used by ordinary folk. An interesting contrast between good and bad research into what was needed comes from two well-known British clothing manufacturers. The first set out to sell a household brand name of men's shirts without doing their fieldwork adequately. The brand name, of course, meant little to the Japanese, but the real problem lay in inadequate study of design to be compatible with local habits. The shirts didn't sell in spite of being of excellent quality and value. What the British firm had not observed was that the Japanese climate and the influence of American customs have combined to lead office workers to work in their shirt sleeves and if you're not wearing a jacket you need at least one breast pocket for pens, pencils etc. Once this was realised and the product modified to suit, sales started rolling in.

In contrast, a British brassiere manufacturer sent an expert for six months to the Far East literally to study 'form'. Centuries of wearing the traditional 'obi' have evolved a nation of small-breasted Japanese women for whom a modified product range was designed. It sold with great success. Costly market research paid off and, no doubt, the company keeps a watchful eye on further changes in the female Japanese figure resulting from liberation from the obi and dietary changes (see Chapter 13).

Bureaucracy in Japan is no worse than in the West but has resulted in a considerable volume of legislation relating to such matters as machine safety, plant pollution levels and consumer protection. To ignore the relevant rules is to court failure in a sales campaign in Japan. Clearly, once a working partner is found in Japan, he can be relied on to advise on such legislation but finding a good partner will be facilitated by the potential exporter taking the trouble to check that his products comply with the local laws and requirements. Few Japanese distributors, for example, are likely to discuss seriously the import of a make and model of car which doesn't conform to the government's exhaust emission legislation. Summaries of much of the legislation for machinery, consumer goods and pollution are given in booklets published in the excellent JETRO Marketing Series (Nos. 13, 14 and 15). If these give insufficient information, either JETRO's local office or the B.O.T.B. will give further advice, but it is up to the foreign exporting company to get the facts before making serious attempts at entering the market.

So far we have merely considered selling to Japan through indigenous companies of different types. For the more ambitious, wealthy and self-confident exporter, other methods are available which involve different degrees of investment, control and participation. Until 1967 close government controls existed, but in the past decade the majority of these have been lifted so that there are few restrictions today on foreign capital investment in Japan. Foreign participation in retailing may now be 100% of the equity in retailing. What are the other alternatives open to the prospective exporter today?

You may set up an office with your own representative without any registration requirements, though such an office may not engage in trading directly but must carry out business through a Japanese partner, ie agent, trading company or distributor. If one has been found, such an office may be a useful temporary measure to accelerate progress in the early stages of cooperation, particularly if some closer connection is envisaged such as a joint venture company. Salaries etc. are paid from the home base and Japanese income tax is only liable if the office steps over the line and gets involved in commercial activities. All its income then becomes taxable. If plans for future development exist, this type of operation is a useful way of introducing foreign staff to life and business in Japan and helping them to get to know your Japanese partner's people.

Overseas companies are also permitted to set up their own registered sales offices in Japan, their income there, of course, being taxed, with its costs offset against this. You can also set up your own company with no Japanese investment, although generally this is an expensive and not very effective arrangement. If it is to operate successfully, it will necessarily have to recruit a high proportion of its staff and employees in Japan. Though attitudes are slowly changing, the Japanese are reluctant to work for foreign companies, even if these are run on Japanese lines. They have difficulty in identifying with a non-Japanese organisation, do not feel 'at home', and are generally suspicious of their security in the hands of 'gaijin' bosses. As a result, you are likely to obtain only 2nd or 3rd grade employees, who have tended to be misfits in their previous jobs and companies, although, with higher unemployment, the situation is becoming easier. There are notable exceptions of course such as the Dodwell and the Houlden trading companies and Olivetti in manufacture, but the success of such firms has been hard won over many years. Setting up your own firm is by no means impossible but it is no way to instant success. The Bank of Japan acts as both counsellor and supervisor of such ventures involving the influx of foreign investment while the aspirant to this type of project would do well to select a major Japanese bank to act for him.

Usually a joint-venture with a Japanese company shows better prospects of success, and it is not unusual for this to develop out of previous cooperation with a manufacturing company who have been successful in selling your products and with whom you have established the necessary rapport. It is even possible to establish such a company without even having to deplete your own bank account, your Japanese partner paying your company a fee for your designs and know-how which you at once re-invest as your share of the equity in the new venture. The value placed upon your contribution will, of course, influence the proportion of the total shareholding capital that your company holds and hence the degree of control that it will have in the joint venture company. Even if, however, you inject your own additional capital, it is unlikely that you will be able to achieve more than a 50:50 balance of power, and even at this level, relations must be based on a high degree of mutual trust and confidence. Should this approach appeal to your company, your Japanese partner will usually take the necessary steps to obtain government approval, registration etc., normally completed almost automatically within a few weeks though it may be much longer before you are jointly in business. Depending on the percentage of your ownership of the new organisation you will have proportional representation on the board of directors. How frequently your directors attend board meetings is up to you. It is possible to nominate a British resident in Japan to act for you in the capacity of a director, but once more it comes back to how closely you know your Japanese partners and how your mutual trust and understanding has been established. I have mentioned previously the Japanese viewpoint in which success tends to be meas-

ured more in terms of growth than in profits and variance between their objectives, and yours must be harmonised from the
start if harmonious co-existence is to be achieved in the long-
term.

If you decide to attend board meetings more or less frequently,
you will be well advised to arrive in Japan some days before they
are due. I have never seen a Japanese managing director adopt
the steam-roller tactics that happen in some western Board-
rooms but, as with other types of 'kai' or meetings in Japan, the
Torishimayaku-kai tends to be a rubber-stamping affair for the
automatic approval of matters that have been chewed over at
many less informal meetings and on which decisions have already
been made. If you want to take part in the decision-making, be
there in time to have friendly talks with your Japanese co-
directors singly or in small groups, possibly over a drink or a
meal, to find out what lies behind the agenda. This way allows
you to express your opinions without too much disruption of the
harmony when you eventually sit down with the green tea round
the Boardroom table.

You will sometimes find that, in the early years of a joint
venture with a Japanese company, your partners would like you
to appoint a resident director to stay in Japan. Apart from
denuding your manpower at home, this is clearly to the advantage of both sides, particularly if you have a Nippophilic personality that you can possibly spare. He will probably already be
known to your Japanese friends and, if willing to go and cloaked
with sufficient authority, he can solve problems, help and make
decisions on a day-to-day basis and thus accelerate considerably
the progress of your joint venture scheme.

This can only be a brief summary of the ways to enter the
Japanese market. You must have the right product at the right
price and the right delivery. You must make promises about
them all — AND keep them. You must build up and maintain
confidence for, even with modern communications, Japan is a
long way from Britain. Most of all, you must establish and
maintain personal friendships, relationships, trust and confidence with a people very different in thought and culture from
your own but with a people who can be the most friendly and
trustful in the world. To do so, you must have a deep understanding of Japan, the Japanese and the spirit of Japan, which, after all,
is the main objective of this book.

CHAPTER NINE

Ordeal By Blackboard

Let's assume that you've reached an agreement with a local company to represent you as agents or distributors in Japan. Note that it is against Japanese law for any company to have exclusive rights and any other Japanese firm can legally import your products if they can obtain them at a competitive price and on suitable delivery terms. Delivery on time is an absolute essential in dealing with Japan and delivery promises must be maintained. You will clearly do your utmost to satisfy your appointed agents or distributors in this respect for, if you fail, it is they who will lose face with their customers to whom they may also be selling other products. One cannot over-emphasise the importance of this question of delivery on time

I might add here that in coming to this agreement, if your company follows normal British practice, you've probably spent quite a lot of money with your lawyers drawing up a legal contract and they'll have spent a good deal more of it having the whole thing checked by their legal associates in Japan. No doubt your Board of Directors is happy and your lawyers are happy, but that's not really what counts in succeeding in business in Japan. I've nothing against feeding starving solicitors — though I've yet to meet one — and I've nothing against giving the Board of Directors (or the stay-at-home types if you're the globe-trotter amongst them) a comfortable sense of euphoria, but, to Japanese minds, the legal contract is barely worth the paper it's written on.

What matters vitally to the Japanese is the spirit of the agreement rather than all the legal formalities. Agreed, you must set down a clear *modus operandi* to ensure who is to be responsible for what and how everything is to be done between you and when, but this is better done in plain English language, the language of Sir Ernest Gowers' *The Complete Plain Words*, for example. In fact, even if you've signed a legal agreement, it is wise to back it up with an unemotional but warm letter, explaining what the agreement means and expressing your own spirit, your own goodwill and your desire and determination for mutual success.

If you reflect on the complexities of the Japanese language which we discussed in Chapter 3, the comparatively small number of Japanese who can understand plain English and the probably even smaller number of British businessmen who can understand lawyers' English— if it can truly be called English— I think you will see what I mean. The expensive legal jargon may serve its purpose but, as a means of communication between your company and your new colleagues in Japan, it is merely the erection of a stone wall in front of a bamboo one that already exists in the linguistic communication barrier. (Bamboo is, of course, notably stronger in that it has a resilience rare in the material world. Its ability to bend before the storm and then return to normal is a characteristic much emulated by the Japanese people.)

The spirit of your new agreement is the crux of the matter and, if you are to represent your company in Japan, it is this spirit that you must display both to agents or distributors and to prospective customers. It is not that the Japanese are any more distrustful than any other nation: it is just that they need to have some visible sign of the good qualities of the organisation in which they are putting their trust. After all, apart from some sales literature and probably some sample products, they have little else to go on. Thus the man or men who go out to represent their companies in Japan bear a heavy responsibility to nurture mutual faith and trust and to cement an embryo but growing friendship. As we have seen in earlier chapters, the whole of Japanese business, and in fact Japanese society, is founded on personal trust and friendship and on the inter-reliance of people. If this is the general condition of life between one Japanese and another, as well as between Japanese companies, how much more important must it look to Japanese eyes when they are dealing with foreigners from 7000 miles away on the other side of the globe?

Whether it is part of your legal agreement of not, it is important to back up your new agent, particularly in the initial stages, with one or more visits to Japan. These should be of reasonable length — the longer, the better — and I have always found that less than a month achieved little and was uneconomic. A visit from an overseas principal is always a help to an agent in any country, to assist in training his staff, to boost morale and to visit prospective and existing customers. It is visible proof of the principal's interest in the agent's success. It similarly convinces customers of the foreign principal's concern with doing business with his company, and of his anxiety to learn first-hand what he, the customer, wants. Such visits are advisable in any export venture. I believe that they are more significant, more useful and more necessary in Japan than in any other country of which I have experience.

Naturally both politeness and efficiency require that you give your agent plenty of notice of your impending visit. He will have a good deal of spadework to do before you arrive in arranging an effective programme of visits to customers as we shall see below. It amounts almost to pick-and-shovel work and cannot be done without much time and effort. Above all, don't forget, when writing, to define as clearly as possible the objectives of your visit. You will find that, if your company is of any size and your products are of any complexity, that you will need to spend much of your time in giving lectures or talks to groups of salesmen, sub-agents and technicians in your agent's organisation. This will be time well spent but, unless you state that you want and are prepared to make a tour round prospective and existing customers if you already have any, your agent may not realise this. This might appear self-evident in Western circumstances but the Japanese do not always think along the same lines as we do. As Ruth Benedict wrote in her fascinating book, *The Chrysanthemum and the Sword*, "We had to put aside for the moment the premises on which we act ... and to keep ourselves as far as possible from leaping to the easy conclusion that what we would do in a given situation was what they would do." It is essential to be precise in all your communications.

It is possible that you may have appointed different agents to deal with different parts of your product range, a course to be avoided if possible but sometimes unavoidable. If this is so, precise definition of your visit proposals to each of your agents becomes even more vital and should include an idea of when you can be with each of them and how much time you have available for each. Otherwise you are likely to find yourself disembarking from your aircraft at Tokyo's Haneda airport to be met by delegations from both agents who, tired though you may be, will vie with each other for the honour of your immediate entertainment and refreshment. The initial ceremonies of hospitality being concluded, you may well then find that days may elapse in useless and expensive idleness while schedules are worked out for you, both the agents being under the impression that the main purpose of your trip was to visit the other one! All this may sound too obvious to need stating but I confess to having fallen into this trap myself on one of my earlier trips to Japan. Mistakes may be useful if you can learn something from them — but they can be costly.

It will become apparent when we get down to the details of what may happen to you when you arrive at your customers' premises, that whoever goes out to act as your representative must be a man of some consequence and standing and must be well briefed in every aspect of your business. If your company is big enough to send a number of specialists in different fields, so much the better, but I imagine that most businesses that have sought guidance from a book such as this will not be in the big league and will be sending a lone representative to promote their sales. He'll need to know the facts, ALL the facts, as we shall see.

Before such a sales tour is proposed or planned, it is, of course, vital that an adequate supply of suitable sales literature is available in Japan, ie leaflets or catalogues in Japanese, and good Japanese at that. Some experts advise that all that is necessary is to provide literature in English with an abbreviated insert in Japanese. The logic behind this ploy is that the customer will be flattered that you expect him to be able to understand the full English text. In fact the matter depends to a great extent on what the product is and to what level of executive the sales process descends. Top people in Japan can no doubt cope admirably with English but, if you are selling a technical product where it is desirable that your catalogue should be beside the board of every draughtsman, then it needs to be in Japanese as fully as possible. Engineering drawings and data sheets are, of course, almost international and do not need to be converted into Japanese.

While there are a few excellent companies who can handle translation and even Japanese printing in the UK, their services are naturally far from cheap and a good agent in Japan can get the job done much more easily and at lower cost out there, assuming that you supply him with the right material and, so far as possible, check any proofs that he may send you and return them promptly. As I have said in Chapter 7, the collective nature of the Japanese decision-making process is a slow one, but, once the decision to work with your company has been made, everyone on the Japanese side will have been convinced that it is a desirable course of action. If you've got the right agent, everyone concerned will be determined to do their best to ensure the success of your cooperative venture and things are likely to move fast — faster in fact than you may find comfortable. Probably one of the best known of Japanese pictures is a wood-block print by the artist Hokusai, one of his *Thirty-six Views of Mount Fuji*. It is the view through the waves off the coast of Kanagawa and depicts a huge, towering wave with claw-like foam breaking in the centre and dwarfing the famous mountain. It characterises the elemental power of nature. Perhaps it is a fanciful concept but, to me, it also symbolises the dynamic energy of the Japanese people, of Japanese business and industry. Such a wave threatens to engulf the embryo British exporter once an agreement to work together has been reached. The demands of the Japanese in terms of detailed information wanted are liable to swamp him, sweeping in daily, by letter and by Telex, and these demands need to be met diligently, promptly, fully and accurately if the newly established partnership is to flourish. Emotion playing a bigger part in Japanese life than logic, the Japanese, whose zest, enthusiasm and hard work are second to none, can easily become disillusioned and lose heart if their European partners do not match up to their own ebullient activity. In the early stages of my own work, after the first contract was signed, I sometimes wondered what sort of uncontrollable force I had unleashed on myself and my colleagues in almost every department of the company. Our Japanese friends seemed to have an insatiable appetite for both the expected as well as the most abstruse information on products, prices, applications, sales figures, markets, competitors ... There were days when I thought that the only way of avoiding being swamped by their avidity for knowledge, of being drowned in the ever-encroaching sea of paperwork on my desk, was to buy a larger wastepaper basket! I resisted the urge and did my best to satisfy our Japanese friends' hunger for facts and figures — and little by little, the waves subsided and the sea receded.

I might add that it was nothing for the phone to ring in my office two or three times a week at 3 p.m. One or other of the departmental managers of our new agents, having worked perhaps until eight o'clock at night and spent a convivial hour or two in a bar or club with his colleagues (see Chapter 5), had just arrived home by train to suburban Tokyo. He would like the answers to one or two little problems and queries. It would be midnight in Tokyo!

Getting back to the business of visiting your agent and, assuming that you have primed him well, it has to be appreciated that, only if you have chosen a good agent, will you obtain appointments to see the right people in the right customer companies. More than in any other country, business in Japan is based on mutual respect and trust, both between companies and between individuals. It is also a country in which cold canvas calls are virtually non-existent and visits are preceded by numerous lengthy sessions on the telephone. If your agent has a good reputation, the right doors will be open to you, though it is very much up to you to make the most of what happens when you pass through them. The agent's reputation, which he is now largely entrusting to your care, depends on his integrity, his level of success and his ability to satisfy the multifarious demands of his customers. The standard and quality of his staff, and the business rating of his other customers, are also of great importance. The same aspects of you, or your representative, and your company will shortly come under similar, detailed scrutiny and will be of equal significance to the customer if he is to accept you as a potential supplier. For this reason you must be fully prepared for the forthcoming 'inquisition', for that is what most sales meetings amount to.

In spite of their undoubted success in almost every business they tackle, there is, as with so many other aspects of Japanese life, a curious element of vagueness about visit plans. If you have given your agent precise instructions and sufficient time, he will doubtless present you with an efficiently detailed schedule in writing on your arrival. This may present an alarming prospect for it will probably confront you with a five-and-a-half or six day working week, each day involving ten or twelve hours of work and travel, not to mention the extramural activities after the labours of each day are finished officially! However, it can only be hoped that this is what you came to Japan for. You will need Herculean stamina. Nichiyobi (Sunday) is officially a day of rest, but it is unlikely that you will have much time to rest for the Japanese are today the kindliest and most hospitable of people and they will put themselves out to show you the beauties and wonders of their country. Sunday will thus turn out to be twelve hours of driving, eating, drinking and sight-seeing. If you're in Japan for any length of time, there will be bound to be a National

Holiday on which it is impossible to go visiting customers. For several years I have looked forward to a good rest on Old People's Day (15th September), but I have invariably found that my enthusiastic agents refuse to admit that either they or I come under this heading, hence I usually find myself having to give talks to sales or technical staff. So far I've avoided 10th October which is Physical Education Day. I'd hate to think whàt relaxations might be in store then!

You will note, by the way, that your schedule will leave you no time at all in which to write notes or reports of your visit. Unless you have mastered the art of Oriental detachment and have the ability to write legibly in the uneven motion of car, train or plane, I recommend taking along a pocket tape recorder. I post my half-hour tapes home every few days as they fill up, and a good draft report is thus ready when I get back to the office. My secretary used to be put off by sudden interjections of drums and shakuhachi (a sort of Japanese flute) when people were dancing in the streets at the Autumn Equinox Festival. The curious Utai chant of our agents' Vice President recorded late at night as his whiskied tones filled the back of the taxi upset her equally but she soon got used to it. At least the essentials get recorded along with the less important sounds.

As I said, that visit schedule looks precise but it doesn't usually work out to be quite like that. Things change in an unpredictable way because suddenly Kaji-san of Sotoso Kaisha (Company) whom you were to meet has been called to his Yokohama factory, or Yamanaga-san has had to attend the funeral of an old University colleague. Somehow, though, another appointment seems to get fixed up instead.

Then there is another vagueness to be taken into account in your plans— the vagueness of time in Japan and this is a two-way business. One of Japan's finest products is the Seiko watch. (Seiko is a curious homophonic word. With four different kanji ideogram spellings but with exactly the same pronunciation, it can mean success, delicate, accurate, steel manufacture or sexual intercourse!) Yet in spite of the universal presence of accurate timepieces, if your agent says he will pick you up at your hotel at 8 o'clock, he is very likely to ring from the lobby or knock on your door when you are still in the bath at 7.30. It is as well to be prepared for this sort of embarrassment. Nearly all Japanese hotel rooms, Western style at least, have a built-in alarm clock, even if they did keep you up late the night before.

If your agents are a firm of any size or consequence you will probably find that you are accompanied on your visits to customers by quite a retinue. This is not so much a retention of the customs of olden days when foreigners were never allowed to wander abroad without an extensive escort of Japanese to see that they didn't get lost or into any mischief. It is rather a reflection of the present day Japanese desire to learn and particularly to extract the maximum possible advantage from your visit, an opportunity not to be missed by either party. A director, a manager or section chief may head the team with a branch manager or representative if you are away from Head Office; one senior salesman at least and, if there is room in your transport, perhaps some bright youngster who is learning the ropes. With luck — and the right sort of agent — at least one of these will speak English. If not, you must add the "Tsuyaku", the interpreter and, of course, senior Japanese management rarely sit behind the steering wheel, so you'll need a driver, unless one of the salesmen does the job. Well, that's too many for the company limousine, even if it's a posh Nissan President with digital clock, hi-fi stereo, air-conditioning and white seat covers and anti-macassars on the headrests. So someone, the junior salesman probably, dashes back into the office to phone for a private-hire taxi. You sit for five minutes, the engine ticking over to keep the air-conditioning going, looking at your Seiko and wondering if you'll ever get started, let alone get there on time. Don't worry there are other frustrations ahead of you. Someone has to find your destination.

This is an integral part of Japanese life that should be conducive to hypertension, coronary thrombosis, nail-biting, ulcers and excellent business prospects for the local psychiatrists. In fact, it is treated with the utmost good humour and merriment. No-one, except perhaps you — and I strongly advise you not to — gets at all worried. Finding — and losing — the way is almost a national sport, a hobby, in which the course rules are set up by the fact that all but the most major routes and main streets are unmarked. Few street names sully the landscape and, if you are in a city, the numbers of the buildings do not run along the streets but round the blocks. (You may have noticed in addresses the frequent use of the suffixes, '-cho' and '-ku': -ku is a city ward or district; -cho is a block of buildings.) Tales are often told of taxi-drivers stopping and hopping out frequently to ask the way from postmen, policemen, grocers, schoolchildren and noodle shop proprietors and, on finally succeeding in delivering their passenger to the correct destination, embracing him with the jubilation of an Olympic Gold medallist.

For the visitor, this business of finding the way can be traumatic but, since there is absolutely nothing he can do to help, and I assure you it always turns out all right in the end, there is no point in getting agitated. You'll probably arrive about a minute before you're due, for all this has been taken into account in planning your schedule. You have, in fact, a comfortable seat in airconditioned luxury and a little time to spare to brush up your homework. Unless you are one of the giant memory men of British industry, you can well make use of that time. You are approaching the testing period where, like a car in the manufacturers' test-house, you will be subjected to every kind of jolt, stress and impact that can be dreamt up by the mind of man.

So finally your convoy arrives at the offices of your important prospective customer. The environment differs if you're calling on some small back-street firm backing onto the Sumida River or an 'Ichi-ryu' or first grade company like Mitsubishi, Hitachi or IHI. Likewise, if you're trying to sell into the prestige purveyors of consumer goods, but all in all the procedure remains the same. After the initial barrier of Reception is passed, you reach a table, either a small canteen-type with matching chairs which may be one of a row in an office discussion area or, a vast U-shaped affair in a separate room that could accommodate a lunchtime reception for a hundred and fifty wedding guests. Tables, chairs and a good supply of 'haizara' (ashtrays) usually make up the furniture, except for two other items, a glass case full of shields and trophies won for safety and productivity, and maybe an elegant traditional Japanese doll that seems to have no right to be there at all. The other item of furniture is of much greater significance to you — a blackboard. Just like being back at school, only this time you're to be the teacher. This ubiquitous piece of equipment, found in every Japanese office, can become your enemy or your greatest friend and succour in the time of need to come. It depends which way you look at it. You may not be a trained lecturer but, if you adopt the right attitude, you can get plenty of practice in Japan.

The scale of the meeting will vary with the size and the status of the company you're visiting, but the principles and procedure remain much the same. I will go to the upper extreme and describe one of the most exhausting and harrowing three-hour periods I've ever had to spend. This was on a visit to one of the many offices of one of the engineering giants of Japan. I won't mention the name but I can assure you they were well up in the industrial hierarchy. The journey to their prestige factory and offices, not far from the centre of Tokyo, was much as I've pictured it above, and the interview room was huge. We were there on time, six of us, and smoked nervously — at least I did — while awaiting the opposing team. Our appointment was for 10 o'clock and, almost to the minute, they began to file in. One, two, three, four, I counted ... until there were no less than twelve of them. Short Japanese, tall Japanese, senior Japanese, junior Japanese and finally the Section or Group Chief to whom all paid due respect.

The 'meishi' or visiting card is an essential tool of Japanese business life, as indispensable as the pen in your pocket or, in fact, your trousers. You can no more do business in Japan without an adequate supply of properly printed cards than you can without those vital nether garments. You are equally naked and vulnerable without either. If you have heeded my advice in Chapter 1, you will have come properly prepared.

The business of presenting and receiving cards is a lengthy and time-consuming affair, but it is important to the Japanese. At this meeting, with six of us on our side and twelve on theirs, no less than 144 cards changed hands, were read with care and studied with due solemnity. The procedure, which has the air of an elaborate ceremony about it, cannot be hurried, for each participant scans the cards he receives in order to assess the exact rank and standing of each person from the other company so that he can accurately estimate his own position on the business-social scale in relation to each of the others. Until these assessments have been made, there is a sense of tension and no-one can be comfortable. As each mental calculation is made and everyone becomes conscious of his proper status in the assembly, bows of different degree and gravity are made, places are taken appropriately on each side of the table and a noticeable relaxation of manner becomes apparent.

Two points for the 'gaijin' or foreigner are worth noting here. First, many of the cards that you receive will only be printed in Japanese. Only the senior men will have their identification and company details on the obverse in Roman script. I have found it advisable to get my agent to translate the names and positions on all the unidentifiable cards either during or at least immediately after the meeting. It is, in fact, not impolite to have this done right at the start: rather the opposite for, though it may delay the proceedings for a few moments, it shows that you are as interested as your hosts in knowing the names and job-status of everyone present, which is no more than common sense and courtesy.

The second point is a minor one of manners. Japanese who are sufficiently senior in the business scale and some of the juniors who have learnt one or more foreign languages have become attuned to our Western custom of shaking hands on meeting or being introduced. To others, at least to look at, it is as comical as it is to us to observe the complexity of their trial-and-error of bowing to the correct depth until both parties are satisfied that they have established their relative ranking in society. But there is another aspect of the handshake. The physical contact involved in the shaking of hands is distasteful if not actually repulsive to the untrained Japanese. Hence the proper course of action is not to offer your hand, or worse, to seize the hand of the Japanese you are meeting, unless he offers you his first. If he doesn't, you just simply bow. Of course, the Japanese do not expect foreigners to understand the complex ritual of the bow, a sort of unspoken respect language. All that is needed is a slight forward inclination of the body from the hips to acknowledge the other person's presence.

You will generally find that, if you are visiting an industrial concern and particularly if there is an adjacent factory, that most of the representatives of your customer are wearing para-military clothes — battle-dress of grey or soft blue with which peaked caps are worn in the workshops. Identity badges, sometimes insignia of rank or qualifications in First Aid (Green Cross in Japan) are prominent. Nearly everyone, except possibly the most senior men, will be carrying some sort of notebook. Everything that you say or your agent says for you will be taken down and may be used in evidence either for you or against you, depending on how well you impress your listeners. At least you can be assured that they will listen.

At the meeting I was describing, a high proportion of the customers' team could understand a good deal of English — particularly if spoken slowly and clearly. Five of the twelve, I discovered, were Doctors of Engineering but they had also brought along an accountant, a commercial man, someone from their sales office and a couple of people from the shop floor where my products could conceivably spend part of their lives. To be confronted with a multifarious team like this could be nerve-racking for they could and did ask the most wide-ranging questions with the greatest of expertise at finding the awkward ones.

The company for which I was then marketing director was a member of a substantial engineering group in the UK and it is significant to record this unwitting piece of one-upmanship. The size of a business or an industrial organisation is something inherently admirable to the Japanese. The fact that I came from a 3500-strong group was far more interesting and far more in my favour than the 200-man company that I was representing on this visit. If your company is in a group or has associate companies, don't be shy about it. You will gain far more respect in Japanese eyes than if your organisation is small and independent, however inventive, successful and prosperous. The lone wolf, either as a person or as a company, is not admired in Japan, but size is equated in the Japanese business mind with success.

On the other hand, if you mention membership of a group of companies or some other larger organisation, you must know all about it. You must have all your facts ready and be prepared to talk at length about its history, its financial record, its shareholdings, its product range and applications, its subsidiaries apart from your own company, its markets, market shares, sales outlets, export percentages, location and equipment of factories, its sales offices and its agents overseas. There is no aspect of your parent group that may not come under scrutiny. It is self-evident that you must be able to answer detailed questions on all the same aspects of the company you are representing. The demand for information, sometimes of the most unlikely kind, appears to be insatiable. If you haven't done all your homework and there is some question that you can't answer, it is best to admit your failing with due apology and say that you'll find out when you return home or, better still, get the answer by telex or letter or phone while still in Japan, and pass it on to your agent. This can be an excellent lever for him to contact the customer again and suggests also that your organisation is an efficient one. Even more important, you will have proved to the customer that you are a man of your word and that you can be relied upon. This is a most important aspect of business relations with the Japanese.

I mentioned the blackboard, a ubiquitous feature of all Japanese interview rooms. Much of the conversation, the questions and answers, may be carried on by your agent or interpreter, a slow, laborious and sometimes misleading procedure. You may from time to time find it advisable to take the bull by the horns and seize the chalk before someone puts it forcibly into your hand and starts to pull your chair from under you. Organisation charts, financial figures, statistics, graphs, system diagrams, simple engineering sketches ... all these and a host of other ideas can be more easily and more quickly conveyed visually with blackboard and chalk than by a thousand words that may have to be translated and are hence, liable to be mistranslated and misunderstood. There is the fact, too, that the Japanese have a graphic, a pictorial side to their character — their very writing is done in ideograms — and they will gain both instruction and pleasure from an efficient visual presentation. Incidentally, they are a totally metric nation (though not always thoroughly familiar with S.I. units should you be in an industry that employs them) and, if you've got to go into prices, sales turnover, profits etc — and I'd be surprised if you get away without such financial figures — it will save time if you convert roughly into Yen or at least into US dollars before your visit. No doubt there will be someone with a pocket calculator or a soroban (abacus), but you'll impress them more if they don't have to use them and errors will be obviated at the same time.

Not only does the use of the blackboard simplify and speed up communication, but I believe that a degree of kudos can be obtained from its efficient use. I don't advocate rehearsing at home necessarily but confidence in graphic presentation of facts and figures, even a little panache, will go down well with the Japanese customer. After all, he has faith in your agent or you wouldn't have got in the front door. Now he wants to make sure that he can equally safely trust your company and the only way he can judge so far is by assessing what faith he can put in you. If a dozen or so executives and staff will spend two or three of their valuable working hours trying to find out all about you and your company you've a golden opportunity to impress them — without the flannel of sales-talk or bare untruthful claims which won't get you anywhere — and you should be glad you've found an agent who can open the door for you.

On the occasion I write about, we went through all the preliminaries at length, history, finance, markets etc. Then, as it was , a technical product that I was selling, the time came for the big guns to be turned on me — the Doctors of Engineering.

For some time they plied me with intelligent, technical questions and my replies were duly noted down. I should mention that our agents had done an excellent job in producing an attractive short-form catalogue of our products in Japanese, and almost all the customers' people at the meeting had either a copy of it or a photostat set of its pages. Where this was not detailed enough, our English data sheets with outline and sectioned drawings of the products were perfectly intelligible to engineers without the need for translation. We were doing fine and I was wearing out chalk at a great rate when, imperceptibly, at first a sort of Alice-in-Wonderland influence seemed to creep into the proceedings.

We had been talking about fairly complicated mechanical equipment until then. Although a good deal of thought goes into the design of the oil tank that is associated with it, it is the simplest and most basic component and more or less universally understood by quite junior draughtsmen in the industry. Suddenly I found that I was being cross-examined by these mechanical pundits on this very elementary piece of equipment. The questions were deep and searching. My agent handed me a piece of chalk. "They would like you to draw a hydraulic reservoir, please," he said. I obliged, describing the details as I sketched it. Huddled conversations took place between the members of the Brains Trust opposite. Sketches were made in notebooks. Further consultations ensued ... a long pause ... and then everyone smiled.

Talking to my agents later did little to elucidate the reasoning behind this curiously naive set of questions. I've had similar experiences since then elsewhere in Japan and have, I think, worked out the only possible motivation for experienced and highly qualified engineers asking junior technical college-type questions. It is really quite simple. There were only two answers to the type of question put to me. Either I would give the correct reply and would sketch a conventional design which everyone present would at once recognise. This would, if nothing else, prove that I knew what I was talking about. There was also just the barest possibility that I could come up with something quite new and unconventional, something unknown to Japanese engineers from beyond their shores. If this was a nonsense, they would know that I was not the type of person for them to be dealing with: if it wasn't, they would have acquired useful new knowledge. Either way, they couldn't lose!

An extraordinary aspect of these big sales meetings is that the timing of the end of the appointment seems to be almost more important and more precise than that of its start. A skilful agent, aware of this, will time his part of the sales talk neatly so as to finish just as the customers' team are about to close up their notebooks and pocket their ball-points. A lesser light may be caught in mid-speech and have to bow his thank-yous and his goodbyes with a sentence literally left in mid-air. No sign appears to pass, no-one seems to be glancing at his watch, but always the meeting seems to close sharp on the hour or the half-hour.

There is one Continental business custom, not usually adopted by British firms, that can pay dividends in Japan when visiting customers. I refer to the Reference List. On a recent visit to Tokyo, I was trying to introduce a product, new to our agents, about which we had not long before sent out a direct mail shot in Europe. This had included a reference list of customers to whom we had previously supplied this type of special equipment. Foolishly, I did not take a copy with me but, during the meeting with our first prospect in Japan, while my agent was talking, I jotted down some of the names from memory. I put down six British and six overseas firms to whom we had supplied and slipped the list across to my agent. He explained what it was to our customers' team, this time a mere six of them, and passed the paper across to them. It was eagerly picked up, studied, passed around and eventually impounded, no doubt to be photocopied and distributed to all concerned. During that trip I repeated this performance four times and always with the same result. I should have thought of it before I left London — but at least I learned a valuable lesson. Where and to whom you have already sold the product you are discussing is of prime interest and importance to your prospective Japanese customers.

You will note that I have assumed that your agents have provided at least one Japanese who is competent to act as an interpreter between you and the customers you are visiting. If not, I'd be very doubtful if you've picked the right agent! If you have to employ a professional interpreter — an expensive and somewhat risky business that may cost you £40 to £50 a day — there are a number of points to remember.

You must make sure that you leave plenty of time for adequate briefing. So far as possible, explain your product range, its purpose and application. Maybe this raises few problems in the consumer goods field but, however brilliant little Miss Kitamura may be at English, she's not likely to become an expert in the intricacies of electrolytic decoders, underwater knitting machinery, or whatever you make, in half an hour, or even half a year. Give the interpreter, too, as much background information as possible on all the data mentioned earlier in this chapter and explain your motives in the meeting that he or she's been hired for.

Whether your agent is doing the job or you're hired a professional interpreter, remember the points made about language in Chapter 3. Cut your speech as far as possible into short sentences, each of which can stand by itself. Remember, the shorter the sentences, the easier is the translation and hence the better chance you have of getting your message across correctly.

One last comment I would like to make is that the Japanese seem to have a surprising inclination for wanting something very near to the product that you've been trying to sell them but with just that little bit of difference. Bearing in mind what I have said earlier about the Japanese desire never to disappoint you and the extremely rare use of the word "No", one could easily be led to believe that this is a polite way of saying, "We're sure you've got a splendid product in what you've just shown us but it isn't of the slightest use or interest to our company." In my experience this has sometimes been the case but it would be foolish to assume that it is always so. If the figurative whistle has been blown and your time is up, there is nothing more that you can do on that visit. However, you can and should drop a broad hint to your agent and suggest that he should call again and get a more precise specification of the customer's requirements. Sometimes this works and with a relatively minor modification the product can find a market in Japan. I will revert to the question of product modification in Chapter 12.

Another possible motive behind this matter of wanting something slightly different from what you are offering is this. It is unlikely that, even when you have had discussions with a large group on the buying side, they will want or be able to come to an immediate decision. They will want to discuss the product and the implications of buying it between themselves and probably with others in their company. Hence, however enthusiastic they may be, politeness will lead to evasion. Much will depend on the ability of your agent to understand these reflections of national character and to know what course to adopt next. In any case, that's why you took an agent on, or wasn't it?

CHAPTER TEN

Soya Sauce And Geisha Gaiety

I read recently in a London newspaper that Tokyo is now the most expensive city in the world in which to live. The paper omitted to state whether their evaluation took into account the current rates of exchange. Without benefit of statistical back up, I'd formed roughly the same opinion when I visited Japan for the first time about nine years ago. At that time you could get around 820 Yen to the pound: the latest figure I have from the *Financial Times* is 381 Yen — 46.5% of what it was when I first hit Haneda Airport. Only the other evening a 'bookmark' fell from one of the books in my small library on Japan. It turned out to be a bar receipt for one gin and tonic from the Ginza Tokyu Hotel — and that's no Hilton or Ritz, but suited my requirements. At the current exchange rate a gin and tonic cost about 75 pence almost a decade ago.

I'm not trying to put you off. Far from it, but, before we look into how you and/or your hosts can spend money and on what, I just want to come face to face with reality. The relative sinking of our so-called 'floating pound' in these years means that a trip to Japan needs more than a dip into the kids' piggy-bank. It's far from cheap but, conversely, the embryo exporter should be cheered that his prices in Japan should, at least F.O.B. or C.I.F., be recipocally reduced and hence exporting should be that much easier.

Well, that's a rather serious vein in which to start a chapter of far less gravity than most that have preceded it and bearing the light-hearted title I have chosen for it. So let's look at the bright side and see what the bright lights of Tokyo, Osaka, Hiroshima etc. have to offer — with a few cautionary notes.

The Ginza district of Tokyo (Gin = silver, za = place and the G is hard) is the city's equivalent to Soho but, though only embracing eight blocks, it contrives to make London's square mile of vice look like a Lilliputian kiddies' playground, reputedly having some 300 varied Japanese restaurants, 150 serving Western cuisine, 75 Chinese and over 1200 bars, clubs and cabarets. A funny thing happened to me in this expense account playground the first time I went to Tokyo.

Three sararimen from a company with which I was negotiating had been detailed to entertain me for the evening. Evenings can start early in Japan and by eight we'd dined superbly on Kobe steak and saké up in Akasaka (if you've lots of money to spend and want to eat the world's most succulent beef, try the Misono Steak House there). Someone suggested, as someone always does, that we go to a 'club' and drink some whisky. In no time a taxi had whisked us at nightmare speed through the crowded 'dori' or main streets and decanted us in a Ginza side street where every floor of every building above shop level seemed to be a separate club. We took a lift up to one and were plied with scotch-on-the-rocks (or 'locks') and tit-bits by slim long-legged bunnies supervised by a matronly madame in kimono and obi. Empty glasses were banned by both my hosts and the management and the bottle went down fast. Someone suggested after an hour or so, that we go to another club and try some Japanese whisky. My three guardians, only one of whom was previously known to me, soon had me swigging down the Suntory Imperial and very good it was. (Both Suntory and Nikka produce excellent whiskies but avoid their cheap, unmatured blends which can be pure fire-water!). An hour and a bottle passed when someone suggested ...

I was still sober enough at the fourth club to spot an unfamiliar face among my hosts. I looked at the others through an alcoholic haze to realise that none of the three had started out the evening with me. The original party had been completely changed! Each time we'd moved clubs one of them had dropped out and a waiting replacement had stepped in!

At first sight one might assume that the objective was a deliberate attempt to get me drunk (yotte) without chancing hangovers (futsukayoi) themselves, but this is an uncharitable view. As it was, I decided it was time for me to call a halt and go back to my hotel and question them later. I did so, but no-one would confess to, nor explain the shift-system of entertaining. My personal conviction is that they wanted to ensure that I could drink my fill always accompanied by at least one perfectly sober host to see I didn't get into trouble and got safely back to my room. I don't say this happens to every foreign visitor but I do record the incident as both a warning and, I believe, a true example of the Japanese as the most painstaking and thoughtful hosts.

Both cuisine and service are usually superb in Japanese restaurants of reasonable standing and, even behind their 'noren' curtains, most of the little timber yakatori and soba shops are neat and clean if not luxurious. Customarily if you are taken out to dine, beer or grape-wine (budoshu) may precede the meal, accompanied by a glass of cold water and a hot towel, sealed in plastic, with which to refresh your face and wipe your hands. Beer or saké goes with the food, each diner having his own supply, and o-cha (green tea) concludes the meal. It is polite to fill your companions' cups from your own saké jug while they will do the same to yours. Thus if you're not very nimble, you again will probably end up with the lion's share but that's hospitality! In some Ryori or Japanese-style restaurants, the domestic custom of taking off your shoes in the ante-room prevails but these places are in the minority. Anyway your hosts or the joshu-san, the waitress, will soon put you right. Similarly, seating arrangements vary from eating at a bar or Western style table to getting down on the floor. Knowing the gaijin or 'foreigner's' inability to squat in the Japanese manner— with the buttocks resting on the heels— both in restaurants and in some homes the low table is so positioned that, while the Japanese may squat on zabuton cushions, the visitor has a position at the same level in which there is a lower space for his awkwardly inflexible Western legs. Every consideration is given to the visitor. As mentioned elsewhere the Japanese are great fish eaters and much of it is consumed raw as sashimi, slices of various kinds of fish or sushi, such slices wrapped in rolls or balls of rice. Japanese rice, by the way, has a glutinous consistency which makes the grains adhere to each other, otherwise it would be almost impossible to eat with hashi, or chop-sticks! Being considerate, Japanese rarely introduce Europeans to the pleasures of sushi, unless they are known to like it or ask for it. Scandinavians are, of course, the exception as they are familiar with raw fish on their own menus whereas most of us go no further than smoked salmon or roll-mops or oysters.

While on the subject of chop-sticking gohan, the honourable rice, into your guchi or mouth, I would mention that it is quite polite to raise o-sara, the bowl, to your mouth and to use the chopsticks like the boom of a high-speed earth-moving machine.

Similarly, soup is supped directly out of its lacquered bowl with none of our nonsense about spoons. In a commercial hotel bedroom in Hiroshima, I was interested to find amongst the guidance to visitors, the English translation of instructions to Japanese guests on how to use Western eating utensils! It is anomalous that, while UK cutlery manufacturers are complaining about the cheapness of imported Japanese knives, forks and spoons, the use of such barbarian metallic tools is unattractive to the Japanese generally. After all, the soft swish of hashi is much more restful than the incessant clatter that we make with metal on china! On the other hand, you may slurp your soup in Japan as noisily as you like. The local expertise in this auditory exercise can be upsetting to the Westerner, especially at breakfast time! While not in use and at the end of a course or meal, you should leave your chopsticks on the little rest provided, not on or in your plate or bowl.

As with almost every aspect of Japanese life, there is a big element of formality in meals and eating. Seating arrangements are directly related to rank so that Number One (Dai-ichi) guest generally has his back to the best part of the room, the 'tokonoma', a recess in which some objet d'art, in the widest sense (see Chapter 12) is placed. On the other hand, with his back to it, he won't get food down the back of his neck from high-speed waitresses coming in from the kitchen if that's the sort of place he's being entertained in. In fact, in a big proportion of restaurants, as well as in the Japanese home, should you graduate to being a visitor there, most of the cooking is done right in front of you on the bar or table you're sitting at.

Japanese restaurants tend to specialise and serve only one type of food. There are travel books, such as Fodor's *Guide to Japan and the Far East* in most public libraries which have space and motive to go into much more detail, but I would mention a few traditional dishes generally welcome to the Western palate — avoiding such curios as Fugu, the blowfish, only available in specially licensed restaurants as, if the chef doesn't know his job, he may omit to remove certain poisonous anatomical organs, which, if consumed, may cause death within five minutes. (In spite of the regulations five or six people die from this every year.) I would keep you off Ebi-kok, small shrimps eaten alive, and an exceedingly rubberish dish of shredded and fried jelly fish, edible but very difficult for the chopstick novice to get into his mouth. The pasta world of Italy is childsplay in comparison!

Fish, but not raw fish, is superb as 'Tempura' where mouth-sized portions of different fish and vegetables (including, when in season, Matsutake, the 'phallic' mushroom) fried by your own chef in batter and served in individual pieces as they come from the post. Tenpanyaki — literally "cooking on an iron plate" — happens on your table, the centre of which is a heated iron plate (originally a plough-share). Tenpanyaki beef, said in Kobe to be fed on stout and massaged every day, is unbelievably tender, served with onions and bean shoots. Sukiyaki and Shabu-shabu are again meat dishes, the meat sliced razor-thin and cooked in boiling water with vegetables on your table. Rather like the French-Swiss Fondue Bourgignonne, after the joshu-san has launched the table into orbit, you just go on cooking and eating for yourself.

Practically everything is eaten with Soya sauce, which you may mix to suit your own taste in the little saucer-like dish provided with raw egg yoke, mustard, powdered radish or garlic, with the tips of your chopsticks. Each mouthful is dipped in the sauce before eating. Not only does the sauce add flavour, but it obviates the risk of burning your mouth with an excessively hot morsel.

One could fill a whole book with this sort of gourmet gossip, so I will leave the rest of it to an appendix listing common and useful food words and definitions of dishes (see Appendix E). One can always survive, at least in reasonable Western style hotels with a substantial English or American breakfast in the 'Coffee Shop' — or some such name — without even having to bother about chopsticks! A matter of perhaps greater import is that of getting about in Japan on your own. But first, if you are travelling by yourself and dubious about your linguistic capabilities on the food front, all you have to do is to look for one of the many Japanese restaurants that deck their windows out with plastic replicas of the dishes they serve, often with a duplicate set by the cash desk. It sounds terrible but they're realistically fresh-looking, dusted daily, and, in all but flavour, do resemble what they represent.

If things are going well and a warm friendship begins to develop socially with your Japanese friends, you may, almost literally, be asked to sing for your supper. You may not consider that you have the voice of a Caruso, a Gigli or even Bob Dylan but if ever at the rugger club, the school choir or just in your local, you've exercised your lungs in song, you have a talent that may be exploitable in the cause of 'kokusai yujo' or international friendship. Social evenings in Japan tend to develop, when gaijin guests are about, into song. Often the start of it comes when a senior Japanese starts making a continuous noise that makes you wonder whether you should call for a doctor or a vet. In fact he is not in pain and, as you listen, the music of 'utai', the strange chanting of an ancient Samurai song, strikes the Western ear with its movingly plaintive tones. The applause is followed by other offerings of songs from East or West. Don't think you can escape easily. Your turn will come!

Faced with this unexpected situation, as a Scot by birth, the best I could do, in my early days when a good performance would have been to my best advantage, was an imperfect rendition of "Glasgow belongs to me". I knew lots of traditional folk tunes but could never remember the words. Since then I learnt the lyrics of songs like "Widdecombe Fair", "Clementine" and "Early One Morning" and believe me, the small effort has been worth it in cementing personal relations with Japanese friends and associates.

The first step in making any but a pedestrian journey on your own is to get someone to write your destination out in Kanji for you. Front hall staff in hotels are usually obliging and efficient at this though I often wonder if they don't write "Please take this foreign idiot to the British Embassy at 1-Ichiban-cho Chiyoda-Ku" or something equally impolite! However, it works and at least you have a hope of your taxi driver getting you there. Don't, by the way, try to open the door of the taxi to get in. In spite of their kamikaze image at the wheel, Japanese taxi drivers are sensitive souls and suspect anyone who so much as touches the door handle of intent to assault. The driver will open the nearside rear door by an ingenious mechanism from inside the cab. It is also advisable if you're staying at anything but the top hotels to take one of the hotel's cards to get you home again. There's usually a stack of them at the desk, often with a location map if the establishment isn't on a main street or 'dori'.

As noted in the last chapter, city taxi drivers are notoriously uninformed about the local geography. The big taxi companies seem to go out of their way to hire country yokels as drivers to ensure the maximum difficulty in reaching the right destination. Perhaps the longer drives are good for business. "Isogaba Maware", as the proverb says, "if in a hurry, go round"! If you get a choice, pick a cab driven by a Ko-jin, an owner-driver. He must be experienced — 10 years or more — and have a 'yu' or 'excellent' record, signified by a gold or silver and red plastic card inside his windscreen. Some non-Ko-jin drivers also have such licenses displayed, indicating a good safety record and experience. If the pace has you nervous or you spot the place you want, 'yukkuri' means 'slow-down'.

You don't, by the way, tip your taxi driver. The fact that tipping is not part of the Japanese way of life makes the country all the more pleasant. Instead a service charge is nearly always imposed and tips are neither given nor expected. Airport and railway porters have a fixed charge per bag. Barbers may accept a tip and hired car drivers may take 1500 Yen or so for a day's work and you may drop something at the cloakroom of a high-class "Naito" or night club. If you really want to recognise some particular service, sealing your bank note in an envelope converts it from a tip into a present and no-one loses face — or you can give a small gift instead, in the unlikely event of your having one, suitably wrapped, in your pocket or briefcase!

A land without tipping sounds like something out of paradise but there is a snag in it. Depending on the places you go and the company you keep, the Japanese have other ways of parting you from your money. In many bars and clubs, you'll certainly find that keeping at least the hostess is your job — apart from enjoying yourself — and keeping her is far from cheap! She gets commission not only on your drinks but on the highly-priced fruit juice disguised as champagne, that she knocks back at the same rate as she fills you up — and she'll expect a tip of one or 2000 Yen. The same applies to other establishments in the demi-monde of entertainment where 'sessu-appiru' or sex appeal has any significance.

Another point in visiting such places is that detailed bills are not the general order of things. You have your fun, you get a lump sum bill often including non-existent taxes conjured up by the imaginative proprietor. It may include an 'uncover' charge as well as a cover charge! The trouble is that, in the same situation, a Japanese is doubtless paying out of his lavish expense account so he's not all that bothered. On top of that, he would probably lose face if he questioned the bill so there's little chance of such audacity. And if you want to argue, you've got the language problem to deal with unless you know your Japanese guests well enough to let them take up the cudgels for you. I don't say Japan is any worse than other countries when you are dealing with this class and level of society but it's certainly no better. It boils down to that, if you're a greenhorn and unless you've an expense account to match the Japanese, you'd best keep away from the bright lights. Entertaining in your own hotel will be expensive, but at least you'll know what you're getting and how much you'll have to pay for it.

Except during the rush hours when 'shiri-oshi' or 'hip pushers' are employed to cram 400 passengers into 100 passenger carriages, the 'chikatetsu' or subway is a quick way of getting around Tokyo. A red circle on the wall-map shows where you are at the start and the Yen prices to other stations are marked in other circles. Directions are marked up in 'Romaji' that you can read and if you count the number of stations to the place you want to get out, you should be able to make it. At each station, too, the names of those before and after it are marked up in smaller letters than the station name. Subway station entrances, sometimes concealed in subterranean basements of hotels, shopping precincts or railway stations, are marked above by a blue S, and the station name.

Japanese trains, both of JNR and the private lines, have the great virtue of being on time — except when Japan National Railways have a strike — and they are relatively cheap. Apart from local trains there are the 343-mile New Tokaido line super express Shinkansen or Bullet trains, (also running on to Hakata, as far again; 3 hours and 10 minutes from Tokyo to Osaka), expresses, and limited expresses. 'Itto', first class, is definitely worth it for 'nito', (second class) is often very crowded and seats can't be reserved. If there isn't a restaurant car, 'o-bento', a standard packed lunch, of Nippon Ryohri or Japanese food can be bought at most stations, and is very palatable, though containing a bit of that raw fish! On the bullet trains and some other expresses, waitresses rush continually from one end of the train to the other with refreshment trolleys. Unfortunately at the 'eki', or station, few of the staff speak English, though more and more are obtaining a smattering of it. You may be lucky at the first class ticket office but it's safest to get the hotel people or a Japanese friend to write out a note of what sort of ticket you want and your destination. Platform signs are marked up in English but trains come and go with very short periods between them so you need to be sure you get the right one. The destination of the train is marked in small letters on each carriage, usually in 'Romaji' but it's a good idea to have a note of it in Kanji to be on the safe side. The whole business of travelling round Japan is simpler if you get the Japan Travel Bureau to help you. If the itinerary is complex, they'll need a few days notice but can book hotels, train tickets, buses, boats and even tickets for visits to tourist sights — if your schedule allows you the time! The Japan Travel Bureau then give you for a single payment a set of travel coupons for the lot and you should even get a discount! As each coupon is used up you've only to show the next one to anyone local and they'll send you on your way without any need to speak Japanese. That's what they say, but don't blame me if you get lost!

The Japan Guide Association can provide guides who speak English (and other European languages) fluently but the cost is around 12,000 Yen for an 8 hour day and, if you want them to travel with you, it's a costly exercise paying all their fares and expenses too.

Six Japanese cities have international airports, although only those at Tokyo and Osaka serve Europe and the USA. On the other hand there are over thirty towns with airports for internal domestic flights. While JAL fly some inter-city flights, the majority are hauled by All Nippon Airways (ANA) or Toa Domestic Airlines (TDA) to which Nippon Kinkyori Koku, the Japan Short Distance Airline, has been recently added. All have their own airport and terminal booking offices but flight planning is probably most easily arranged through the Japan Travel Bureau. Overall, the internal airline service is excellent apart from some rather primitive airports in the remoter parts. Plane seating, too, tends to be designed round the smaller-framed Japanese form, compressing the Western passenger rather more than is comfortable. However, unless you want to go to distant Okinawa, there are few flights of over an hour and a half.

A minor aspect of travel that once caused me trouble is a question of manners. We had to board a semi-express train at Gifu and something had gone wrong with our seat reservations so we had to travel in a somewhat overcrowded second class carriage. Among other passengers getting in was a little gnarled old country woman in grey kimono, her back bent nearly double with decades of working in the rice fields, and carrying her belongings tied in a heavy bundle. There was one unoccupied seat in spite of many people standing and I signalled to her to take it. I won't go into the pantomine that followed as I tried to get her into the seat while my Japanese travelling companion was equally adamant that I should take it. In the end he and local custom won and, of course, the old lady squatted quite comfortably on her heels in the corridor. No matter how old or deserving she may be, male supremacy in Japan dictates that you don't give up your seat to a lady!

While culture-hunting, the same problem has become even more apparent to me. Ever since I asked a simple question when being shown round a Shinto Ṣhrine at Kamakura that my cultivated and educated Japanese friend couldn't answer, they've been suspicious of me and determined not to be caught out by this inquisitive 'gaijin' again. Whenever we go shopping or sight-seeing, they protect themselves from the possibility of losing face by not being able to satisfy my curiosity about Nippon history and culture by bringing along an expert. The expert is a 'she', a most cultured Japanese lady who travels the world lecturing and demonstrating as one of the top five Ikebana (flower arranging) specialists in the country. When I was first introduced to her in a 'Naito', she was wearing an expensive version of that 'little black dress' that British wives find 'so useful'. Her English isn't all that good so we conversed in French. I'll call her Mrs Ichida.

The next time I met her, my hosts had arranged to take me to a very special shop to buy paper, brushes and ink such as are used in Japanese calligraphy and 'sumi-e', water colour painting. In the front of the chauffeur-driven Nissan President with its air-conditioning was Mrs Ichida, dressed that day in the most exquisite embroidered kimono and all the trimmings. She was a delight to the eye as well as to the mind. After the shopping trip, she was to take me round Tokyo's remarkable Folk Art Museum (which, incidentally, has a wonderful collection of the pottery work of the Englishman, Bernard Leach, who worked for a long time in Japan).

It was a day to remember; the people, the weather, the places were perfect but that's not the most memorable aspect of the day. It started when the car stopped outside the art shop. The elegant, cultured, beautiful Mrs Ichida and I seemed irrevocably locked in a struggle to open doors for each other and to let the other go first. In the end I got the message. No matter how splendid a creature she may be, the Japanese woman knows her place and that is not in front of any man. In everything (except perhaps the household budgetting mentioned in Chapter 5) she takes second place.

Most Western males have the misguided idea that a Geisha is something you take to bed with you. You don't. Only her patron does, if she has one. Literally Geisha means 'art person' and the exquisitely formal ladies of this dying race (there are only some 50,000 in Japan today) are highly trained artistic entertainers, their services being accordingly highly priced. Their accomplishments include Eastern and Western dancing, a knowledge of foreign languages, the social graces, how to fill saké cups and an unusual ability to giggle politely. They are also experts in party games and tricks, the art of conversation, singing, playing the samisen or koto or the small taiko drum. In spite of the Japanese capacity for providing comprehensive statistics, no-one has yet been able to tell me the capital investment needed to take a young girl through the Maiko (apprentice) stage through to the fully fledged Geisha. A single kimono, however, with accessories, can cost up to a quarter of a million Yen (about £650 at today's exchange rate), and a Geisha may have a dozen or more in her wardrobe.

Geisha are thus high class, expensive, professional performers, hired by the hour to look after the upper crust of the Japanese business world when they have people to entertain. Their function is to divert and amuse host and guests, to nurse them into a state of relaxation. They are social ice-breakers paid highly, if I may mix metaphors, to oil the wheels of inter-company and inter-personal relationships. Prostitution is outside their duties — so far as you're concerned.

If you are invited to a real Geisha party, you may consider yourself honoured, but don't expect that it will be all fun. For a start it won't be an attractive little novice that's detailed to look after you. As a guest and a foreigner, you'll need the attention of an expert who knows all the answers. Don't believe Ian Fleming's description in the James Bond book *You Only Live Twice*. Experienced Geisha tend to be a bit long in the tooth, and even with the younger ones, it's difficult to find the real face beneath the black wig and heavy mask of white make-up. There's a further problem too, in that, while most of the antics are just plain boring, the 'relaxing' process is usually so successful that the initial formality ends in Bacchanalian revelry where almost everyone — except the Geisha who are watching the clock preparing to dash off to their next engagements — look like the aftermath of a drunken strip poker game. Ah well, Mama-san knows best — and how much to charge!

Should you be invited to a Japanese home, protocol is much the same as being entertained in a hotel, restaurant or club except that it is customary to take with you a small gift, properly wrapped as I've previously mentioned, particularly if you've already received an 'okurimono' from your host. Gift-giving in Japan isn't like in some Moslem countries in the Middle East where, if you admire your host's house, horse or harem he smiles and gives it to you. The Japanese have a saying: "Do not repay a sea-bream with a minnow", but they understand that your expense allowance may not be the same as theirs, so a smaller sea-bream will be adequate. The Japanese love to receive something typically British, not some kitsch plastic model of Westminster Abbey or St. Pauls, but something tasteful. I've had great success giving away small English landscape paintings of my own in oils but if you're not an artist, little framed historical prints are popular, if a little difficult to transport by air. Small items of china such as Wedgwood, replicas of Magna Carta (obtainable from HMSO), sets of coins or even commemorative stamps will be received with pleasure. On a relaxed evening, I've even had to give away my tie, that of a British technical society which must remain nameless! Gifts needn't be extravagant but they should be original and of good quality.

It may be worth while to talk of crime. In spite of student violence, and such exuberances as television shows of the demonstrations against Tokyo's new airport at Narita, the Japanese are one of the most law-abiding nations in the world. Petty crimes like mugging and theft are rare, but they do occur. When the walls of your house are made of paper, there isn't much point in bolting the front door, but it would be foolish to leave your hotel room unlocked. If you do have trouble, the police have 110 as their emergency telephone number. (119 will get you an ambulance.)

Japan is a land of festivals, both national and local and, while you shouldn't miss them if you happen to be there at the time, a knowledge of their dates can save you wasted days of valuable time in your work. (The principal public holidays are listed in Appendix F and in B.O.T.B.'s *Hints to Businessmen Visiting Japan*, while the Japan National Tourist Organisation publish a leaflet *Annual Events in Japan* detailing local 'matsuri' up and down the country). If your hosts or Japanese colleagues suggest going to one of the festivals, don't miss the opportunity. A few of the Buddhist temple festivals are imbued with pomp and solemnity, but most of these special Japanese celebrations are fast-moving scenes of jostling activity and fun, the religious significance generally having been forgotten by most of the participants and the spectators.

Festival activities include moon- and cherry blossom-viewing, usually with the consumption of much saké, kite-flying battles, fireworks, archery on horseback, and gaily coloured costume processions pouring sweet tea over an image of Buddha on his birthday which is the Flower Festival or Hanamatsuri. Huge processions of giant floats may be involved, or the streets may be filled with groups of chanting and perspiring youths bearing heavy, glittering portable shrines or 'Mikoshi', and wearing little but sweat bands on their foreheads and 'fundoshi' loin cloths below. There are ceremonies honouring the Emperor's birthday, spring and autumn equinoxes, the iris and chrysanthemum seasons, ancestors, old people, youth, labour day, culture day, the cremation of unwanted dolls, and even to pray for the souls of discarded sewing needles. There is one in which beans are thrown to drive out devils. Many of the ceremonies, appearing more like orgies, involve the spectators in long lines or circles of dances in which your participation may be welcome and encouraged. Even if it's hard work, it can be fun and helps to improve cordial relationships. It may help you towards understanding the people of Japan and suitable refreshment is bound to follow!

A word for the solitary just in case you do find some time to spend on your own which, in my experience, isn't very likely. Apart from the risk of getting lost, the only danger about adventuring out on your own is to your pocket book rather than your person. No-one's likely to steal it but Tokyo and other towns abound with touts to draw you into expensive establishments where the Mama-san and the hostesses are poised to lighten you of the load of Yen notes you're carrying. Don't be taken in by the touts. Avoid also any place where the doorway is decorated by an inviting young hostess or two, unless you and your company have a passion for parting with pounds. You're better off in a 'stand bar', oddly named as you sit at a bar stool, but at least you don't have to fork out for a 'hostess drink' every time you have one yourself. The Beer halls, too, are reasonably priced and lively, with food available, and modelled along the lines of the German equivalent.

In most of the main hotels, you can obtain a free copy of the Tokyo *Tour Companion*, a weekly paper comparable with

What's on in London. Although it plugs places that advertise in the paper, the *Tour Companion* gives reliable suggestions on where to go and not be fleeced excessively, as well as other useful information of a practical nature like subway maps, how to ˙ telephone, and charts of Japanese coinage, currency conversion, shopping and entertainment news and advice. Many of the restaurants and other places mentioned or advertised give prices so you've some idea of what you're in for. The *Tour Companion* also details the programmes of the unique JCTV system.

Colour TV is almost universal in Japanese hotel rooms, even in Ryokan or Japanese-style hotels, and there are many channels to choose from but naturally in the Japanese language. (Programme details are given in the four daily English language newspapers — the *Mainichi Daily News*, the *Japan Times* the *Asahi Evening News* and the *Daily Yomiuri*). JCTV, however, although not on all day, is broadcast in English. It is Japan Cable Television and is available in a number of the main hotels and a few apartment blocks. Programme quality is variable but JCTV's worth watching for the news and some of the programmes about Japan.

Incidentally, although that's not what it's for, JCTV can be a sales aid for some products if they've a cultural or newsy angle. There's a programme in which 'interesting' visitors to Tokyo are interviewed. I once appeared on the programme, talking about something quite apart from my engineering export work. The other person interviewed in the studio was an angular American lady over from the States as agent for a group of artists whose products she was exhibiting and selling. She had a number of samples of their modernistic daubing on the studio walls and pumped the microphone with a stream of esoteric jargon as the camera panned on to them. Her commentary doubtless got her some good free publicity within the limited scope of the Channel 2 programme. If you're selling anything rare, newsworthy, cultural, historical, artistic or fashionable, a phone call to JCTV in the Asahi Shinbun building may be worth a try. They even pay your expenses getting to and from the studio.

CHAPTER ELEVEN

You Can Bank On These

To 'bank on' something or someone generally means that you can count on them or rely on them, and this chapter is mainly concerned with fixed and reliable elements that you can depend on in the whirlpool of the Japanese business scene. There is, however, another side to it, too. Just as you can back the favourite in a horse-race and 'bank on' its winning, you can equally well bank on a number of other horses than can be relied on not to win. Some such beasts are bound to intrude into this chapter for, if not unreliable, there are certain aspects of Japanese business that are likely to provide problems, at least if they are not understood. To include them under the same heading is perhaps showing an element of Japanese logic but it seems sensible to me. There's not much problem with the banks but, if anyone expects the Law— in the broadest sense— in Japan to bear anything but the most superficial resemblance to its solid, immutable English counterpart, he needs to think again.

Banking in Japan, as mentioned in Chapter 3, originated in its present form in the Meiji era and was based on European models. The Bank of Japan, which is at the peak of the financial pyramid, occupies much the same place as the Old Lady of Threadneedle Street as being the only issuer of banknotes and as the Ministry of Finance's main channel for controlling monetary, interest rate and investment policy. Through BOJ the government retains tight control over the yen, at least internally. Both internal and external economic policy are in fact drawn up by the Bank's Policy Board which has seven members representing the Ministry of Finance, the Economic Planning Agency, the city banks, the local banks, industry and commerce, agriculture and the Governor of the BOJ. The dependence of most enterprises on banks for investment and working capital, already mentioned, makes it clear that this is a highly effective method of financial control. The influx of foreign banks into Japan and their subsequent activities in the money market has had some diluting effect on the influence of the BOJ but, as they in their turn have to comply with many of the BOJ's edicts, the effect is minimal. The importance to the Japanese economy of the selective financing of industries that the government wishes to encourage for their potential future profitability, as opposed to those that should be reciprocally discouraged, has already been discussed. It is through the BOJ that this type of policy is put into practice. Interest rates and total borrowing are similarly controlled, regulation of the level of loans being under what is known as 'madoguchi kisei' or window guidance. In spite of the stress that is laid on the independence of the BOJ, it is interesting to note that the non-government members of its Policy Committee are elected by the cabinet.

There are many other banks and government financial institutions which I will touch on only briefly. Cooperation with them is more likely to be the preoccupation of the Japanese partner in any joint venture than of the British partner. In any case they have been described in detail in such publications as JAL's booklet, *Japan's Banking and Investment Systems* by Dr Hoshii Iwao, and, at least in the case of the Bank of Japan and the commercial or city banks, information can be obtained about their services for the British exporter from their London branches listed in Appendix A. The same applies to British banks having branches in Japan. At least fourteen are represented in one form or another in Japan.

There are thirteen main commercial or city banks in Japan, some bearing the same names as the groups and trading companies with which they are associated. Government-backed financial institutions include the Japan Development Bank, the Japan Export-Import Bank, the Trust Fund Bureau, the Small Business Finance Corporation and the People's Finance Corporation. The government licences the Foreign Exchange banks, among which the Bank of Tokyo has a somewhat special position in matters concerned with foreign business. Other banks include the local, ie provincial or regional banks, the Long Term Credit banks and the Trust banks.

I would mention that many of the last have the same primary names as some of the commercial banks, though having to keep their assets and liabilities quite separate for the two types of banking business. I have special reason to be aware of this personally. Many years ago, apart from running my own affairs, I was appointed stand manager for a Joint Venture stand at a trade exhibition in Tokyo. The trade association involved arranged with their bank in London to send me the necessary funds to pay for furniture hire, stand cleaning, interpreters, etc in the form of a Letter of Credit and with great ingenuity found that Sumitomo had a branch conveniently near the hotel I was staying at. Whether they got the right address and the wrong name or the other way about, I never discovered, but I imagine it was the former. Neither did I find out what the postman did with a letter addressed to the Sumitomo Trust Bank at the address of the Sumitomo Trading Bank. All I know is that I wasted many fruitless hours and an exorbitant sum in taxi fares chasing round Tokyo banks looking for my money. The other British exhibitors tut-tutted sympathetically but, to a man, kept their wallet pockets firmly buttoned. Luckily I had local friends who were kind enough to loan me the thousand or so pounds needed, or I might still be languishing in some Tokyo gaol and this book never written! After this lesson in the need for properly addressing correspondence, I invested heavily in credit cards against future emergencies. Apart from a number of local cards, such as JCC, American Express, Diners Club, Carte Blanche, Master Charge and Bank Americard are fairly widely accepted in Japan.

From one of James Kirkup's books I learnt a useful tip about Japanese banks. Kirkup, who was Professor of English Literature at Tokyo Women's University and has years of experience of living in Japan, points out that, if at any time during banking hours that you are overheated or tired, most of the banks are air conditioned and very helpful to foreigners. If you've lost your way or just want a rest, they try to help you, at least let you enjoy the luxury of their deeply unholstered furniture and even ply you with refreshing green tea. Another tip is that if you really want to transact any business in a Japanese bank, leave plenty of time for it. You may get a better rate for your travellers cheques at the bank than at your hotel, but generally the hotel will do the job much faster. At the bank even the simplest transaction calls for a multitude of forms in many copies and their reference to any number of the clerk's seniors, sometimes located as far away as the building will allow, all of whom have to give the paperwork lengthy consideration and reverence before approving it.

You can bank on the Law in Japan but the chances of your

having to do so are small, except insofar as it controls your commercial activities. Doubtless before signing any agreement or contract with a Japanese company or partner, you will be placing due reliance on your own lawyers in the UK or your company's legal department if it has one. I would repeat, however, the advice already given, ie, that to the Japanese the written contract is of minor importance compared with that of the spirit behind it. The mutual trust that should and must develop for any sort of sucess to be achieved in your working with a Japanese company can in fact receive a serious initial setback if you will go on harping about all the details of the fine print. It just makes it look as if you don't trust them and, if that's the case, so far as they're concerned, they might just as well forget about the whole thing. Compared with the Law in England, in Japan it is far less clearly defined. Government departments, for instance, have much wider powers of interpretation within the framework of any piece of legislation than is to be found in the West. Their 'administrative guidance' must generally be accepted for there exists no proper court of appeal against their decisions. On the other hand they are almost always fair in their dealings, particularly with foreign companies for loss of face could result from any blatantly unfair decision and could be to the detriment of both the ministry or department concerned if not to the image of Japan. The same applies to the Bank of Japan which, I should mention, is the ultimate arbitrator in all matters relating to foreign cooperation and investment. All proposals for international cooperation have to be submitted to the BOJ in many copies, many of the simpler affairs being automatically rubber-stamped with no undue delay. More complex matters take longer but the BOJ is a quick and efficient organisation which doesn't waste time. The same can be said of the Fair Trade Commission who are also generally involved in anything concerned with international contracts. The appropriate papers have to be filed with the commission and rarely do they even comment, let alone ask, for any modification of a contract which will in the normal course of affairs be drawn up by the Japanese partner involved who should know the rules and play according to them. This may be an over-optimistic view but businessmen going abroad are 'salesmen' and salesmen are optimists!

The Japanese legal profession is, in fact, one of the smallest in the world for the size of the population. It didn't exist until the early years of the nineteenth century and other methods of settling disputes had been used for many centuries before and have persisted until today. Japanese law, as it stands today, originated on western patterns evolved during the Meiji era and subsequently modified to conform with the new Constitution drawn up after the last war. Generally the Japanese do not fly to their lawyers to obtain counsel's opinion at the drop of a 'boshi' or hat. Only when litigation seems inevitable do they call in lawyers and this is fortunately rare. Most disputes are settled by conciliation quite apart from the Law profession. The parties involved agree on an independent arbitrator who is quite unofficial and is generally chosen for his age, experience and wisdom rather than for his knowledge of the Law which may be non-existent. Thus, while arbitration clauses may be written into most contracts and the legal arbitrators to be used are specified therein, such clauses and arbitrators are rarely called on, the dispute being settled out of court. Incidentally, international contracts with Japanese companies can be drawn up in accordance with the laws of any country so long as these do not conflict with the laws of Japan.

An important point regarding the law when dealing with a Japanese company is that their reaction to a change of circumstances is very different from that in the West, and here lies a great risk of misunderstanding. With their far greater concentration on the spirit of an agreement than on its strict wording, the Japanese, if changing circumstances appear to call for it, are likely to ask for a change in the terms of contract. This can lead to suspicion on the part of the Western company involved and a decline in the trust they have put in the Japanese. Should you be faced with such a situation, think twice before rejecting the Japanese proposals out of hand. Their motive is likely to be simply to preserve your cooperation in the state in which it is likely to be most effective under the new circumstances whether these have changed internally or for external reasons. They will be acting for the best as they see it and you should try and see it their way. My own plans for progressive cooperation with one Japanese firm were drastically changed with the OPEC price 'hike' on oil in 1973. In fact it did not call for any contractual modification, no more than a deference of a further contract that we had proposed to put into operation, but the principal was the same and the vast change in the world economic situation brought about by the action of the OPEC states was such that it would have been foolish not to have agreed to the Japanese proposals. The Japanese were not trying to evade their responsibilities but merely trying to face up to a new situation in the most practical way for both parties.

Should you decide that you do need the services of a law firm in Japan, a list of possible contacts is given in the appropriate B.O.T.B. *Hints to Businessmen* booklet. However, if your legal affairs are normally handled by one of the major British company law firms, it is possible that they have an association with a Japanese firm and their advice should obviously be sought first.

Patent and trademark law is a specialised subject requiring the engagement of experts conversant with the field. The protection of industrial property rights in Japan is much the same in Japan as elsewhere, with a comparable range of legal protection and procedures. The risks of not taking advantage of such protection are no more nor no less than anywhere else. The main difference is that applications for patents, trademark, trade name or design registration in Japan not unnaturally have to be made in Japanese and, in spite of the wizardry of the experts in Southampton Row and thereabouts, not many of them are well versed in 'Nihongo', and hence the employment of a firm in Japan may probably be necessary. As with solicitors, many UK patent agents have their own networks of overseas affiliates so your first approach should clearly be to your UK expert. As with the Law, B.O.T.B. supply a list of suitable Japanese firms if your own man isn't in touch with a Japanese professional of the right calibre.

Two minor points I would like to make in this connection. First is the need to register trade names in Japan before starting into the market. I have not personally found a special need for this but it is a point of policy that has been made to me by many more experienced people in the market. It seems that while the copying of products is no longer a prevalent habit in Japan, it is still not uncommon for another company to start selling quite a different product under your trade name before you've even got off the ground. Hence you must protect your trade name at the earliest possible moment. Second, there is in the patent system a class of invention entitled a 'Utility Model' which, while still retaining a degree of novelty as in a patentable product or process, does not involve quite the same degree of inventive capability. Such a patent is easier to obtain than for a fully patentable invention. Further details of this and other details of the patent laws are to be found in the B.O.T.B. booklet, *Trading with Japan, Import Procedures and Industrial Property Rights in*

Japan, which you would be well advised to read.

A fixed point on which the exporter can set his sights with confidence is the other side of the law that protects the Japanese citizen, and which can be categorised under the headings of Consumer Protection, Industrial Safety and Anti-Pollution Laws. In principle these are the same as in our own country, but in detail they may be very different. In these fields the Japanese are probably more advanced than any other country. It is useless to grumble about these laws. They exist and apply equally to Japanese products and manufacturers. The important thing is to obtain the fullest possible information about the relevant regulations and to ensure that your products conform to them in every way. Japanese law can be particularly harsh in respect to the compensation that must be paid to persons suffering in any way from manufacturers' infringements of any of the many laws enacted. Even penalties for the prime offenders can be severe: a motorist exceeding the allowed limits for exhaust noise, for example, can be sent to prison for up to a year. In the Minamata mercury poisoning affair mentioned in Chapter 2, compensation of 640 million Yen was demanded for 109 plaintiffs and the defendants were later faced with several hundred more claims. The Japanese approach is a long way from the half-hearted lukewarm British approach exemplified by the Thalidomide tragedy of the 1960's.

Legislation is rarely a static affair. The JETRO booklets on this important subject have already been mentioned but, for most products, the potential British exporter would be advised to obtain the most up-to-date information from the nearest JETRO office, in this case from Baker Street, London, and to make sure that his products conform.

Spend an evening or an hour or two in front of the colour television ('terebisu') and you might think (unless you are in the business) that advertising in Japan is no different from that at home, but there are some important facts that must be recognised. On the face of it, the same sort of sing-songs and jingles seem to accompany the same sort of inane smiles on the faces of ostensibly satisfied housewives as they do in Britain and to an extent this is true, while in other advertising media, radio, the press, direct mail, etc. there are similar parallel features.

For a start, the function of an advertising agency in Japan is generally quite different from that of its UK (or Western) equivalent. The Japanese agency exists largely to finance the media by purchasing space or TV time in advance and then re-selling it in the manner of a broker in other fields. While such agencies are willing to undertake a total sales promotion campaign for a client, it is likely that in most cases they will farm out most of the work, including the so-called creative side, on a sub-contract basis. Such an extension of the lines of communication is unlikely to appeal to the foreign business concern, already faced with the problems of distance and language but that's the way it is. The selection of an agent thus becomes a primary problem. There are, in fact, a number of Western advertising agencies with branches or subsidiaries in Japan such as McCann, Erikson and J. Walter Thompson, a strong American slant originating from the days of the Occupation.

A great deal of account must be taken, too, of the difference in outlook of our two peoples. Due to their ideographic writing, the Japanese are a far more visually-oriented nation than most while, at the same time, they are far more influenced by emotional criteria than by pure facts. On the other hand where facts are stated as facts as in statistics, the Japanese are far more likely to accept them at face value than with the scepticism that many Europeans may regard the nine-out-of-ten-dentists-recommend-Toothyclense approach, implying, but by no means proving, that ninety per cent of all dentists approve of the dubious product. The importance of the written word has to be taken into account from another aspect, for the visual character of kanji symbols, instantly recognised by the reader, means that greater impact may be obtained with a more briefly encapsulated message. The Japanese, too, are generally much more impressed by the recommendations of public persons in advertisements. While we may sceptically wonder foremost how much a well-known TV or film personality is getting for his or her sponsorship of 'Indigestibrek', the Japanese are more likely to really believe that their favourite star loves nothing better.

These are but some of the differences, small but relevant, in advertising in the two countries. The important thing to realise is that, with two cultures so different, what is right for one is not necessarily right for the other and it is only sense, if one has put one's affairs in the hands of a Japanese advertising company, to, at least in the initial stages, take things to a great extent on trust. It is no use trying to impose the outward aspects of one culture on another, although with many products success has been achieved by the use of Western actors or models in advertisements in

Japan. This is particularly effective if one is trying to put over the image of a product which has predominantly Western characteristics that are likely to appeal to the Japanese.

The media choice is wide. There are five major newspapers in Japan with circulations of from one to six million and representing two-thirds of all newspaper circulation, the rest being made up of fifty-eight local papers. There are twelve sports magazines, fifty-one weeklies and over thirteen hundred monthlies, apart from some eleven hundred and twenty trade, technical and commercial papers and journals. In addition to radio, there are eighty-two commercial television stations. This very plethora of choice only tends to make the problem more difficult for the 'gaijin' tyro. With consumer goods, too, comes the added problem of the extensive and complex distribution system, entailing a large number of people who have to be convinced of the quality and viability of a product before they will throw themselves into the job of selling it. This almost requires a separate advertising campaign in itself to get the wholesalers and retailers on your side. Another point is that the very size of the market means that the cost of saturation is bound to be high although the potential rewards are, of course, in proportion.

A small point that is worth noting is that Japanese advertising agents, acting as they do more as space-brokers than anything else, are not averse to taking on more than one client in any product field, an attitude that would be contrary to the ethics of any agency in the West. It seems that nothing can be done but to accept this but, if you can obtain the information, try to ensure that you are the first on the agency's list for the particular product that you are trying to sell.

Where market research is concerned, the situation is very different. There is a wide variety of choice in the organisations you can employ, and this includes a number of companies of British origin but which have long experience of Japanese affairs. Again the B.O.T.B. have a list from which to choose. This is a field in which the Japanese excel. I was once at a luncheon in London where the position was summarised succinctly. The guest of honour was Kato Tadeo-san, the recent Japanese ambassador in Britain, who gave an entertaining speech liberally larded with statistics on Anglo-Japanese trade. Lord Limerick rose to reply. "You, sir, have statistics," he said to the ambassador, "statistics which purport to be accurate." He paused significantly to allow this apparent diplomatic insult to sink in and then with superb timing continued, "We have none and therefore ours are suspect." There is a harsh reality behind his Lordship's humour for that is just how the matter stands. When it comes to trade, commercial or other figures, we are kindergarten kids compared with the Japanese in spite of the vast number of government forms that firms are legally bound to fill in every month or more often. Market research in Japan may not be cheap but it is efficient and one of the fields in which American business expertise seems to harmonise with Japanese thought and method. You shouldn't have any trouble here as long as you can pay the price. You can certainly bank on your market research company.

These are a few of the reliable and unreliable aspects of the business scene as things stand today. In Chapter 13 we'll take a look at the overall social picture and try to see how things are changing in some fields while remaining more or less static in others.

CHAPTER TWELVE

Culture Condensed

Is it really necessary, you may ask, for the hard-headed, practical British businessman to be versed in the complexities of Japanese poetry, painting, pottery and similar unbusinesslike pursuits? I can't prove that it is but I'm firmly convinced that such knowledge can do him and his company nothing but good. Quite apart from its intrinsic interest, it must at the same time deepen his understanding of the country and its people and broaden his mental horizon in a practical and businesslike way for, in spite of change, much of the national character today is based on the cultural background.

Looking at it from the other side, I know a number of Japanese business friends who can come to England and recite more Shakespeare than I can and give the dates of his birth and death. (1564-1616, in case you've forgotten.) This isn't one-upmanship. They just happen to learn it at school — and remember it. At the same time some 40,000 British exporters leave London Airport each year, optimistically euphoric about the prospects of selling their wares in Japan, but I doubt whether one in a thousand of them has ever even heard of Chikamatsu Monzaemon. I hadn't when I first went to Japan and yet this playwright, who lived from 1653 to 1725, is generally acclaimed as the Shakespeare of Japan.

We've had a look at the language question in Chapter 4. It must be admitted that it should be no more difficult for a Briton to learn 'Nihongo' than it is for a Japanese to learn English but there is one difference in their favour, at least since 1945. Since then, ie for more than the last thirty years, English has been taught as the second language in Japanese schools. Few British businessmen can claim to be fluent speakers of French, a language which has a structure not much different from that of our own, but we do have a basic knowledge upon which we can build if we want to, just as the younger Japanese have at least a start in 'Eigo'. But what about 'culture'? It seems to me that only laziness, lack of interest and indifference can account for our lack of any grasp of the culture of Japan and our resulting ignorance seems hardly likely to endear us to the Japanese when we visit their country.

To condense some thousands of years of Japanese culture into a short chapter seems an almost impossible task. If only culture in Japan was confined to cultured pearls, such a condensation might not seem so difficult! However, the divergence between our two cultures is such as to make the endeavour all the more worth while. If I do nothing else, I hope to stimulate the reader's interest, and the Bibliography in Appendix H is designed to point him in the right direction. Even if I only succeed in interpreting some of the terms involved and producing a short 'name-dropping' guide, I shall have achieved something. To know at least the names of some of the great Japanese writers and artists is surely better than never to have heard of them at all? I believe that it will be appreciated by the Japanese and, if British Nippophilic scholars should deride my efforts, they are only debasing themselves to the level of critics. As Sibelius said, "Pay no attention to what the critics say: no statue has ever been put up to a critic."

Culture and history are so inextricably interwoven that this chapter must be closely related to Chapters 2 and 3. To refresh your memory and present a proper perspective Table 4 gives a summary of the main historical periods of Japan with a comparison of what was going on in Britain at the same time. Most cultural activities can be related to these periods of history. What do we have to consider under the heading of culture?

Broadly speaking, a summary for any country would include architecture, art, possibly some artefacts, drama, literature, music, pottery and sculpture. Japan has a few additional specialities which cannot be ignored as they are closely inter-related: Ikebana (flower arrangement), Cha-no-yu or tea ceremony, and the special nature of gardens where bare sand and rocks may replace the lawns, shrubs and flowers, conventionally essential elements in the West. There is the art of growing miniature Bonsai trees, of Bunraku puppetry to say nothing of the much admired and practised art of calligraphy. As in other cultures, the relationship between the plastic and the graphic

Table 4.   HISTORICAL PERIODS IN JAPAN AND BRITAIN

JAPAN		BRITAIN	
The Ancient or Kodai Era			
JOMON Period		Iberian & Celtic	to 55 BC
Hunting & Fishing	1500 BC – 0AD	Romans	55 BC – 407 AD
YAYOI Period		Anglo-Saxons	300 – 1066
Agriculture. Villages	0 AD – 250	Early Christian	400 – 800
TUMLUS Period	250 – 500	Viking Invasions	800 – 900
ASUKA Period.			
Introduction of Chinese			
influences (Buddhism 522)	550 – 710		
The Middle Era			
NARA Period	710 – 794		
Early HEIAN Period	794 – 857		
Late HEIAN or			
FUJIWARA Period	857 – 1185	Normans	1066 – 1189
KAMAKURA Period	1185 – 1336	Plantagenets	1189 – 1399
ASHIKAGA Period	1336 – 1573	Early Tudors	1399 – 1485
(Muromachi Period	1392 – 1573)	Late Tudors	1485 – 1603
AZUCHI – MOMOYAMA			
Period	1576 – 1614	(Elizabeth I	1558 – 1603)
TOKUGAWA Period		Stuarts	1603 – 1702
(Capital, Edo)	1614 – 1867	Hanoverians	1702 – 1837
		Victoria	1837 – 1901
The Modern Era			
MEIJI Period	1867 – 1912	Edward VII	1901 – 1910
TAISHO Period	1912 – 1926.	George V	1910 – 1936
SHOWA Period	1926 –	George VI	1936 – 1952
		Elizabeth II	1952 –

Note on the Names of the Japanese Periods   The Nara, Heian and Kamakura Periods are named after the locations of the capitals of the time, Heian-kyo being the earlier name of Kyoto. The Ashikaga, Tokugawa and Fujiwara periods take their names from those of the ruling Shogunate families. Muromachi was a district in Kyoto, while Azuchi was the site of Oda Nobunaga's castle on the shores of Lake Biwa and Momoyama was that of Toyotomi Hideyoshi's villa. Edo (or Yedo) was the old name for Tokyo, the 'Eastern Capital'. In the Modern Era the periods are called after the names chosen by the emperors for their regimes.

forms of art are generally apparent, the same spirit pervading practitioners using either two or three dimensional materials and techniques. In Japan there are additionally links between different cultural fields. Calligraphy with kanji ideograms, for example, has a graphic, pictorial quality closely allied to painting while, at the same time, being the visual component of poetry and prose, it is inherently an element of literature. Such links tend towards a simplification of artistic concepts which can be deceptive for, in Japan, hidden formalism and symbolic significance abound to confuse the uninitiated, though these need not worry the foreign visitor. Most Japanese are aware of the three fundamental elements in ikebana — heaven, earth and man — though they may not immediately recognise them in their wives' flower arrangements. I have mentioned the use of rocks both in gardens and as ornaments in either home or office. In gardens rocks of different shapes are usually placed in groups of two or three, apparently according to the aesthetic conception of the garden designer. In fact there is much more to it than that. There are five basic forms of rocks used, the body rock, the reclining rock, the branching rock, the heart rock and the rock of spiritual form and there is a complex symbolism in the way in which these are combined in groups, which probably few Japanese could define today. Similarly, while most will probably know of the four 'paragons' — the orchid, the bamboo, the plum and the chrysanthemum (the last an Imperial symbol) — few know of the 'Emon ju hachi byo', or Eighteen Rules for Drawing Lines in classical art. These range from the Floating Silk Thread line to the Nail Head or Rat Tail, the Gnarled Knot and the Whirling Water lines. They were used in olden times for sketching clothing, the lines distinguishing between people of different classes and occupations and being a reminder of the historical hierarchical nature of Japanese society that persists, if in different form, to this day. I mention them to stress the underlying complexity of Japanese life and thought that is often concealed by the apparent simplicity on the surface. You can even find similar symbolic formalism in the way a dish is laid out in a restaurant, each component representing some element, typically of a season, for the Japanese set great store by seasonal changes and bring them into their daily lives more than most.

Literature is clearly the most direct and communicable of art forms as well as being the one in which Japanese material for study is most readily available to us, thanks to the work of such translators as Arthur Waley, Donald Keene, Ivan Morris, Geoffrey Bownas, Edward G. Seidensticker and E. Dale Saunders. Those, like myself, who wish to savour either classical or modern Japanese literature owe an immeasurable debt to these and other scholars who have spent their lives disentangling the complex wilderness of Japanese thought and writing.

Though all over the world tales have been told long before the invention of writing, literature as such depends for its existence on there being some means of recording it. It is thought that the Chinese script was known to a few scholars in Japan as early as the 1st century A.D. but its official adoption is considered to have taken place about the middle of the 5th century. A Korean monk is known to have been teaching Chinese writing to the Emperor of Japan's son in 409 A.D.

The first written books in Japan were the 'Kojiki' or *Record of Ancient Matters*, largely a collection of legends and dated 712, and the 'Nihon Shoki' or 'Nihongi', the *Chronicles of Japan of 720*. The same period brought the 'Man'yoshu' or *Collection of Ten Thousand Leaves* which recorded some 4500 ancient poems. It is interesting to note in comparison that *De Tempore Ratione*, the first major written work in England, by that schoolboy favourite, the Venerable Bede, dates from 725 while the *Anglo-Saxon Chronicle* was initiated by King Alfred who lived from 871 to 900. The 3200 line poem, *Beowulf*, is dated 715 A.D.

The emergence of Japan into the Chinese-influenced glory of the Heian period (794-1185) brought about a remarkable flowering of Japanese literature in which a predominant characteristic is the contribution made by ladies of the Imperial Court. One of the greatest and earliest novels in any language, the 'Genji Monogatari' or *Tale of Genji* is also one of the longest and was written by the Lady Murasaki Shikibu who is thought to have lived from 987 to 1015. She wrote it in the first decade of the 11th century and later wrote her own diaries or 'Nikki'. Sei Shonagon (b.965), another lady-in-waiting, wrote her remarkable *Pillow Book* a little earlier — a piquant observation of the court life of her time. It is interesting to note that these ladies, upper-class servants of the court, wrote in Japanese, mostly in hiragana script, while their male counterparts were still occupied in composing poems in the Chinese. Another well-known writer of the period is the Lady Sarashina whose diaries date from 1037 onwards. The literature of the period is almost exclusively concerned with court life while its contemporary readers were members of the court.

Before pursuing the thread of literary history further, let's look briefly at other art forms up to this period. Though it may not directly affect your business, you should know of the word 'Jomon', the name of the Japanese period, roughly the equivalent of our neolithic, which lasted from about 4500 to 250 B.C. Jomon pottery is characterised by being imprinted with patterns of cords. While the Bronze Age in Britain dates from around 2000 B.C., the first significant use of metal in Japan, introduced from Korea with rice and the potter's wheel, did not occur until the first three centuries A.D. From the ancient or 'Kodai' period, too, originates the use of red ochre as a pigment, to be seen all over Japan today. The style of decoration of bronze mirrors and bells (some up to 3 feet high even in these early centuries A.D.) was adopted in the pottery of the time and known as the Yayoi period. Other features were tumuli burials and wooden coffins. It had been the custom when entombing an emperor to bury a number of his retainers up to the neck alive to escort him into the next world but clay effigies known as 'haniwa' were later substituted for these luckless warriors. (Four such figures were buried with the Emperor Meiji as late as 1912.)

Early Japanese painting was mostly of religious subjects and there was little until the Korean monk, Doncho, introduced a whole set of innovations such as paper and the art of colour preparation in the 7th century. Apart from a few frescoes, pigments mixed with glue and water were painted on silk or paper, outlined without modelling or perspective and much in the Indian style. Throughout Japanese history, ink painting or 'Sumi-e' has been one of the strongest and longest lasting trends. ('Sumi' literally means charcoal, 'e' is painting). The same medium is used in calligraphy.

The Heian period saw the first 'Emakimo no' or horizontal scroll paintings, often of such subjects as the life of the Buddha. Like the Bayeux Tapestry, these scrolls depicted series of events, rather like an early version of today's strip cartoons. (In contrast to Emakimono, the vertical hanging scroll such as would ornament the 'tokonoma' recess in a living room, is called 'kakemono'. 'Mono' literally means 'thing'.) Buddhism had a strong influence on art from the 8th century onwards right through the Kamakura period. An interesting variant on the religious scroll paintings is that of 'emakimono monogatari' which depicted scenes from the books of stories or tales already mentioned. Lady Murasaki Shikibu's *Tale of Genji* was a favourite subject.

The Kamakura period continued the pursuit of elegance in art, if not so much in court life, and saw the beginnings of literature for and about the warrior class, rather than just for the nobility. Typical is the Heike Monogatari, Heike being another name for the Taira clan. These Tales of the Heike, whose author is unknown, were put together from the stories related by ballad singers and tell of the struggle of the Taira against the conquering Minamoto clan. It should be noted that the Samurai warriors, though acting as they lawfully should in a very overbearing and lordly manner, were in fact only the servants of the 'Daimyo' or great land-owning lords — the word samurai literally means servant — but they were becoming more numerous. At the same time natural disasters, always present in Japan, combined with civil strife, led to the retirement of many nobles and officials into hermit-like or monastic seclusion. Their writings such as the *Essays in Idleness* of Yoshido Kenko (1283-1350) and *An Account of my Hut* by Kamo no Chomei (1153-1216) are typically filled with sadness and the woes of the time.

Poetry has always been a condensed form of literature, a distillation of observation and experience into a magical minimum of words illuminating some aspect of life, except in the case of a few more long-winded poets. Until the Kamakura period, Japanese poetry had been mainly based on the Chinese as a model, rarely wordy but often of some length. There were and are longer Japanese poems such as the 'choka' but a respect for brevity emerged in the Kamakura period when the 'waka' or 'tanka' form emerged. Metre and rhyme are generally absent from the Japanese poem, stress on different syllables being as in ordinary speech, equal and even. Hence a Japanese poem is generally structured in lines and syllables, waka and tanka having fine lines of five, seven, five, seven and seven syllables. Later, in the Muromachi period, this was to develop into what was known as linked verse, almost a conversation between poets in which the first writer would give the first three lines, the remaining two coming from the second and so on. The form and its execution was rather like a game of chess with strict rules but with different objectives. One of its best known masters was Sogi (1421-1502). From this type of poem the ultimate in brevity, the 'haiku' of three lines of five, seven and five syllables grew in the 17th century.

The Muromachi period saw two other innovations of note. First the beginning of the form of drama, highly stylised and known as No drama (or Noh). Probably the most noted playwright of No was Zeami Motokiyo (1363-1443). Such plays are deeply concerned with death and the world of the dead, and to offset this, brief comedies which are sometimes parodies of No were performed with them, these being known as 'kyogen'. 'Otogi soshi' or children's tales also began in this period.

By now painting had moved a long way from the purely religious subjects, and landscapes of seasons and places were becoming common as well as scenes depicting the ordinary life and work of common people. Animals, some in caricature, and plants, the essences of nature, were depicted in both paintings and in writing. With the inception of the Tokugawa Shogunate, which was to last from 1600 to 1868, a new style of literature began which was both about and for the merchant class. After the years of turmoil of the internal wars of Japan, an element of frivolity and humour, sometimes even bawdiness, came into the work of writers. There was a release of spiritual tension somewhat akin to events in Britain when the Restoration followed the period of the Civil War and the rule of the Puritans. The early years of the Tokugawa brought about the novels of writers such as Ihara Saikaku (1643-1693) like *Tales from the Provinces* and *Five Women who Loved Love*. Drama, in the form of Bunraku puppet plays, flourished with the work of Chikamatsu Monzaemon with a high poetic content and concerned with either heroic historical themes or simple domestic activities. Bunraku is still to be seen today and is well worth the effort. The figures, some four feet high, are operated by three men each, all in full view of the audience while musicians and a story-teller recite and play. It sounds an improbable form of entertainment but is highly successful both with Japanese and foreign spectators. The development of music and musical instruments such as the samisen, the koto and the shaku-hachi owes much to the demands of drama in No and Bunraku form and later in Kabuki. This was a more popular, exciting and realistic form of theatre art that began in the 17th century and was originally performed by women actresses. On moral grounds, however, it was banned in 1707 but later revived with male performers. It is in this form that it is still to be seen today, the 'onnagata' or men who play female roles being highly skilled and much admired. Kabuki performances today last anything up to four or five hours, the audience either bringing their own food with them and eating it in their seats or coming and going as appetite and the other needs of nature need to be satisfied. It's advisable to take your own cushion too!

The early Tokugawa years were also those of the full development of the 'haiku' form of poem, Matsuo Basho (1644-1694) being perhaps the best known, followed by Yosa Buson (1716-1781) and Kobayashi Issa (1763-1828). Basho who wrote such accounts of his constant wanderings up and down the country as *The Records of a Well-Exposed Skeleton* and *The Records of a Travel-Worn Satchel*, concentrated on and wrote about common things and people, and the sights, sounds and smells that he experienced on his travels. At last the willowy warblings of the court poets about falling cherry blossom, blighted love and the watery moon were replaced by stark realism. With Basho writing such verses as:

> "Plagued by fleas and lice
> I hear the horses staling.
> What a place to sleep!"

it is not surprising that the scholar R.V. Blyth, who published four volumes of collected haiku in 1952, wrote: "The aim of the haiku is not beauty ... It is significance."

The observant reader will have noted that I have referred to the poet as Basho, his forename, rather than as Matsuo which was his family name. This is the common way of referring to writers and artists and the like in Japan and does little to simplify life for the foreigner. The situation is further complicated by the habit of such worthies to change their names as often as they changed their houses, if not more so. Basho had at least three names before this last while the artist Hokusai, the self-styled 'mad old man of art' who died at the age of ninety, moved his place of residence ninety-three times and changed his name twenty times!

Before reverting to the art scene I must comment that, in case you think I have concentrated too much on the esoteric topic of poetry, I have reason to do so. Poetry is a living tradition in Japan, even today. It is a part of everyday life. The Emperor Meiji is said to have composed over 100,000 poems in his lifetime. I do not know how many Emperor Hirohito has written but he is responsible for the annual New Year poetry prize competition which attracts tens of thousands of entries. Haiku and Tanka clubs with their own journals proliferate throughout

Japan, their members and contributors being ordinary people from politicians and company directors to taxi drivers and farmers. These people write and declaim their own verses as well as being familiar with the vast store of poems that go to make up the poetic legacy of Japan's past. There is even a card game in which the contestants have to match successive lines of well-known classical poems. One does not have to be in love to send a poem to a friend or to receive a reply in verse. In Japan, as in the West, the art of drawing has largely decayed in the face of the march of the camera but both calligraphy and poetry are very much alive as the pursuits of Everyman and his wife.

To revert for a moment to the Kabuki stage, one of the most popular plays is an action-packed drama based on historical fact and still often acted today. This is the *Tale of the Forty-Seven Ronin*, 'ronin' literally meaning wave-man, being a Samurai warrior who has no lord. Some of these became mercenaries, hiring out their fighting skills wherever they could. Others, like the followers of the Lord Asano in the tale were not so fortunate.

As the story goes, in 1703 in the Shogun's castle in Edo, this daimyo, Asano, wounded another, the Lord Kira, who had insulted him, and for this minor infraction of the strict social code of the time, Asano was condemned to commit hara-kiri or ritual suicide. Naturally he obeyed the command and did so. Since Asano's death had basically been caused by the behaviour of Lord Kira, his followers, now ronin, became intent upon revenge. After long planning, led by one of their number named Oishi, they broke into Lord Kira's house early one snowy winter morning and killed him. They cut off their victim's head, presented it at the grave of their late master and then gave themselves up to the authorities.

The Shogun, Tokugawa Tsunayoshi, was at a loss to know what should be done, for while the 47 ronin had certainly committed a breach of the peace, on the other hand in defending the good name of Lord Asano, they had acted properly in accordance with Confucian ethics. They had behaved correctly according to the code of 'bushido', the way of the warrior.

Tsunayoshi himself was a bit of an oddball character. Born in the 'Year of the Dog' in the old calendar, and his only son dying young, he was unable to beget an heir and attributed his failing to the wrath of the gods for the sins of his ancestors which could only be expiated by a national policy of kindness to animals and especially to dogs. Deaths of animals had to be reported and officials carefully investigated the circumstances which could result in the imprisonment or even the death of a guilty owner or other person. The Battersea Dogs' Home had nothing on Tsunayoshi, since for twenty years stray dogs were carried to the kennels he set up in the luxury of palanquins! When faced with the problem of the 47 ronin, the Dog Shogun, as he was later known, took advice. The law would not punish them but they were ordered in their turn to commit 'seppuku' as their Lord had been. They did so and were buried beside his grave. Their tombs stand in the Sengakuji temple in Tokyo and a memorial service is still held for them every year on 14th December.

As with literature, the influence of the court in painting gradually declined over the centuries, the Tosa School of court painters practically alone keeping up the traditions of excessive mannerism and refinement. Even the Buddhist priest artists studied, and depicted more realistically an increasing number of landscapes and the everyday occupations of all types of people. Sesshu (1420-1507) was perhaps the greatest of these, with Sesson and Keisoki, both Zen priests and amateur artists. All these and many others worked in Sumi-e for which demand was growing so that a professional school of painters, the Kano School, was founded by Kano Masonobu. Its style and tradition were to continue well into the Tokugawa era. Under Hideyoshi and Ieyasu and their successors, these painters were kept well-occupied at providing painted screens such as were essential features of the houses of the wealthy and into which they introduced much more colour than their Sumi-e predecessors. Sotatsu and Korin were among other famous artists of the late 17th century.

The continued state of peace under the Tokugawa Shogunate brought with it a prosperity that Japan had not known for many years and, at the same time, a broader and more even distribution of money (in coin rather than rice, the earlier form of currency). Craft industries developed together with the growth of mineral extraction, and commerce thrived, the merchant class now beginning to rival the Samurai in status. Concurrently, the cities spread and their populations expanded with a great growth in the number of people demanding and enjoying objets d'art, artefacts and entertainment. It was in this climate that the 'Ukiyo-e' genre of painting originated, 'ukiyo' literally meaning 'the floating' or the 'passing world'.

Printing had been known in Japan for many centuries and

wood-block prints, generally in monochrome, of religious subjects had existed since the 13th and 14th centuries. The 18th century saw such a demand for pictures that the art of wood-block printing developed both in output and in technique almost beyond recognition. Much of the success of these prints depended, of course, not only on the artist but also on the skills of those who carved the blocks and those who printed from them for, with a full range of colours being used, a multiplicity of blocks was required for a single print and register had to be precise to achieve quality. Only in rare cases did the artist involve himself in the craft side of print-making.

The list of artists that one could mention is formidable but one of the most prominent and best known today is undoubtedly Kitagawa Utamaro (1754-1806), famous for his prints of courtesans and lovers, not excluding a number which can only be called erotic, but whose first volume was his charming *Book of Insects*. His contemporary, Sharaku, was among those noted for pictures of the current actors of the day, which were in growing popularity as social life expanded in the cities and more and more people went to enjoy No and Kabuki performances. Perhaps best known of all outside Japan are the colourful volumes of topographical scenes by Katsushika Hokusai (1760-1849) such as his *Thirty-six Views of Mount Fuji*, his *Scenes of Edo and the Sumida River* and his *Famous Bridges and Waterfalls*. Hokusai, who added 'mad artist' to his name wrote at the end of his later *One Hundred Views of Mount Fuji*: "From the age of six I began drawing the shape of things. By the time I reached the age of about half a hundred, I began to produce quite inept pictures, and even at the age of seventy I produced nothing of any worth. When I became seventy-three I began to be able to understand the basic form of animals and plants. By the time I become eighty, I will have made some progress, at ninety I will be able to know the secrets of the art, at one hundred my work will be praiseworthy, and many years later I will be able to produce true living likenesses. I only hope I will live long enough to accomplish this. Written by the Mad Old Man of Art." This was in 1834 when he was seventy-five. He died in his ninetieth year, his fame by then eclipsed by Ando Hiroshige (1749-1858), best known for his series *The Fifty-three Stages of Tokaido*. These stages were the prominent crossings, guard-posts and staging posts on Tokaido, the road between Edo, the seat of the Shogunate government and Kyoto where the Emperor's court still retained its capital, which was the most travelled thoroughfare in the land. Some of the prints are purely scenic but most are packed with detail of human activity and give a fascinating picture of the times. Starting with an early morning scene of a Daimyo and his entourage crossing the Nihonbashi (bridge) in Tokyo, every facet of people, places, seasons and times of the day and night are included. The first publishing was in 1834. A set of the 55 prints is one of the writer's most treasured possessions, a constant source of interest and delight and a memory of the friendship of the Japanese business friends who gave it to him. Hiroshige was also known for his 'Jinbutsu' or human figure pictures but it is for the Tokaido series that he is immortal.

I have said little about architecture, the most practical of all the arts. It is difficult to give any picture of the subject in a few words but the first distinction to be made is that between basic Shinto and Buddhist styles. Shinto architecture derives from the design of the simple primeval hut in which many of the roof structural members were exposed. Even in quite large structures the rafters form an external cruciform pattern resting on the ridge log that ran the length of the building. The structural members of the original style were straight, the graceful curvature of Buddhist style roofs being an inheritance from Chinese culture. In looking at historic buildings in Japan today, it must be remembered that, apart from the massive square stone foundations of the profusion of castles which are a feature of every town and also found in remoter country parts, permanence was not the main objective of the 'architect'. The prevalence of earthquakes and similar acts of the gods were something the builder couldn't beat and he knew it. The last major earthquake was the one that destroyed some two-thirds of Tokyo in 1923, and since then architects and engineers have learnt new methods of combating seismic disturbances and moved into the skyscraper age. A large proportion of the 'old' temples, shrines, pagodas and castles that exist today have been rebuilt at least once if not more often.

Buddhist architecture is generally much more elaborate in concept and more highly decorated in detail than Shinto but is restricted to larger buildings as listed above. The structure of the ordinary Japanese house on modular lines has already been mentioned, timber being the material of construction until recent years. Even the modern house retains much of the traditional features such as the 'shoji' and 'amado' sliding panels which could open it to the space outside, integrating the living space with nature. Similarly, 'fusuma' and 'karakami' opaque paper screens inside could be removed to turn two smaller rooms into one. The ingenuity and craftmanship employed in the work was considerable but still did not always combat the effects of winter. "A house should be built with the summer in mind," wrote Yoshido Kenko in his *Essays in Idleness* about 1330. "In winter it is possible to live anywhere, but a badly made house is unbearable when it gets hot." To some extent this attitude persists today. No doubt it accounts for the comment of the shivering insomniac diplomat, quoted by Basil Hall Chamberlain, who, after a sleepless winter night spent in trying to block up the chinks in the screens and windows, remarked, "Mais les Japonais ADORENT les courants d'air!"

The sweeping generalisation that there was a decline in quality in almost all the arts as the Tokugawa Shogunate tottered towards its doom exaggerates but is fundamentally true, but the new release of energy and intellectual activity that accompanied the Meiji Restoration quickly reversed the trend. Among the shiploads of study groups in technical, economic, political and other fields that sailed for Europe and the United States, the arts were not entirely neglected. It was not only commerce and industry that were to be opened to Western influence but almost every facet of life including literature and art. This was by no means a one-way affair. *Madame Butterfly* and *The Mikado* swept opera-goers into raptures, and the craze for Japanese lacquerwork and other objets-d'art swept the West while Vincent Van Gogh, alone in his studio in Arles in 1888, wrote to his brother Theo, "I envy the Japanese the extreme clearness which everything has in their work. It is never wearisome, and never seems to be done too hurriedly. Their work is as simple as breathing, and they do a figure in a few sure strokes with the same ease as if it were as simple as buttoning your waistcoat." Little did Van Gogh know the trouble that learning to button a waistcoat had given a generation of Japanese gentlemen who had been forced into Western dress by the new regime!

One of the most remarkable of writers of the Meiji era was Natsume Soseki (1867-1916), the son of a minor official, who started engineering studies at Tokyo Imperial University in 1881 but transferred to the English department. After a period as a teacher, he was sent on a scholarship course by the Ministry of Education to London University in 1900. Living for three years in a succession of delapidated lodging houses and hardly ever meeting any English people of his social standing, he spent his time reading English literature in solitude until his return to Japan in 1903 to succeed Lafcadio Hearn as a lecturer in English literature at his old university, before putting his pen to writing in Japanese. My own introduction to Soseki was in a Tokyo taxi (like so many others were!) where I had told a young Japanese graduate that I did not think that modern Japanese literature was a true reflection of modern Japanese life because it seemed to be totally lacking in the sense of humour that I had found almost everywhere I went. Next morning a copy of Soseki's first book, *I am a Cat*, was delivered to my hotel room and, if you concede that a book published in 1905 can be called modern, I certainly had to take back my words. The nameless cat of the story which writes in the first person has a truly Marxian view of life, by which I mean Groucho of the Marx Brothers rather than comrade Karl. *Botchan*, Soseki's second novel, based on his experiences as a provincial school-teacher, has the humour toned down to second gear but, once one has entered a little more into the Japanese mind, is full of laughs. Soseki's masterpiece is probably 'Kokoro', a title also used by Hearn, and meaning 'heart', 'spirit' or 'soul'. In a survey in four universities among professors and students, Soseki's *The Heart of Things* was rated second to only Dostoievski's *Crime and Punishment* as the book that had the greatest influence on their thinking.

Born in the Meiji era, but writing more in the Showa, were such authors as Tanizaki Junichiro, probably best known for his *Diary of a Mad Old Man* or *Dairy of a Lunatic*. Dazai Osamu is an author evidently of some significance to Japanese who have mentioned him to me, but I have not found his work in translation so far. Kawabata Yasunari, whose works, *Snow Country* and *Thousand Cranes* are available in English, must especially be mentioned as, for these two comparatively short books, he was awarded the Nobel Prize for Literature in 1965, being the only Japanese writer to receive this honour. In *The Sound of the Mountain* one of his characters comments, "I am an old man and I have not yet climbed Mount Fuji," seemingly expressing a feeling of the sadness of life that permeates the work of many Japanese writers. Yasunari must have had similar sentiments for, in his seventies, he concluded that he had written everything in him that was worth writing and took his own life. Another who did so much earlier in life, and with a flamboyance that brought him as much fame as his prolific writings, was Mishima Yukio.

Here was a man cloaked in success but disillusioned with the materialism of post-war Japan, who formed his own small private army dedicated to the protection of the emperor and the revival of the samurai spirit. In 1970 he completed the third of a tetralogy of novels, and dressed in his para-military uniform as commander of the Shield Society, with his followers forced his way into the Defence Forces H.Q. at Ichigaya. From a balcony he harangued a thousand soldiers on the parade ground below but with little effect. He then retired to the C.O.'s office where that officer had already been tied to his chair and in the traditional white loin-cloth disembowelled himself with his favourite sword. According to custom, one of his lieutenants dealt the final blow that despatched him by cutting off his head, unfortunately only at the fourth attempt. So ended the life of the forty-five year old author and film-maker who might well have been the second Japanese Nobel Prize winner.

Mishima's many books give a vivid picture of modern Japanese life, though hardly a balanced one since they are frequently concerned with sexual deviation and the shadier side of life. As a writer he truly spanned the literary traditions of both East and West and his death is a loss not only to Japan.

As with classical writers the work of many modern Japanese writers is characterised by a poetic quality in its prose (even in translation), and displays a finely developed sense of perception of detail both in inanimate objects, both natural and man-made, and in the world of emotions. A quality of introspection is often present, sometimes oppressively so, while the macabre and the grotesque are not shunned as subject matter. An example is Abe Kobo's *The Face of Another* which, while not a thriller, has elements that are far more spine-chilling than H.G. Well's *The Invisible Man*. The tautness, detail and controlled pace of his *The Ruined Map* is such that figuratively the reader can hear a pin drop on almost any page.

As one who is at a loss to understand modern art in the West, I do not feel qualified to make any statement about contemporary painting and sculpture in Japan. I would mention though that it appears to be thriving and popular and that it can easily be seen. One of the more charitable functions of some of the big departo stores is that of bringing art to the people in the huge galleries on their upper floors. Some excellent exhibitions are staged at Mitsukoshi in Tokyo's Nihonbashi. You can judge for yourself.

The Meiji period, in importing Western influences, did not

neglect architecture and for a while Japanese cities went Victorian in spirit. Few buildings of the period have survived. In Tokyo the 1923 earthquake destroyed a high proportion of them while, today, the pace of change is so great that any remaining have fallen to the bulldozers of the developers. The process continues on sites of commercial value so fast that even quite modern buildings are torn down every year to make way for something bigger, better or more prestigious. However, a fine selection of Meiji buildings have been saved and are preserved in a spacious park of great beauty and interest, the 'Meijimura' or Meiji village that lies some way out of Nagoya. There merchants' houses, a post office, a railway station, a telegraph office and many other buildings have been removed and faithfully reconstructed.

Modern city architecture in Japan follows the pattern, that seems almost universal today, of slab-sided boxes and pillars of concrete metal and glass. There are, however, some impressive ones among them, usually spoiled by being cloaked or topped with giant neon advertisements. Among the welter of the mediocre, there are few buildings of outstanding originality. The National Gymnasium and swimming pool, part of the complex of buildings erected at Shibuya, Tokyo, for the 1964 Olympic games, is a prime example and the work of the noted architect, Tange Kenzo. Similar in some respects, in its application of modern reinforced concrete construction to forms of modified traditional character, is the vast curving roof structure of the headquarters of the new Soka Gakkai sect of Buddhism. The whole complex of buildings that comprise it can be seen in the foothills of Mount Fuji, the graceful form of the giant main hall in pale grey standing out against the green of the countryside. Soka Gakkai whose political wing, the Komeito, or Clean Government party, has some 50 seats in the Diet, literally means 'Value-Creating Society' but it is not clear what values it intends to create. The sect, founded by a Buddhist schoolmaster, with its paramilitary methods of mass enthusiasm, appeals largely to the younger Japanese and generally to the underdogs and the downtrodden of today's materialistic society. The temple is not easily approached for it lies in vast grounds, every entrance of which is controlled by healthy young smiling guards with walkie-talkie radios. In Soka Gakkai may lie the seeds of a new Japan but of what sort it is difficult to guess. The sect is said to have over ten million adherents today.

What importance the Soka Gakkai sect places on meditation, I cannot say, but it is an important element in other Zen sects including Nichiren, the sect founded by the saint of that name in the 13th century to which Soka Gakkai owes its inspiration. One aspect of 'Za-zen' or meditation has been crystallised into the formalism of 'Cha-no-yu' or tea ceremony, still practised by many Japanese for its intrinsic value but today also something of a tourist gimmick. Cha-no-yu is intended to induce a calmness of spirit through its stylised form and the deep contemplation of the beauty and functional simplicity of the various traditional utensils employed in it. Baseball and ten-pin bowling may have intruded into Japanese lifestyle but they have never supplanted the timeless conventions of Cha-no-yu. Viewed at its face value, it may be nothing but a bore to the visiting 'gaijin' but, approached thoughtfully and with consideration for its meaning and antiquity, it is a worthwhile experience contributing towards an understanding of the dichotomy that still exists in the Japanese today. Far from being purely a tourist attraction, it is actively practised by many families. I have visited a company president, wealthy and able to afford such luxuries, whose home is a modern house of ample size and mainly of Western style. Protruding into the peaceful garden from a wing of the house is an exquisite traditional-style room specifically for the performance of the ritual of Cha-no-yu. This V.I.P., who relaxes in a cotton 'yukata' after the cares of the working day in industry, doesn't just have his tea ceremony room for show. He uses it, regularly. The garden that surrounds it is formal too, based on a number of traditional elements, carefully disposed so as to suggest a miniature of a natural landscape, much use being made of stone and water in addition to growing plants. In his novel, *Headlong Hall* the English humourist, Thomas Love Peacock in 1816 mocks the art of the English landscape gardener. "I perceive," says his Mr Milestone, "that these grounds have never been touched by the finger of taste." Would that Peacock had had the chance of seeing gardens touched by the finger of Japanese taste, for here, even in the confines of city or suburb, the Japanese mastery of creating beauty on a small scale, contrasting so sharply with their ability to produce ugliness on a large scale, can induce a deep sense of inner peace such as is inherent in the tenets of the Buddhist religion. Only seeing and sitting quietly in a Japanese garden can give any conception of this exquisite Japanese three-dimensional art form. A restful microcosm of nature is the result of the Japanese landscape gardener's efforts. William Blake wrote in his *Intimations of Immortality* of "seeing beauty in a grain of sand". That is one of the supreme achievements of the Japanese, an inherent characteristic of their nature, exemplified not only in their gardens but also in their esoteric art of growing miniature or 'Bonsai' trees. 'Bonsai' is literally a 'plant in a tray' or shallow receptacle. The results are astounding in their realism of nature on a small scale, but irritatingly difficult to achieve as I have found from some years of trying to emulate the Japanese!

I am very conscious that in hardly any topic in this chapter have I done more than make the merest scratch on the surface but that was inevitable from the start. It would take several volumes to do justice to the vast field I have tried to cover, but I hope I have done something to whet the reader's appetite and to suggest the fascinating vistas that lie behind the artful, surface simplicity of nearly every facet of Japanese life and art. Should I have succeeded in this, a list of references for further reading are given in Appendix H.

CHAPTER THIRTEEN

A Gentle Breeze of Change

So far we have largely treated Japan as if it were a static society with a fixed economy, but such a concept is clearly far from the truth. We live in a world of change and one in which the rate of change is accelerating yearly. It is no part of our business here to predict whether and how, in the long-term, this rate of change will slow down and even halt, for this would involve distant global political and economic forecasting. It is sufficient to observe for the moment that Japan, while peppered with anomalies and anachronisms, is as subject to change from both internal and external pressures as the rest of the industrial world. We should note in passing that the Japanese as a nation, however, are generally more adaptable to change than most other peoples. While retaining much that is traditional, they thrive on change, adapting both themselves and the elements of change to their own advantage. It would not be going too far to say that the successful perception and realisation of what is static and will remain so, what is changing and what is likely to change in the future in Japan is to a very great extent the key to success in the Japanese market in the years to come.

Much of the final outcome is dependent on political issues and pressures that the percipient exporter can and should absorb from the news media, in particular in the UK from the *Financial Times* and *The Economist*. Perhaps, with faith, a study of the great American prophet, Herman Kahn's *The Emerging Japanese Superstate* (Pelican Books, 1970) may be relevant to future forecasting. Though it is a little out of date today, it does give alternative scenarios in several fields which are worthy of consideration. Kahn certainly stretches the mind in a useful way and his book shouldn't be missed. By the time this book is in print, Mr Kahn's latest work on Japan, *The Success and Failure of*

Economic Success, should be available to the reader.

The imponderabilities of forecasting are illustrated by the following instance from the book by Kahn and the Hudson Institute, one of the most experienced teams of crystal ball gazers in the world. Kahn describes how, in the post-war years, the Japanese classified industries according to whether they wanted to compete in them and whether such competition was likely to be successful, the process including the ruthless pruning of uneconomic activities. (It seems that the Japanese are doing a re-think on this today and, in spite of comments that the cooperative attitudes of government and industry are steadily weakening, it seems that further 'administrative guidance' may soon initiate a new look and further changes.) Much of the success of the Japanese 'Economic Miracle' was due to this practical approach which was, however, somewhat influenced by a desire for prestige. "Thus," writes Kahn, "simple cotton textiles, sewing machines, bicycles and pottery might be suitable for Egyptian or Indian manufacture but 'they are not for the Japanese'." By some uncanny quirk of fate, however, Japan has become the second largest manufacturer of bicycles in the world, making some 10 million machines a year! I have no iconoclastic intent in pulling the skids out from under Mr Kahn. I just want to show that even the best of us can be wrong some of the time. Anyway he was only quoting from a study by *The Economist* and that's a pretty reputable source. Writing in 1968 Peter Drucker in *The Age of Discontinuity* commented as follows on the Japanese post-war approach to their problems, "What the Japanese realised twenty years ago was that they had to make sure that their productive resources would go into tomorrow's rather than yesterday's work. They further realised that it is the world economy that indicates where tomorrow is likely to be. For the past twenty years the Japanese have therefore systematically projected the trends of the world economy on to their economic policy, both domestic and international." While the Russians have political purges and the Chinese indulge in cultural revolutions, the Japanese quietly rethink their economic and technological forecasts and collectively change to the most favourable national course. The process continues today.

By an odd coincidence, two days after I wrote the above paragraphs, new recommendations from Japan's Industrial Planning Council were published, regarding policy changes in export aimed at "improving industrial structure and correcting

Japan's trade surplus." Among eighteen items whose export the report recommends should be "stabilised" or reduced are bicycles. "The classification," reports the *Financial Times* "was largely on the basis of whether the industries were the high-·value-added, low-energy-consumption which are deemed appropriate now that for the first time since the 19th century, Japan can be 'completely free from the spell of the export-first principle'."

It is the purpose of this chapter to look at some of the changes in Japan that can be seen today, some factors that seem likely to remain more or less static and, if our stamina sustains us, to attempt to look a little into the future. If in the process my prognostications should be inaccurate, I hope, at least, to suggest some useful clues and some verifiable facts and to stimulate the reader to follow profitable lines of thought. I am reminded of the apocryphal Confucian analect "To prophesy is very difficult — especially with respect to the future," related by Alvin Toffler in *Future Shock* (Pan Books, 1971). At the same time as attempting the difficult feat of prophecy, I hope to illuminate the theme of what may possibly be exported to Japan with notes on some earlier and existing British and European export stories. They must necessarily be brief and not entirely consistent but, where possible, I shall give references to sources where the reader can obtain fuller details of how these firms achieved success. Here lie ample clues for the would-be exporter to ponder over. Here lies gold for the intelligent and contemplative prospector.

Politically Japan has had comparative stability for the three decades since the war, with the Liberal-Democrats holding over 50% of seats in both Houses of the Diet, ie over twice the number held by the next most successful party, the Socialists. We have already noted the close relationship between the existing government and 'big business' and while the Communists with some 8% and the Komeito (7%), supported by the ever-growing new Soka Gakkai sect of Buddhism, continue to make inroads, their gains are small and likewise their overall influence. I believe, therefore, that a continuation of Liberal-Democratic party government, with its strong influence on and by industry and the financial world, is to be expected in the foreseeable future. Major policy changes then are not likely; minor ones, like the declared — but so far ineffectual — encouragement of the import of more finished products rather than simply of raw materials for conversion, will doubtless continue. Whether the slight but perceptible growth of the old militaristic spirit of Japan will become significant is hard to say, but the possibility seems slim. (If it did, the British Defence Exports Association should have a ball!) Antinuclear sentiment in Japan is extensive and intense so the opposition to peaceful nuclear devices is practically and positively inhibiting development. The possibility of nuclear militarism seems nil.

The likelihood of little major change in the political field for quite a few years validates many of Kahn's assumptions and predictions, and accordingly narrows the margins of the reader's basic field of speculation. Changes there will be, but these will largely be made against a stable political background. Economic stability with growth can also be anticipated except insofar as Japan is dependent on the import of raw materials and on the rest of the world to absorb its exports.

It would be quite untrue to say that Japan is economically 'at war' with the West or with other parts of the world. The fact is that, apart from the economic disruptions caused in the world economy by the activities of the OPEC countries, Japan is, to Western eyes, an intruder in the consumer-durable goods field, and an intruder in a big way. Historically, Europe and the USA have had the field of industrial production and sales to themselves for the last century and a half and now the emergent Japanese economy is making an uncomfortable dent in the ego of Western industrialism. What's more, other Far Eastern countries such as Korea and Taiwan are not being slow to learn a lesson from the Japanese way of going about it, but that is a different kettle of 'sakana'!

It has, however, a significant influence on the Japanese for in some labour-intensive industries such as steel, shipbuilding and textiles, these countries as well as Hong Kong and Singapore with lower labour costs are able to undercut Japanese prices and contribute towards the decline of these industries in Japan. In some cases Japanese investment, intended to take advantage of the cheaper labour, has aided in the process and accordingly contributed towards the present unemployment problem in Japan.

An intruder, in the economic scene, 'in a big way' is what I have said above. Is this true? No! Just because anyone poaches on what we consider to be our preserves and because they have wisely concentrated their efforts in a few selected fields, we assume that the economic assault on our Western bastions is 'big'. I have already pointed out that the Japanese export a smaller percentage of their GNP than either Britain or Germany. A further sign towards a realistic perspective of the present trading situation has been published as I am writing. Professor G.C. Allen, London University's expert on Political Economy, has just produced a study (published by the Institute of Economic Affairs), *How Japan Competes: A Verdict on Dumping*, in which he writes of the "almost hysterical comments over Japanese activities" and explains that imports in recent years from Japan "made up less than 3% of Britain's total imports and less than 4% of the EEC's." (Our trade deficit into Japan is only half of the one we maintain with Holland, yet few voices are raised against those 'aggressive Dutch traders'!) What I believe to be most relevant to the economy of the West, and particularly to Britain, is that Japan has whole-heartedly and enthusiastically set about the problem of exporting to the Third World, the developing countries and, where advisable, investing there too. Starting with the oil-producing countries of the Middle East and many parts of South America, I believe they have a commanding lead now in many of the deeper parts of Africa. As a British exporter, I used to visit Iran for a couple of weeks, once or twice a year. My Japanese associates weren't interested in such half-measures. As soon as HM Shah-in-Shah Reza Pahlevi emerged as a major power in the world economy, they set up their own offices in Teheran, admittedly small and staffed initially by only one lonely Japanese 'manager'. But there he was, 365 days a year with his ear to the ground and his finger on the pulse of Iranian politics and economy.

I'm sorry if this spirited defence of Japanese export methods has intervened in my disquisition on how and what to get into the changing Japanese market, but it would be regrettable to ignore the way the Japanese export for it must inevitably reflect on their own view of how others try to sell into Japan. The Japanese have, in many fields, become the export experts and are hence critical of amateurism when they are the prospective buyers. Such attitudes bear thinking upon. Why suffer fools lightly, when you're not stupid yourself?

Meanwhile, back in Japan, while one cannot predict, beyond unreliable graphic extrapolation, what will be the future population growth trend, there is no doubt that apart from minor land reclamation, excursions into the sea, the land area and the area of 'usable' land will remain constant. 'Minor' was the adjective I used, and it may be appropriate to date, but nothing would surprise me less than seeing Japan increase her area of usable land substantially by building out into the sea that surrounds her should such a construction policy be desirable or necessary. All Japan's six major steel producers — and Japan is the second largest steel-making country in the free world — have been building their latest plants on artificially reclaimed land giving the advantage of deep-water berthing. At the marine 'Expo '75' on the Island of Okinawa, an offshore structure, 'Technopolis' showed what could be in terms of extending the land for living. A complete paper-mill was recently exported from Japan including the sea-going floating platform on which the whole plant was erected. Imaginative thinking of this kind allowed the whole integrated plant to be delivered thousands of miles away in tested and commissioned state and obviated the need for foundations and buildings to be put in on site. At the same time a 'new town' is currently being built on a man-made island in the Bay of Kobe, the first of its kind in the world, while the Japanese are experimenting with artificial reefs to attract migrant fish to swell the declining catches of her trawlers.

For the British exporter, the import of the Japanese concentration on and success in selling large-scale turn-key engineering projects to developing countries lies in his chance of contributing to, and hence sharing in, the project. Their hard work can be to your benefit if you let your Japanese partners have their lead. Whatever happens, don't be so stupid as one UK company I know of, who heard that their agents were selling their machines to a Japanese group who were quoting as main contractors for a plant in India. That, said my British ex-friends is outside the terms of their agreement with us and declared war. I never found out who won but I'm sure it wasn't the British firm. If the Japanese sign a sales agreement with you, you can put in all the limitations and provisos you can think of but, if they scent business, they'll go for it — not on your own doorstep, maybe, but anywhere else in the world they think fit. As things are going these days, you ought to be glad to let them do the legwork and give you the business.

To get back to life in Japan today, what are the obvious observable trends? Well, affluence for a start! The odd thing is that, apart from a small upper bracket in industry and finance, the realisation that they're now one of the richest nations in the world hasn't yet penetrated to the average Japanese. Years,

Table 5.   HOUSEHOLD OWNERSHIP OF CONSUMER DURABLES

Percentage of total households owning:

washing machine	97.5
refrigerator	94.7
stainless steel sink	64.4
food mixer	40.9
electronic range	7.5
dishwasher	0.6
fan	91.8
kerosene stove	87.7
gas water boiler	57.9
electric blanket	50.3
ventilation fan	46.7
gas heater	20.2
electric heater	19.3
air conditioner	12.9
central heating	1.4
wardrobe (Western)	93.8
wardrobe (Japanese)	92.8
rug (for floor)	46.9
kitchen table and chairs	37.9
Western-style bed	35.5
three-piece suite	27.4
sideboard	24.5
colour television	75.8
black & white television	65.4
radio	72.4
camera	72.1
bicycle	71.3
stereo set	44.4
tape recorder	42.2
electric organ	22.8
golf clubs	10.2
piano	9.7

Many households may of course own more than one of many of these items.

Similar sets of figures to those above are to be found in different published sources. Some are more recent but not so complete while others may list more items but for earlier years. I have compromised with this list for February 1973 from 'The Japanese Market in Figures' (JETRO Marketing Series Booklets No. 10) decades, centuries of comparative poverty have so ingrained themselves in the nature of the people that they are still generally frugal beyond reason which, of course, is a good thing as their vast personal and family savings, stored in their efficient banking system, is largely the fuel that fires the unbelievable rate of investment that goes into industrial research and development and into efficient, labour-saving manufacturing plant. This, in turn, it is reported, allows a Japanese car worker to turn out a car a week compared with his British counterpart's one car per month (More recent figures suggest a ratio of 9:1 rather than 4:1!)

But affluence is slowly beginning to have its effect. Much of Japan's staggering export performance springs from having a strong and healthy home market, photographic and electronic equipment being typical leaders in the field. It used to be said that the Japanese had three coveted desires, the three Cs — car, room cooler and colour TV, whereas later, having largely achieved these, they went on to the second three Cs — cottage, central heating and concubine! This is, of course, a travesty of the facts, but is based upon an element of truth. The sarariman, for instance, is taking on more and more consumer durables (see Table 5), as well as arranging his own holidays instead of going on the company organised and subsidised packaged tour, but a major obstacle to further growth of the trend is the backward state of housing in Japan in general. The comparative trend of UK and Japanese private income and expenditure is shown in Table 6.

Japanese architects have achieved marvels in vertical development where hotels and office blocks are concerned, but

Table 6.   PRIVATE CONSUMPTION IN UK & JAPAN
(*1976-8 per cent change on year*)

	Real Disposable Income			Impact of changes in savings ratio on real private consumption			Real Private Consumption		
	1976	*1977*	*1978*	*1976*	*1977*	*1978*	*1976*	*1977*	*1978*
UK	−0.4	−1.8	2.3	0.8	1.2	0.4	0.4	−0.6	2.7
JAPAN	3.7	4.0	3.7	0.7	−0.2	0.5	4.4	3.8	4.2

(OECD figures published in *Financial Times* 17.4.78)

for one reason or another, though they do exist, tall flats or apartment blocks still have not caught on to the extent they have in the West and form a comparatively small proportion of the total dwelling accommodation. Even where the 'high-rise' concept has been accepted, the floor area per person is still restricted, for the traditional concept of converting a day-room into a bedroom at night by merely unrolling the 'futon' mattresses onto the floor is persistent. In an overcrowded country it's also logical. The dual-purpose nature of the Japanese room saves an enormous investment in furniture and space. If you only need something to sleep on for eight hours out of every twenty-four, why let it take up some 22 square feet for the whole time? In spite of this the Western bed is moving into Japanese homes, even if slowly, and has a long way to go before it gains the popularity of the Western style 3-piece lounge suite now to be found in 27.4% of Japanese households. Such suites, I would add, have been successfully exported from Britain by Ercol Ltd. I haven't checked but suspect that this was another instance where the product had to be adapted to the market. Any settee or armchair I've ever used in Japan has been much lower than those in Europe, with the result that it almost needs a crane to get me out of it again! You'll appreciate the difference in size and flexibility when you've tried the baths in not quite top class hotels in Japan!

Here, however, is an interesting trend of change. Traditionally considered to be much smaller than us, it seems that steady improvement in diet in the post-war period is having a significant effect on the Japanese physiology. Apart from a new breed of tall, willowy night-club and bar hostesses whose figures never cease to dazzle me, the Japanese of the present younger generations are becoming steadily taller. The change, it seems, must start quite young for not many years ago the Ministry of Education produced a new standard for school desks, making them 5 cms higher than before — and that's quite an increase. You will no doubt notice that the calves and thighs of most Japanese girls are, on average, much more substantial than those with which we are familiar in the West. This physiological difference arises from the inheritance of many centuries of adopting the squatting position when at rest. Now that most girls use chairs at their work and in public places, and chairs are becoming more common in the home, one could predict a change towards slimmer legs in the future. This is obviously of direct relevance if you're in the rag trade export business, but it is also one of the likely changes that could and should be of interest to any manufacturer whose products involve ergonomic considerations. The first thing you do when you're thinking of buying a car is to sit behind the wheel of the model that attracts you. If it doesn't fit, you try another make. Foreign car manufacturers are always complaining about their lack of success in selling to Japan. I don't know if they send out standard Western models or if they've studied the Japanese anatomy from the ergonomic point of view. The Japanese have largely sized us up that way! Maybe, here again, we need to adapt the product more carefully to the market.

Changing diet is not just a matter of positive thinking in dietetics and family shopping. In spite of Western moans about the cost and complexity of the traditional Japanese distribution system, particularly for foodstuffs (previously mentioned in Chapter 5), there is no doubt that scope for the import into Japan of new food experiences is widespread today. A British company which had had some success in an agreement for local manufacture of ice cream with their brand name, has had further success in negotiating with a Japanese company to produce and bake their fruit tarts. Special machinery is needed to make them on an economic production line, which in turn has led to the export from Britain of complete production machinery for these comestibles. Changing food fashion can be seen, too, in the chain restaurant business. A jocular Japanese friend once told me that the greatest influence that the American Occupation of 1947-52 had had on Japan was the intrusion and adoption of baseball, Coke and hamburgers. In spite of the last you may find franchised Wimpy bars in places like Roppongi in Tokyo. Similarly, Berni Inns, with their quick service restricted menu, are to be seen not far away, having now sold out to their Japanese partners. What's the secret of success? I'd say value-for-money and something a little different from traditional Japanese fare. Maybe the Wimpys and the Bernis won't be culinary giant killers, but they've got their foot in the door. The Wimpy is competing, not so much with the Japanese, but with the Americans for the McDonald hamburger chain is strongly established.

The JAL booklet of six business case studies explains how the Austrian confectionery firm, Pez, have become the largest selling single brand of lozenges in Japan. Apart from the good fortune of coming into the market at the right time, there was nothing magical about the Pez success story. It involved hard work, good planning, the proper use of marketing techniques from research to advertising and point-of-sale promotional aids, and putting over a national image of Austria to even the youngest consumer whose taste-buds Pez wanted to tickle. Picking the right partner in Japan was, of course, a crucial part of their marketing plan.

Traditionally tea (o-cha) tends to be of the green type in Japan but in the quest for variety and new experience for the palate, black tea, as the Japanese call it, is making its impact. Coming from the terraces of India, Ceylon and China, no doubt some is bought direct, but a major exporter of tea to Japan is the firm of Twinings of London. Their success is doubtless due to good packaging and their long history in the business which leads to their products having what can only be described as 'snob value'.

'Snob' should be interpreted loosely to include almost anything that is novel to Eastern senses and where at least in its home-grown state, isn't 'Kitsch'. Apart from the Wimpy -Bernie brethren, you can find in Tokyo such institutions as 'Scotch Pub' and 'Tartan House York'. They may sound a bit silly but they exemplify the Japanese desire for something with a novel flavour, a scent that hasn't assailed their senses before.

From Scotch Pub it is no great mental step to St Andrews. A Japanese business syndicate paid dearly for permission to reproduce that famous seat of the 'Royal & Ancient' on Japanese soil, I am told. The course, constructed after a costly survey trip to Scotland, is no doubt an example of bad Japanese marketing for the company went bankrupt. We've already dealt with some aspects of the game of 'gorofu' in Japan. Golf courses and golf driving ranges are only one perceptible sign of the influence of affluence on the growth and potential prospects in every aspect of the leisure industry. Think up something new and you should really be in business.

I don't know how the skateboard craze has worked out there but take hang-gliders for instance. In 1975 there were an estimated 1000 of these devices in Japan. A year later another 2500 had been added, while the British Hang Gliding Association estimate that by 1982 there will be nearer 200,000. Costing around £800 to £900 apiece, this is no mean market. The recently reported development in the UK of a mini-engine for hang-gliders could find a big market in Japan. Japanese geography, with its high percentage of hilly and mountainous country, is ideal for such a sport while similarly the sea-girt isles are made for water sports. (A British company, Submarine Products Ltd of Hexham, has had some success in selling underwater breathing apparatus in Japan on the basis of its being technically more advanced than indigenous products.) You might think that the Japanese could produce all the necessary gear themselves, and maybe they can. The climate and the mountains give ample opportunity for skiing, but do the Japanese make all their own skis and skiing equipment? No! One of the classic export stories is that of the French firm, Rossignol, as related by Charles Smith, Far East Editor of the *Financial Times*. Rossignol, who sell through the trading company, Mitsui, compete mainly with Yamaha, but in 18 years have captured about a sixth of the Japanese market. This may not sound a shattering story of success, but if you're selling 100,000 pairs of skis at up to £200 a pair into the Japanese market, you've something to write home about!

Japanese music in my experience is not nearly as overladen with discordant cacophony as some of the modern European stuff that the BBC push out on my Radio 3, but it isn't easy stuff to appreciate. It is thus always a surprise to find how many Eastern, and particularly Japanese, musicians have got to the top as performers or conductors in the field of Western classical music. There are many clues to the matter in the earlier text of this book, but the predominance of the piano must have a profound influence. I don't know what the equivalent figure is for the UK but it's reported that 14% of Japanese households have a piano — that's one in seven! No doubt most of these 4.2 million pianos were made in Japan, but at the upper end of the social scale there must be a market for top foreign makes of piano and the same applies to most other types of musical instrument.

In their race to catch up with the West — and overtake it economically — the Japanese have undoubtedly fallen behind in what can best be termed the social services in the widest sense, and attention to this gap could well benefit potential exporters in a number of fields. While the mountainous topography of 70% of the land may partially account for the fact that the Japanese motorist has only half the length of paved road to drive on that his British equivalent has, the same cannot be said about main drainage. Perhaps its underground invisibility accounts for its omission from the modernisation of the Meiji era and the fact that, today, a high percentage of Japanese homes are still served by the night-soil cart.

Technically and scientifically, Japanese medicine is among the best in the world and this is a field totally receptive to new ideas and technical developments. Professor Robert White, director of Neurosurgery at the Metropolitan General Hospital, Cleveland, Ohio, has been quoted as saying, "The Japanese will be the first to keep an isolated human head alive. I will not because I haven't resolved as yet this dilemma." Thus, while suggesting a variance between the ethical standing of the Americans and the Japanese, the professor is at least praising the medico-surgical abilities of the latter. In trying to analyse the export potential for medical equipment, a curious feature emerged. Whereas, per head of population, the number of doctors and hospital beds in Britain and Japan is roughly equal, we have 5.2 nurses per 1000 population while the Japanese have only 1.42. Whether this means a lower standard of nursing care, more help from patients' relatives, or more advanced medical equipment, I don't know, but the market for medical equipment is worth exploring.

Allied changes are taking place in Japanese attitudes both towards the elderly and the disabled. In the case of the former there is a move away from the traditional acceptance by the eldest son of the responsibility of looking after his parents, and a corresponding need for the State to provide more facilities such as geriatric hospitals, homes and day centres. At the same time, society is beginning to relax its rigid attitude towards the physically handicapped. Buddhism has tended to frown on the existence of anything imperfect, including humans, and hence it has been the custom to conceal the presence of the disabled member of a family, shutting him or her out of sight. This archaic attitude is fortunately changing and, therefore, as such people become more integrated into society, there is a growing market for aids of all kinds for the disabled from communication devices for the blind and deaf to outdoor electric conveyances. These are small but significant social changes that suggest new fields of export.

Unemployment and the decline of heavy 'traditional' industries like shipbuilding are raising an allied problem in that those most likely to be thrown out of work are the older blue-collar workers who are the least likely to find jobs in the newer high technology industries. Only in the construction field does there seem much hope for them. It is impossible to say whether the government has plans to cope with the plight of these middle-aged workers.

There is a distinct but slow change in the status of women in Japan, where they reputedly make up 38% of the labour force. At present, women tend to be employed in clerical and service occupations as well as in precision and electronic industries or manual work. More and more girls, however, are receiving the benefits of higher education (18% of school-leavers went on to college in 1970; 32% in 1975). The bastions of pharmacy, medicine, design, teaching, computer programming, consumer consultancy, law and even management jobs are increasingly being stormed and captured by women in Japan, and the trend seems one that will continue as they become more liberated, better organised and less satisfied with their lot as somewhat second-class citizens. The import of this to the exporter takes some thinking out.

These are a few surface indications of social change that appear likely to continue. But social changes cannot be considered in isolation. They are one aspect of the whole matter of the quality of life in Japan and, while the Japanese are now a wealthy nation, the total concept of their 'quality of life' leaves much to be desired. Its improvement and up-grading to a level comparable with the best in the West requires — and will probably receive — heavy investment by government in an overall improvement in the infrastructure of Japan. A national plan for this was put forward by Mr Tanaka Kakuei during his premiership, the Tanaka Plan, and a revival of this or a new plan on similar lines may well appear. Whether it does or not is largely dependent on the politicians, whose direction is difficult to predict. Certainly, today, increased sums are being spent in many fields, such as roads, housing and social services but, on the face of it, expenditure is haphazard, uneven and lacking in any overall cohesive plan.

Social and infrastructural development is dependent on economic and political considerations. It is also closely related to technological progress and we may well look here at some of the directions in which this is proceeding in Japan, particularly in such fields as transport, communications, energy and ocean development in all of which research and development expenditure is increasing both in government agencies and in private industry, often backed by MITI funds and planning.

Some idea of the growth of expenditure on research and development in science and technology in Japan can be obtained from the following figures, the latest Government statistics published. Between 1970 and 1975 expenditure increased at a rate of 15% per annum reaching three million million Yen in 1975 (or about 7792 £million at a current exchange rate of around 385

Yen to the £). Of this expenditure, 70% was investment by private industry while 57% was spent within the companies' own research laboratories, 28% at universities and colleges and 15% at research institutes.

In 1975, 88% of this expenditure was in the physical sciences, and this included 3.6% on nuclear science, 2.8% on space exploration, 0.6% on oceanography, 3.9% on computer science and 4.1% on environmental research. The number of research scientists and engineers employed in 1976 was 404,000, about double the number so occupied ten years earlier. Of these, 54% were at universities, 36% within companies and 10% in research institutes. Expenditure per researcher was 7.5 million Yen in 1975.

By comparison the figure for research and development expenditure in 1975 is 14 times that of 1960, and 6 times that of 1965.

Further development of high speed trains and monorails proceeds, the former led by a new High Speed Surface Transit (HSST) system based on a magnetically-levitated train which has already reached 210 mph and should eventually travel at over 300 mph. At the same time there is great interest in small automatic trains for local transport, of which several were shown in service at the ocean 'Expo '75' in Okinawa. The Vona train may soon go into service. Anachronistically, perhaps, there is renewed interest in the tram for city transport on the grounds of its fuel economy and its freedom from atmospheric pollution. Although the original levels have been relaxed, Japanese regulations on i.c. engine exhaust emission are stringent and relevant to imports of cars, but the determined foreign manufacturer can meet them. The Triumph TR7, for instance, a likely 'prestige' selling sports car, has been approved by the Japanese Ministry of Transport.

Excessive dependence on imported oil is a government headache, leading to a search for alternative energy sources over a wide field, which includes gasification and liquefaction of otherwise uneconomic coal seams and a probable increase in coal imports, calling for suitable terminal facilities and a swing towards more coal-fired power stations. Japan's own off-shore oil exploration has shown disappointing results, but diplomatic talks with China and Korea suggest that cooperation in the East China Sea could tap reserves greater than those of Saudi Arabia. Progress in the nuclear field tends to be slow due to public opposition to the siting of power stations, while preference, not unnaturally, leans towards the Canadian 'Candu' type of reactor which does not need enriched uranium which could be used for military purposes. Japanese ingenuity is apparent in the proposal to increase oil stocks at current prices and storing it in unused tankers.

Expenditure on solar energy research is increasing both for house heating and central generating, for which an 1MW prototype station is planned. The government is encouraging householders to spend on the extra cost of solar heating, about twice that of conventional methods, while introducing legislation on the thermal insulation of new buildings. Progess in the use of sunlight to obtain hydrogen from sea-water is slowed by political problems of the siting of the necessary rafts in the ocean, but this alternative energy source is being explored actively.

Japanese leadership in some aspects of communications, such as Video displays and recorders, is spreading to other fields. Although the world's second largest users of computers, the Japanese computer industry is fragmented and small in comparison with such giants as America's IBM. Concentration, as elsewhere, is on the development to practical use of the '64-Kilobit memory', a 6 mm square silicon chip, the implications of which have been given much airing, even in the UK. In software, peripherals and terminals, the Japanese industry is also progressing, hoping overall to take a larger share of her home market, an essential to tackling overseas markets in a bigger way and hence justifying high research and development investment.

Allied to computer developments is the work going into other fields of electronics such as lasers, integrated circuits for other purposes than large computers, optical fibres and new forms of electron tube. Electronic-powered gas panels, for instance, like liquid crystal displays, would obviate the need for deep, bulky cathode ray tubes. In opto-electronics, the Japanese have succeeded in reducing transmission losses so as to allow the transmission of a pulse code modulated signal through an optical fibre for over 50 km without any repeaters in the line.

Apart from increased cooperation in international space satellite programmes for both scientific and applied purposes, Japan is working on its own contributions and towards having its own space station for the development of the in-space manufacture of materials. The belief that her advanced electronic industry has much to offer, particularly to underdeveloped countries where conventional communications systems are either scarce or non-existent, is related to a deeper involvement in satellite communication systems. Japan, with eight at present in space, is keen, too, to establish a marine communication system network to aid not only the giant tankers of her merchant fleet but the very large number of small fishing vessels sailing from her shores.

The culmination of several of these fields of development is to be seen in a trial communications system now under way in the Osaka-Nagoya area, where over 150 homes have been linked to a computer information centre with audio-visual read-out and two-way communication through optical fibre conductors (comparable in some respects with 'Viewdata' in the UK). This trial installation is a pioneering venture which could lead to extensive business information systems and form the basis of an important new industry. Development of facsimile transmission systems, an extension of the concept of document copying, is also going ahead but, at present, is dependent on aerial wave transmission and hence limited in scope by legal restrictions on the use of the air.

The Osaka communications project, Hi-Ovis as it is called, could link up with Japanese ocean development by being connected to a projected man-made island in nearby Kobe Bay. A prototype, 'Oceanopolis', was a feature of Ocean Expo '72 in Okinawa and mention has already been made of other off-shore extensions of the restricted land area. 'Lebensraum' is but one aspect of a comprehensive long-term plan that the Japan Ocean Development Council is currently putting together at the Prime Minister's request to cover the 200 mile economic zone around the island's shores. Other sections include energy and mineral resources from the sea, food production and safety. Japan's dependence on fish as a protein-rich food has been mentioned before. Inshore pollution and international competition in more distant waters suggest the development of large-scale ocean fish farming. Japan is already active in harvesting manganese nodules from the seabed, in submarine exploration craft and machines (the latest a bathyscaphe to work at 2000 metres depth), while seabed oil-production systems are being studied. Japanese buoys and lighthouses have been powered for several years by wave energy electrical systems, from which basis large-scale wave power plant has been designed and will start trials in the Sea of Japan in 1978.

This brief survey of current and future development in Japanese technology might suggest to the would-be exporter that

Japan has got all the technological ideas and brain-power that it needs, and that he would be wasting his time in trying to sell to them in these fields. This is not so. Many of the developments mentioned above are being carried out in cooperation with other countries and many incorporate know-how purchased abroad under technical licence agreements. Space does not allow for an analysis of the indigenous foreign component ratio in different fields, but it is clear that overall Japan is still wide open to the sale of know-how from outside. In spite of her own high level of education and high standard of technical development, in spite of her increasing expenditure on research and development (which is still far below that of the USA), Japan is still open to buying knowledge if someone has something worthwhile to sell. The Japanese are perhaps the leading nation in the world in the development of innovation from the fundamental idea to the stage of practical and commercial viability, but at heart they are not largely an inventive, innovatory race. Like the Americans, they are superb improvers, developers and producers, but generally behind the British and Germans in fundamental innovatory thinking. Few countries can compete with Britain in powers of invention, even today, yet probably none can be so poor at combining technical, financial and management resources so as to develop her inventors' brainchildren into marketable products. Cooperation between Britain and Japan to make the most of each other's best capabilities shows promise for the future to the advantage of both. In this connection I would make the following points.

First, Japanese industrial and business intelligence, through JETRO, visiting study teams, and businessmen and bankers based abroad, is of a very high standard, and hence most foreign published developments and innovations that could be useful to Japan will be known there and studied. However, no system for information dissemination is perfect and therefore it may not be known to and studied by the right people even in the fields of advanced technology. If you have a technical product to sell, therefore, you must set about the selling yourself. If you've got one of those "better mousetraps" that R.W. Emerson wrote about, don't expect the Japanese to make a beaten path to the door of your house in the woods; not without first taking your better mousetrap to JETRO and showing them how it's better than the others!

Second, while patent trademark and copyright law and its

application is as important in Japan as it is in Britain, it is no more important there. In this sensitive field there are always risks, but they are no greater in Japan than elsewhere. As an author I am far more at risk from having my work pirated in the United States than an engineering firm is of having its designs copied in Japan — unless the USA has tidied up things a lot since Ace Books produced the first paperback edition of J.R.R. Tolkein's, *The Lord of the Rings* in 1964 without any payment to the author of that remarkable and creative work. The Ministry of International Trade and Industry has for years taken the lead in promoting the import of foreign know-how into Japan, but also in ensuring that it is done honestly and under proper technical licensing agreements. I have mentioned before the Japanese desire for acceptance on an equal footing with other nations of the world, the personal and national desire to be liked, if not loved, and MITI's attitude is a reflection of this. The Japanese used to be a nation of copiers and I could quote a case, early in this century, where cameras were made of highly polished wood, held rigid by brass corner-pieces and brackets screwed into the wood. Not understanding the function of the wood screws, Japanese copiers made the cornerpieces without screws but with the recessed heads and slots faithfully reproduced quite uselessly in the brass — but that was three-quarters of a century ago and it is unkind to make more of it than an unfortunate phase in history. Today, the Japanese do not copy. Where they cannot originate, they buy designs and know-how and MITI is hard on any company that infringes the rules. Study teams may swarm round foreign stands at home and overseas exhibitions with Nikons clicking and Sony tapes whirring to record the basis of reports. Studied at technical and management levels in Japan, such reports may produce an initiative from the East, if there's something in them they would like. They'll approach you but it would be very rare for them to copy these days, certainly no more than in any country in the West.

In Table 7 I have listed a number of companies and products where success in exporting to Japan has resulted from good market research and a practical and energetic approach which has taken account of local custom, culture and commercial methods. The list is compiled from several sources and includes both consumer and industrial products.

To conclude, I would quote the curious success of Royal Doulton. Well-known for high-class and tasteful china, they are

Table 7.   COMPANIES EXPORTING SUCCESSFULLY TO JAPAN

Consumer 'Expendables'

Pez: confectionery[1]
Roussel-Velaf: pharmaceuticals[1]
Lindisfarne: liqueurs and foods[2]
Lyons Maid: ice-cream[2]
Lyons: fruit pies
Twinings: tea
Berni Inns: food outlets

Consumer Durables

Dimplex: oil-filled radiators[1]
Philips: household products[1]
Triumph: women's clothing[1]
Norman Hartnell: fashion
Mappin & Webb: jewellery and silver
Ercol: furniture
Rossignol: skis[2]
ICI: Vymura wall covering
Royal Doulton: egg cups (*see below*)
Christie's: Old Master and Impressionist paintings
Submarine Products: underwater breathing equipment[2]
Sinclair: electronic calculators[1]
BSR: record changers for stereo[3]
Volvo: cars[3]
Olivetti: office machinery[3]

Industrial Products

Glacier Metal: marine stern tube bearings[2]
BOC: high vacuum equipment[2]
Hymac: concrete breaking 'Nibbler'
Foseco: chemicals for industry[3]

[1] Further details can be found in *Business in Japan: Six Case Studies* (Japan Air Lines booklet, 1973).

[2] These products are listed in the BOTB's *Into Japan* Report (Trade and Industry, 9 April 1976).

[3] These products originate in a series of articles, *Exports to Japan* by Charles Smith, Far East Editor, in the *Financial Times* June/July 1977.

having, as the *Financial Times* reported, an unusual success in demand from Japan for their 'Bunnykins' egg-cups! Boiled eggs are not a major item of Japanese diet— at least not as eaten from the egg-cup. It's been suggested that they may be ideal for drinking saké! You can never tell your luck; in February 1977, Mitsukoshi departo's buying team started their buying mission with an order for thirty-six galvanised iron buckets and a garden gnome! A final trend may be indicated by the mission in June 1978 of twenty-three leaders of Japan's wedding industry to attend a church marriage in Henley-on-Thames followed by a lecture by the rural dean, and three wedding receptions at Phyllis Court Club. This pioneering study-team is in the vanguard of the new trend for 'English style wedding' in Japan. Confetti (and other wedding appurtenance) suppliers, please note!

You may think I've told only half the story in this chapter. I'd be lucky if I've managed to fit in one-twentieth— I haven't even mentioned aircraft, for instance, but then there aren't very many British suppliers, and, in the whole book, I've only touched on pollution with all its pleasant by-ways of electrostatic precipitation, sanitation and sewage! A friend of mine is successfully exporting a special tapered fishing line to the Japanese, a leisure industry product which, in the overall industrial context, is small fry. However, the special qualities of the product and the unqiue production methods he has developed put him ahead of local manufacturers, and Japanese anglers flock eagerly to their fishing tackle suppliers to buy. There's nothing better than 'Masterline' so that's the line for the Japanese customer! Only you can track down the trends in your own product field and estimate its market, bearing in mind the overall trend for the Japanese, both individually and collectively, to want to acquire the best in the West— using the term 'best' in the widest possible sense. You've got to get up early to beat the Japanese technologically, but fortunately we've still got a few early risers and I wish them well!

One of these, whose activities were publicised almost as this manuscript was going to press, is the Monotype Corporation, which has come up with a masterly solution to the problem of typesetting in Japanese and Chinese ideograms. This is a combination of the firm's 'Lasercomp' typesetter and a special keyboard. The latter is a superb example of logical thinking in design for, instead of having one key to represent each single ideogram in its entirety, each of the keys relates solely to one of the different and separate lines that go to make up the ideograms. A glance at any Japanese book will show how most lines and strokes are common to many ideograms and that the latter can, in many cases, be grouped into families according to these common elements in their composition. Compared to a Western keyboard with only some 50 keys, the new Monotype machine is elaborate with its 240, but this is a considerable simplification and reduction on the 2000 or so which are to be found on a conventional Japanese machine. The process of composition becomes analogous to that of writing the characters by hand with pen or brush. Since meticulous attention to detail in the calligraphic art in the sequence and direction of the brush strokes is an inherent part of traditional Japanese education, little problem should be found in the training of operators for the new Monotype machine. The surprising feature is that the Japanese didn't think of the idea first, although, it must be admitted, the keyboard is said to be the result of five years of research by Professor S.C. Loh of the Chinese University in Hong Kong. Anyway, one up to the Department of Engineering at Cambridge University, the London School of Economics and the Monotype Corporation who cooperated in this outstanding British technological achievement. Let's hope others will emulate their example!

I have called this chapter A Gentle Breeze of Change. Anyone with experience of the country will know how quickly a breeze in Japan can become a wind, a hurricane or a typhoon (Tai-Fun = Great Wind). The people can be as unpredictable as nature.

CHAPTER FOURTEEN

Keeping Up The Pressure

This is a short chapter for most of its content is little more than common sense and courtesy. However, if it acts as a checklist to ensure that nothing is omitted, it will serve a useful purpose. It is written on the assumption that you have finally overcome all obstacles and signed up a partner of one sort or another to represent your interests in Japan. Back at head office you're trying to excuse that last hangover from your send-off at the airport by pleading Circadian Disrhythmia as the medicos call jet lag today.

If you did your stuff right in Japan, you'll have done more than just sign a contract but will have brought back all the information that your company will need to work effectively with your new partners. To obtain from the Japanese such essentials as an Organisation Chart of their company with the full names of all the personnel that will or may be involved in your affairs, is much more easily done while you're in their offices than by a letter request on your return. Many Japanese firms have a strange reluctance to put these sorts of details on paper but you must know who does what out there and to whom different types of correspondence should be addressed. Maybe they will appoint one English-speaking employee to liaise with your company and to channel incoming mail to the right people and departments, with or without having translated it into Japanese. Whichever way it is to be, full details of your joint *modus operandi* are best established while you are in Japan rather than later.

An invaluable help in speeding up communication by mail can also be obtained while in Japan and certainly should be. This, which your Japanese partners can easily supply, is a rubber stamp with their name and address cut in kanji and hiragana characters. Depending on the likely scale of your operations you may need more than one. Of course mail should also be addressed in Roman type or it won't get past the sorting office in the UK postal system, but the use of a stamp like this helps at the other end, making things easier for the Japanese postman who makes the deliveries. After all, you wouldn't expect a British postman to be able to read Japanese!

Again, depending on the nature and scale of your activities, you would have done well to arrange for some personnel from Japan to come to your company for product familiarisation and training, and preparations will need to be made for his or their reception so as to make the best possible use of the time available at your company. Your Training Officer, if you have one, may be able to handle the overall plan, but ensure that he, or whoever undertakes the task, is properly and fully briefed on the objectives and any special requirements that you think your Japanese visitors may have. They should, of course, while with you have the opportunity of meeting as many of your staff as possible, not only during the working day but also socially, for the more each side of the partnership knows of the other, the better relations are likely to be and the smoother will be the flow of business between you. The importance of personal relations to the sarariman and the executive in Japan cannot be over-emphasised and this applies equally, if not more strongly, when he is dealing with foreign partners and suppliers.

Naturally your own staff will need careful briefing, not only about the needs of the Japanese visitors but also about every aspect of the new venture you have initiated with their company. If success is to be achieved and the initial enthusiasm of the Japanese staff is to be maintained, it is essential that you are organised so as to deal with every type of incoming enquiry with the least possible delay. There are obviously many ways in which this may be done but ideally someone relatively senior in your organisation, preferably someone who has been out to Japan, should supervise the whole exercise, at least until you have got your 'kokusai kyoryoku' or international cooperation well under way. It is not a bad thing, particularly in the early stages, to arrange for your Japanese partners to send an extra copy of all correspondence to whomever you appoint to head your end of the operation, and for you to do likewise to their appointed liaison man or the director who will be overseeing the Japan end of the joint affair. This may sound wasteful in postage and paperwork, but it is better to add this small cost if it will ensure that nothing will be neglected or delayed unreasonably at either end of the link.

As things will have an unpredictable way of happening with undue suddenness when dealing with the Japanese, your shipping manager or department should waste no time in familiarising himself thoroughly with freight costs, methods and routes for the new market you are entering. You should, of course, have previously ascertained whether your Japanese agents or whatever they are want quotations ex-works, F.O.B., or C.I.F. and whether they have a preference for any particular shipping line and who acts for them as shipping agents. All this can help in the essential matter of cutting down delivery times in transit. Again, while the Japanese Customs department are no more bureaucratic or inefficient than those in other countries and, in fact, are more cooperative than many European nations, the correct form of documentation must be ascertained and adhered to. There is nothing more damping to the enthusiasm of your Japanese partners, who have been eagerly awaiting goods travelling 7000 miles, than the frustration of having them lying in a customs warehouse, possibly incurring storage and demurrage charges, just because of incorrect paperwork or its non-arrival with the goods. Ulcers and nervous breakdowns are likely to result in Japan, together with loss of profit from delay and wasted telex and telephone costs in pursuit of the proper papers. Your company will lose face, not only with your partners, but also with their customers. I cannot overstress that in many fields British suppliers have let down Japanese customers in the past, and one of the first hurdles to overcome in the export-to-Japan game is to prove that your company is not among the British black sheep in trade or industry. In this connection I would add that, if things inadvertently go wrong as they unfortunately do all too often, and you are forced to be late on delivery of an order, you must let your Japanese partners know as soon as possible. It is much better to face up to the facts and give them as much notice as possible so that they in turn can give warning to their own customers. This may sound kids' stuff and applicable to any overseas market. It is, but it is especially important in Japan, and it is surprising to learn how many British companies appear to ignore or to be ignorant of such simple and self-evident matters.

While they will not want to be overloaded with mail, if you have had help in your negotiations from B.O.T.B. and the British Embassy and Legations in Japan, apart from the courtesy of thanking them, it will do no harm to keep them informed briefly of your progress. Commercial information and intelligence is their bread and butter and very much the essence of their lives. Thus your own experience, whether successful or otherwise, may be useful to them in helping other firms. Sustained contact with them, too, may be of assistance to you on the subsequent visits that you will undoubtedly have to make to Japan if you are to keep the pot boiling and increase your trade there.

What of these visits? Circumstances alter cases, but, in my experience, they must be made at least once a year if not more frequently. When appointing your agent, distributor or whatever, you should have made clear details of the type and frequency of market and sales reports that you require of them. Even if these have been received as specified, they are a poor substitute for going out and seeing and hearing for yourself what is or is not going on. As stated before, due notice of your proposed visits should be given and your objectives defined precisely. Your arrival at your partners' offices, and in those of their existing and potential customers, can be a great potential boost to their feelings and their level of activity on your behalf. If you can get others of your staff out to Japan, so much the better. The more of them that can experience immersion in the environment and culture of Japan, the more they will understand the special problems of the market and the more likely will success come your way. Most of the staff of your Japanese partners will be dealing at long distance with names to whom they cannot even fit a face, let alone a personality. No matter how the doomwatchers predict the takeover of our lives by the computer, and now the microprocessor, business is still very much a people to people activity and nowhere more so than in Japan.

If you are sending new people out to Japan, it should go without saying that you should ensure they read this book. At the same time, if you intend to sustain your own efforts in that country, you won't be wasting your time if you soak up more of the literature of and about Japan such as is listed in the Bibliography in Appendix H. You can't know too much about the country and its people and, even when writing business letters to your Nippon friends, it does no harm to slip in the odd literary, historical or cultural by-line or comment. It shows your interest in them and will go down all the better if it can include an ingredient of humour. Further friendship-cementing to oil the wheels of your cooperation, if I may be permitted to mix a metaphor, can be achieved by letters to the homes of your Japanese colleagues on a personal basis, and the occasional picture postcard from Britain or other places where you travel. This may sound self-evident but I find that Japanese friends in business are far more prone to sending me such communications than any other country where I have done business, and hence I assume that they are all the more appreciative of reciprocal mailings. I would add that, although Christmas doesn't come in the Japanese year as the proportion of Japanese Christians is small, you are likely to receive a substantial bundle of cards, if not calendars, in December, so be ready to send your own out. Christmas or New Year presents to directors, senior executives and special contacts can do no harm. Any of them who have visited Britain, and even those who haven't, welcome colour illustrated books showing the British countryside and suchlike.

Success depends on communication, and communication is a two-way affair. In spite of the time difference between the two countries, or possibly because of it, telex is invaluable. Another Post Office service, not so well known, is equally useful when the occasion calls for it, particularly in the technical products field. That is the service by which drawings can be transmitted quickly, if not instantaneously in the same manner as a telegram. As in other situations a drawing can save a thousand words and once received in Japan can be copied, studied and is far less capable of being misunderstood. This service can greatly cut down errors in communication. Your local postmaster should be able to supply details, and it isn't all that expensive.

The title of this chapter was chosen carefully. As I've pointed out earlier, it is likely that, at least at the beginning, the Japanese will be putting the pressure on you — and very exhausting it can be. It shouldn't always be that way round and, if you want to get ahead as fast as possible, you must communicate with them. Keep them regularly informed of your sales successes in the UK as well as in other export markets. If you've a house journal or news letter, send them plenty of copies. Add to your reference list as time passes and other firms become your customers. Tell them early of new appointments and staff changes, particularly where these affect your Japanese operation. In short, as Mr Micawber would put it, keep up a constant flow of information on everything your company does. It will help to maintain interest until your next visit. Time-consuming it may be, but it will pay dividends.

Lastly, don't neglect the telephone, taking into account, of course, the time difference. The Japanese think nothing of phoning the UK. Times may be hard and money in short supply but, if you've good reason, ring your Japanese friends. You may not have the finest voice in the world, but the sound of it in the Japanese office over the phone can carry your personality out there and rekindle the fire of friendship on which your mutual relationship and your success should be based.

Good Luck, or 'go kigen yo' as they say in Japan!

APPENDIX A

GOVERNMENT AND OTHER OFFICIAL ORGANISA-TIONS IN LONDON

British Overseas Trade Board, Exports to Japan Unit,
Hillgate House, 26 Old Bailey, London EC4M 7HU
Tel. 01-248 5757 Ext. 7162/232

British Overseas Trade Board, Export Services & Promotions Division,
Export House, 50 Ludgate Hill, London EC4M 7HU
Tel. 01-248 5757

British Overseas Trade Board, Commercial Relations & Exports Division,
1 Victoria Street, London SW1H 0ET
Tel. 01-315 7877

Embassy of Japan,
46 Grosvenor Street, London W1X 0BA
Tel. 01-493 6030

Embassy of Japan, Information Centre,
9 Grosvenor Square, London W1
Tel. 01-493 6030

Japanese External Trade Organisation (JETRO),
19-25 Baker Street, London W1M 1AE
Tel. 01-486 6761

Japan AirLines Co. Ltd.,
8 Hanover Street, London W1
Tel. 01-629 9244

Japan National Tourist Organisation,
167 Regent St., London W1
Tel. 01-734 9638

Japan Travel Bureau Inc.,
32 Old Burlington Street, London W1
Tel. 01-437 3601

Japanese Chamber of Commerce in London.
Secretary, Mr. R.S. Milward. Office alternates annually between
the premises of the Mitsubishi Corporation and Mitsui & Co.
Ltd.
For addresses see under 'The Major Trading Companies'.

Anglo-Japanese Economic Institute,
342-346 Grand Buildings, Trafalgar Square, London WC2N
5HB
Tel. 01-930 5567

THE MAJOR TRADING COMPANIES IN LONDON

C. Itoh & Company Ltd.,
The London International Press Centre, Shoe Lane, London
EC4A 3JB
Tel. 01-353 6090

Kanematsu-Gossho Ltd.,
Tribune House, 120 Moorgate, London EC2P 2JY
Tel. 01-628 7901

Marubeni Corporation,
New London Bridge House, London Bridge St., London SE1
9SW
Tel. 01-407 8300

Mitsubishi Corporation,
Bow Bells House, Bread St., London EC2V 7LX
Tel. 01-236 2060

Mitsui & Company Ltd.,
Royex House, Aldermanbury Square, London EC2V 7LX
Tel. 01-600 1777

Nichimen Company Ltd.,
Winchester House, 77 London Wall, London EC2N 1BP
Tel. 01-628 7601

Nissho-Iwai Ltd.,
Bastion House, 140 London Wall, London EC2Y 5JT
Tel. 01-628 6030

Okura Trading Company Ltd.,
Lee House, London Wall, London EC2Y 5AJ
Tel. 01-600 1373

Sumitomo Shoji Kaisha Ltd.,
P & O Building, Leadenhall St., London EC3V 4PA
Tel. 01-281 4931

Toyo Menka Kaisha Ltd.,
St Alphage House, 2 Fore St., London EC2Y 5DQ
Tel. 01-628 2591

Dodwell & Company Ltd.,
18 Finsbury Circus, London EC2M 7BE
Tel. 01-588 6040

Jardine Matheson & Company Ltd.,
3 Lombard St., London EC3
Tel. 01-480 6633

'DEPARTO' BUYING OFFICES IN LONDON

Daimaru
Richard Symes Export Co. Ltd.,
37-38 Margaret St., London W1N 7FA
01-493 9173

Hankyu
Booker Exports Ltd.,
The Adelphi, John Adam St., London WC2N 6BD
01-930 4041

Isetan
Dean Warburg Ltd.,
38 Saville Row, London W1X 2ET
01-734 9421

Matsuzakaya
Associated Merchandising Corporation,
1b Baker St., London W1M 1AA
01-486 4721

Mitsukoshi
Mitsukoshi (UK) Ltd.,
87 Regent St., London W1
01-437 6346 & 01-439 6085

Seibu-Seiyu & Daiwa
Gimbel Brothers,
Ellsley House, 24-30 Great Titchfield St.,
London W1P 8ED
01-637 3931/9

Takashimaya & Keio
Portman (Wholesale & Overseas) Ltd.,
40 Duke St., London W1M 6AL
01-629 8805

BANKS IN LONDON

The Bank of Japan, 27 Old Jewry, London EC2.
Tel. 01-606 2454
The Long-Term Credit Bank of Japan Ltd., 3 Lombard St.,
London EC3V 9AH.
Tel. 01-623 9511
The Industrial Bank of Japan, 14 Walbrook, London EC4N
8BR.
Tel. 01-236 2351
Dai-Ichi Kangyo Bank, P & O Building, 122-138 Leadenhall St.,
London EC3V 4PA.
Tel. 01-289 0929
Daiwa Bank Ltd., Winchester House, London Wall, London
EC2.
Tel. 01-628 4923

Fuji Bank Ltd., Salisbury House, Finsbury Circus, London EC2P 2JH.
Tel. 01-628 0601
Hokkaido Takushoku Bank, 6 Basinghall St., London EC2P '2DR.
Tel. 01-606 8961
Mitsubishi Bank, 6 Lombard St., London EC3V 9AA.
Tel. 01-623 9201
Mitsubishi Trust & Banking Corporation, 8-13 King William St., London EC4P 4HS.
Tel. 01-626 4721/9
Mitsui Bank Ltd, 34-35 King St., London EC2V 8ES.
Tel. 01-606 0611
Mitsui Trust & Banking Co. Ltd., 99 Bishopsgate, London EC2M 3XD.
Tel. 01-638 0841
Sanwa Bank Ltd., 31-45 Gresham St., London EC2V 7DP.
Tel. 01-606 6101
Sumitomo Bank Ltd., 5 Moorgate, London EC2R 6HU.
Tel. 01-600 0211
Sumitomo Trust & Banking Co. Ltd., 62-63 Threadneedle St., London EC2R 8BR.
Tel. 01-628 5621/9
Tokai Bank Ltd., P & O Building, Leadenhall St., London EC3V 4PA.
Tel. 01-283 8500
Bank of Tokyo, Northgate House, 20-24 Moorgate, London EC2R 6DH.
Tel. 01-638 1271

SECURITIES COMPANIES IN LONDON

Daiwa Europe N.V.,
Empire House, 8-14 St Martins-le-Grand, London EC1P 1DR.
Tel. 01-600 5676

Nikko Securities Europe Ltd.,
Royex House, Aldermanbury, London EC2V 7LX.
Tel. 01-606 7171

Nomura Securities Co. Ltd.,
Barber Surgeons Hall, Monkwell St., London EC2.
Tel. 01-606 6253

Yamaichi International (Europe) Ltd.,
St Alphage House, 2 Fore St., London EC2Y 5AA.
Tel. 01-628 2271

LANGUAGE SPECIALISTS IN THE UK

Berlitz School of Languages Ltd.,
79 Wells St., London W1.
Tel. 01-486 1931
Translation Services: 321 Oxford St., London W1.
Tel. 01-629 7360

Eastern Languages Bureau Ltd.,
61 Carey St., London WC2
Tel. 01-242 9267

Japanese Linguateam,
5 Oakfield St., London SW10 9JA
Tel. 01-352 3314/3054

Linguarama Ltd.,
53 Pall Mall, London SW1
Tel. 01-930 7697

Tek Translation & International Print Ltd.,
11 Uxbridge Rd., London W12
Tel. 01-749 3211

Pilot Public Relations Ltd.,
129 Windmill St., Gravesend, Kent
Tel. Gravesend 56544

CBD Associates Ltd.,
77 Park Lane, Croydon, Surrey
Tel. 01-686 7671
Translations and print by offset litho after setting in Japan.

Linguaphone Institute Ltd.,
207-9 Regent St., London W1R 8AV
Tel. 01-734 4347

Stephen Austin & Sons Ltd.,
Caxton Hill, Ware Road, Hertford
Tel. Hertford 4955.
Printing in Japanese.

TRAVEL SPECIALISTS IN LONDON

Japan Air Lines,
JAL House, 8 Hanover St., London W1R 0DR
Tel. 01-493 3831

Japan National Tourist Organisation,
167 Regent St., London W1
Tel. 01-734 4938

Miki Travel Agency,
95 St Pauls Churchyard, London EC4
Tel. 01-248 2020

Nippon Express Co. Ltd.,
Fleming's Hotel, Half Moon St., London W1
Tel. 01-499 1621

MISCELLANEOUS SOURCES OF USEFUL INFORMA-TION IN THE UK

Dentsu Advertising Ltd., 32 St James's St., London SW1. For advice on advertising and the media in Japan.

Economist Intelligence Unit Ltd., Subscription Dept (X1) 27 St James's Place, London SW1A 1NT. The Quarterly Economic Review Service publishes an edition on *Japan & South Korea*. Current price is £30 p.a. for four issues plus annual supplement plus postage and packing.

The Japan Company Handbook, published in January and August, compiled by Toyo Keizai Shinposha (The Oriental Economist) is available through Publishing & Distributing Co. Ltd., Mitre House, 177 Regent St., London W1. 01-734 6534. Current price is 21 dollars per copy or 39 dollars per annum by sea mail. The book gives precise and detailed information on Japan's top 1000 companies.

The Map House, 54 Beauchamp Place, London SW3. Sells every type of map and can supply Japanese city maps.

Overseas Courier Service (London) Ltd., 22 Sussex St., London SW1V 4RW. 01-834 4602 and 6268. Specialists in the supply of Japanese journals and newspapers on a subscription basis.

O.C.S. Book, 67 Parkway, London NW1. 01-485 4201. Associated with Overseas Courier Service. This Japanese bookshop mainly caters for the needs of Japanese living in London and has only a small stock of books in English. Books from Japan can be ordered here.

The Japan Telephone Book, classified edition in English, useful for locating trade association addresses etc. Unfortunately not available in UK but can be ordered from Japan Yellow Pages Ltd., S.T. Building, 6-9 Iidibashi, 4-chome, Chiyoda-ku, Tokyo 102.

International Book Distributors Ltd., 14 Frogmore Road, Hemel Hempstead, Herts. Tel. Hemel Hempstead 58531. Are distributors for Japan Publishing Trading Co. and Charles E. Tuttle Co.

Books from Japan, 13 Milton Road, Pound Hill, Crawley, Sussex, Mail order company for books, periodicals, records, tapes etc and can arrange printing of Japanese business cards.

Nippon Guide Services Ltd., 102 Grand Buildings, Northumberland Avenue WC2N 5EP. Tel. 01-930 6927. Japanese speaking guides: useful if you have visitors who don't speak English.

City Ikebana Services, 34 Queens Drive, Thames Ditton, Surrey. Tel. 01-398 5102. Provide a wide range of translating, guide and interpreter services, including tea ceremony, calligraphy and hostesses in kimono.

THE LIGHTER SIDE OF JAPAN IN LONDON

Before my first visit to Japan I spent many evenings assiduously transferring cigarette butts from one ashtray to another with a pair of slender sticks acquired from our local horticultural suppliers in the hope that I would reach Japan as an experienced controller of chop-sticks. The whole exercise was largely fruitless as I had neglected the changes in muscle tension that occur when the wrist is turned to direct the chop-sticks and their succulent offering towards the mouth. However, if any reader wants to get in a bit of practice before going East, there are a good number of Japanese restaurants in London now, some of which are listed below. On the other hand, if you forget to buy that vital gift, a drip-dry kimono or whatever you promised your wife (or your secretary), all is not lost. Do not despair. There are specialist shops selling Japanese goods in town where you can rectify the error. If the food in Japan really grabs you — and I don't mean in the sense that 'fugu' or the dreaded poisonous globefish can do — you can acquire the necessary ingredients to try your hand at cookery from shops in the same area. Want to study Japanese prints, armour or a real Japanese garden? Probably not, but if you do it's possible. Listed below are the places where you can see or buy the object of your interest. (P.S. If you want to create mayhem, you can even get equipment for the Japanese martial arts here.)

Some Japanese Restaurants

Kyoto Restaurant, Central Park (Tenma) Hotel, 74-76 Queensborough Terrace, London W2. Tel. 01-221 5843.

Suntory Restaurant, 72-73 St James's Street, London SW1. Tel. 01-409 0201.

Sakura Restaurant, 9 Hanover Street, London W1. Tel. 01-629 2961.

Ajimura Restaurant, 51-53 Shelton Street, London WC2. Tel. 01-240 0178.

Japanese Steak House, 22-25 Dean St., London W1. Tel. 01-437 6630.

Japanese Restaurant, Kensington Hilton Hotel, 179 Holland Park Avenue, London W11. Tel. 01-603 3355.

Masako Restaurant, 6 St Christophers Place, London W1. Tel. 01-486 1399.

Saga Restaurant, 43 South Molton Street, London W1. Tel. 01-408 2236.

Fuji Restaurant, 36-40 Brewer Street, London W1. Tel. 01-734 0957.

Hokkai Restaurant, 61 Brewer Street, London W1. Tel. 01-734 2539.

Ginnan Restaurant, 5 Cathedral Place, London EC4. Tel. 01-236 4120.
Kiku Restaurant, 12 Whitehouse Street, London W1. Tel. 01-499 4208.

Apart from trying out Japanese food before you go to Japan, most of these restaurants have traditional Nippon decor and kimono-clad Japanese girls to serve you and are ideal for bouts of nostalgia when you get back home again. They're also useful if and when you have Japanese visitors to entertain in London.

Other Japanalia in England
Mitsukiku, The Japanese shop. For kimonos and happi coats, chinaware, gifts and books. Based at 73a Lower Sloane Street, Chelsea, SW1. Tel. 01-730 1505. Mitsukiku also has branches in London at Notting Hill Gate, Kensington High Street, Old Brompton Road and Victoria Street, as well as in Birmingham, Bournemouth and Brighton.

Nippon Food Centre sells ingredients for Japanese cooking as well as cooking equipment and Japanese tableware. Shops are at 61 High Street, Wimbledon and 483 Finchley Road, London NW3.

Sakura Trading Co., Thornton Road, Isleworth sells equipment for Japanese martial arts.

Japanese arts and artefacts can be studied in the British Museum while the collection of Japanese arms and armour in the Tower of London is admirable and a surprise to many Japanese visitors.

The Japanese Gallery, 66d Kensington Church Street, London W8. Tel. 01-229 2934. Sells, buys and exchanges wood-block prints, books, ceramics and works of art from Japan.

Another print specialist is Milne Henderson, 112 Clifton Hill, London NW8.

Other Japanese food shops are:-
Osaka Ltd., 17 Goldhurst Terrace, London NW6.
Mikadoya, 250 Upper Richmond Road, London SW15 & 529a Finchley Road, London NW3.
Mishuku, 17-19 Pelham Street, London SW7.

If you want to enjoy the beauty of a Japanese garden, there is an extensive one, open to the public by kind permission of the owners, Mr & Mrs F.C. Englemann at the Garden House, Cottered, off the road to Cambridge.

Many aspects of Japanese life, thought and culture can be studied at the Japan Society, 630 Grand Buildings, Trafalgar Square, London WC2. Tel. 01-839 1697.

Finally, by way of complete contrast, at 20 Lisle Street, London WC2, you'll find Kumiko Massage and Baths, Tel. 01-734 7982.

APPENDIX B

GETTING THE GOODS THERE

It is likely that, in the event of your finding suitable business partners in Japan, they will have their own ideas on shipping and forwarding agents and arrangements for freight, probably based on previous experience with other products. You would be well advised to consider such suggestions that they may make. If you are dealing with one of the major trading companies, it is usual for them to handle the shipping side of the business, your responsibilities ending with delivery to their chosen location in the UK, on time of course, and with documentation such as they demand. Whether air or sea freight is to be used will naturally depend mainly on the product, the size of the consignment and the urgency of the delivery schedule. The names and London addresses of the major trading companies are given in Appendix A, while a list of some specialised importing companies in Japan is further on in this Appendix. Their advice and preference on method of shipping as well as the name of any freight agent that they may wish to act for them should be sought. The same applies if you succeed in doing business with any of the department stores or chain stores who may have a set system for the delivery of goods.

Advice on shipping and forwarding agents familiar with the Japanese market and freight routes can be sought from B.O.T.B. There is no doubt that all the major international shipping and forwarding agents have staff competent and well-versed in transport to Japan and a list of some of these is given below. I would mention from personal experience the Ben Line, whose representative is likely to drop his card in or telephone your Tokyo hotel room almost before you've had time to unpack. Their man in Tokyo has an intelligence system that deserves to succeed and he is also a useful and friendly contact for any newcomer to

Japan. I can also speak personally of the abilities of Thomas Meadows & Co. Ltd. and Meadows Airfreight.

Of airlines one naturally thinks first of British Airways and Japan Air Lines, and then perhaps of the other European operators such as Lufthansa, Air France, SAS etc., and anyone with experience will doubtless have his own preferences. In this connection, I would only make two points. First, due to IATA regulations, BA should be able to offer the cheapest rates if the goods are flown via Hong Kong. McGregor Swire should be able to advise on this as, I believe, they operate a special service on this basis. This route may take a couple of days longer for trans-shipment but is worth investigating. Second, I wouldn't omit enquiring into the services of Cathay Pacific who are specialists in Far East transport.

Sea freight container services have been growing on the UK-Japan route as everywhere else. Apart from Ben Line, Mitsui, OSK, NYK and OCL all operate container ship services. I have also heard of a special combined land-sea route run by the Anglo-Soviet Shipping Co. Ltd., reputed to reduce the transit period from some 45 days to 30. I've never used this route but, apart from quicker delivery, it is also claimed to be cheaper than the straight sea route and is hence worth looking into.

Lastly freight can be sent by air to Hong Kong and thence by sea to Japan, the process taking from 10 to 14 days. This is another sphere in which McGregor Swire can advise!

The following list includes only main offices. Many also have branches at London Airport or in its vicinity.

Ben Line containers Ltd. Agents: Killick Martin & Co. Ltd., Crown Linton Road, Barking. Tel. 01-594 7191.

Beck & Pollitzer Packing & Shipping Ltd., Tower Bridge House, Tower Bridge, London SE1. Tel. 01-407 6051.

Thomas Cook & Son Ltd., Forwarding Agents, Riverside House, 41 Berth, Tilbury Docks. Tel. Tilbury 2790.

Kuehne & Nagel Ltd., Service House, 290 Borough High St., London SE1. Tel. 01-407 8844.

LEP Group of Companies Ltd., Sunlight Wharf, Upper Thames St., London EC4. Tel. 01-236 5050.

McGregor Swire Air Services Ltd., Colndale Road, Colnbrook. Tel. Colnbrook 4911.

Thomas Meadows & Co. Ltd., Dale House, Kirkdale Road, Leytonstone, London E11. Tel. 01-556 8811.

Mitsui O.S.K. Lines Ltd., 12 Camomile Street, London EC3.

Tel. 01-283 7081.

NYK International Luxembourg S.A., 10 Bevis Marks, London EC3. Tel. 01-283 5466.

Overseas Containers Ltd., South Regional Office, Box Lane, Barking, Tel. 01-593 8181.

IMPORT PROCEDURES

For many years after the Occupation there were extensive controls and restrictions on imports into Japan but a progressive process of liberalisation has, by now, almost entirely done away with these. Anyone who has kept an eye on the recent history of Japanese economic affairs, as recorded in the *Financial Times*, will have read of the pressures being brought to bear on the Japanese government to reduce tariffs on imported goods, and these have already had considerable effect. No doubt, as the Japanese trade surplus continues to mount, these pressures will intensify to the benefit of the potential exporter. Thus it is today that customs duty over a wide range of product groups has been lowered while the number of 'non-liberalised' and highly taxed products remains very small.

The Japanese Customs authorities work on the lines of the established Brussels tariff nomenclature headings, and permission for the entry into Japan is given for all but a few rare categories such as explosives and tobacco which come under an Import Quota scheme, requiring the relevant Allocation Certificate from the Ministry of International Trade and Industry. Further information on the remaining import controls and the duty rates existing can be obtained from the Overseas Tariffs & Regulations (O.T.A.R.) Section of the Export Data Branch, British Overseas Trade Board, Export House, 50 Ludgate Hill, London EC4M 7HU, Tel. 01-248 5757. Imports into Japan in approximately 15% of the 2600 or so categories in the Brussels nomenclature are duty-free. These are mainly raw materials and fuel and, in fact, add up to about half of Japan's total import bill by value.

Customs Duty (at rates obtainable from the B.O.T.B.'s O.T.A.R. Section mentioned above) is based on c.i.f. values declared. In addition, commodity taxes, which are applied equally to locally produced equivalent goods, may be applicable to some products, such as many types of luxury sports and leisure equipment, alcoholic drinks etc. Again B.O.T.B. can advise on the current situation.

So far as documentation is concerned, the Japanese market differs little from other export fields. Normal requirements to Customs are a commercial invoice, an airway bill or bill of lading and, in a few cases of specific products, a certificate of origin. A few lively items, such as plants, animals and some foodstuffs, may also need an inspection certificate to ensure freedom from disease.

The Japanese Customs will require each invoice in duplicate, signed by the consignor and including the following details: Date and place at which the invoice was made out; consignee and address of destination; details of goods: catalogue/serial reference numbers, etc where applicable, name, description, quantity unit price, value and Brussels nomenclature number; and conditions of contract on which the valuation is based.

Where there is any question of doubt about the valuation, freight, insurance and packing costs may also be required. It may be politic to include these details in the initial invoice. The inclusion of the recipient's telephone number may be a help in case of any query arising.

It is, of course, vital that the proper documentation is also sent to your agent, or whomever is the consignee, in good time. Apart from copies of the invoice, three signed bills of lading should be sent via the bank and at least two unsigned copies to the consignee. I have known cases where the forwarding agent has delayed unnecessarily so that apart from late delivery of an order, the Japanese agent has also had the aggravation of having to pay storage charges for goods he urgently wanted.

SOME SPECIALISED IMPORTING COMPANIES IN JAPAN

American Trading Company Japan Ltd., 1 Shiba Park 7-gochi, Minato-ku, Tokyo (machinery & plant, steel products, chemicals, paints, woodpulp, synthetic rubber and general merchandise).

Chori Co. Ltd., 32 Azuchi-machi 4-chome, Higashi-ku, Osaka (timber, rubber, hides, grain, chemicals and machinery).

Eurojapan (Osaka) Ltd., Kotokuji Building, 6 Nakatsuhama-dori 1-chome, Oyodo-ku, Osaka (electrical and other machinery, instruments etc.).

Ichida Co. Ltd., 2-3 Horidome-cho, Nihonbashi, Chuo-ku,

Tokyo (textile goods, drapery, suitings and dry goods).

Barney T. Jones Inc., Umeda Building, 7 Umeda, Kita-ku, Osaka (raw chemicals for drugs, medicines, insecticides and agriculture, food additives and oils, aromatics, flavours and perfumes, petroleum products and additives).

Kaigai Tsusho Co. Ltd., Gojokai Building, 15-9 Uchikanda 2-chome, Chiyoda-ku, Tokyo (machine tools, communication equipment, transport, chemical, textile and other machinery).

Kanto Gosei Kogyo Co. Ltd., 35-8 Sumida 2-chome, Sumida-ku, Tokyo (moulded plastic products including toys).

Kinsho-Mataichi Co. Ltd., 2-8 Kayaba-cho, Nihonbashi, Chuo-ku, Tokyo (metals, ores, fuels, chemicals, paper & pulp, fibres, textiles, fertilisers, building materials, instruments and machinery).

Koyo International Inc., 11-15 Ginza 7-chome, Chuo-ku, Tokyo (general importers: bearings, sewing machines, machinery, machine tools, electronic products, skis and accessories).

Marusho Industrial Co. Ltd., 11-2 Ginza-Higashi 4-chome, Chuo-ku, Tokyo (chemicals, plastics, machinery, insulating materials and photographic films).

Maruzen Co. Ltd., 6 Nihonbashi-dori 2-chome, Chuo-ku, Tokyo (books and periodicals, stationery, typewriters, calculators and office machinery).

Matsui Commercial Co. Ltd., 4-7 Azabudai 2-chome, Minato-ku, Tokyo (wide range of machinery).

H. Nishizawa Ltd., 8 Bingo-machi 3-chome, Higashi-ku, Osaka (raw cotton and wool, oils textile chemicals and dyestuffs).

Nosawa & Co. Ltd., 4, 3-chome Marunouchi, Chiyoda-ku, Tokyo (agricultural and dairy produce, livestock and poultry, hardwood, herbs and spices, oils, fats, drugs and ores, agricultural machinery, sundry).

Okaya & Co. Ltd., 4-18 Sakae 2-chome, Naka-ku, Nagoya (ferrous and non-ferrous metals and ores and scrap, machinery, tools, hardware and chemicals).

Okura Trading Co. Ltd., 3-6 Ginza 2-chome, Chuo-ku, Tokyo (a very large concern importing almost all types of raw materials, chemicals and machinery, have UK office at Lee House, London Wall).

Shimpo Yuki & Co. Ltd., Shuhosha Building, 6 Nihonbashi Muromachi 1-chome, Tokyo (machinery and general).

F.S. Takahashi & Co. Ltd., 14 Kandaogawa-machi 2-chome, Ukyo-ku, Tokyo (textiles and textile products).

Tokyo Central Trading Co. Ltd., Meiko Building, 7 Ginza Nishi 1-chome, Chuo-ku, Tokyo (automobile accessories and spares, machinery, tools, electronic parts and equipment).
Toyo Trading Co. Ltd., 2, 1-chome Hongoku-cho, Nihonbashi, Chuo-ku, Tokyo (all kinds of machinery and machine tools).
Yokohama Trading Corporation Ltd., 2, 1 chome Sumiyoshi-cho, Naka-ku, Yokohama (timber and marine products).

(It is advisable, wherever possible, to check the addresses of companies listed above. Drawn from directories and the writer's own notebooks of his visits to Japan over several years, their accuracy cannot be guaranteed although they have been checked as far as possible. Tokyo is especially prone to the demolition of existing buildings to make way for something bigger and better and the consequent displacement of their tenants.)

Special mention should be made of two Import/Export companies in Japan which are basically of British origin. Dodwell & Co. Ltd., have already been mentioned and their London address given under 'The Major Trading Companies'. The Head Office in Japan is at Togin Building, 4-2 Marunouchi 1-chome, Chiyoda-ku, Tokyo. They import all kinds of consumer goods and industrial products and act as buying agents for 'departos' and chain stores, as marketing consultants and as shipping and insurance agents.

Housed in the same building in Tokyo is another company active in the import of both industrial and consumer merchandise and as agents for many important UK companies. This is Houlden & Co. Ltd. Founded soon after the war, Houlden have a large staff of English-speaking Japanese, capable of handling both technical and non-technical sales throughout Japan.

APPENDIX C

JAPAN'S OVERALL TRADE BY COMMODITY GROUPS
— 1976

Exports from Japan
Total exports amounted to 55.8 billion US dollars, equivalent to
7.1% of total world trade.

Machinery	58.9
Metals & metal products	19.6
Textiles & textile products	6.3
Chemicals	5.6
Foodstuffs	1.3
Non-metallic mineral products	1.4
Other	6.9
Manufactured goods	95.0
Raw materials	2.0

Imports into Japan
Total imports amounted to 57.9 billion US dollars, equivalent to
7.2% of total world trade.

Mineral fuels	43.7%
Foodstuffs	14.5%
Raw materials	10.5%
Metal ores & scrap	7.1%
Machinery	7.1%
Chemicals	4.1%
Textile fibres	2.8%
Other	10.3%
Manufactured goods	20.0%

of which products of Heavy Industry equal 14.0%, and Light
Industry equal 6%)

FOREIGN TRADE BY COUNTRY OR REGION OF DESTINATION AND ORIGIN

(Million dollars)

	Total value		Asia (total)		China 1	
Year	Exports	Imports	Exports	Imports	Exports	Imports
1965	8 452	8 169	2 747	2 731	245	225
1970	19 318	18 881	6 033	5 553	569	254
1974	55 536	62 110	18 188	29 273	1 984	1 305
1975	55 753	57 863	20 488	28 345	2 259	1 531

Year	(Taiwan)		Hong Kong		India	
1965	218	157	288	35	204	184
1970	700	251	700	92	103	390
1974	2 009	955	1 360	273	595	658
1975	1 822	812	1 378	245	471	658

Year	Indonesia		Iran		Korea, Rep. of	
1965	205	149	58	247	180	41
1970	316	637	179	995	818	229
1974	1 450	4 572	1 014	4 766	2 656	1 568
1975	1 850	3 430	1 854	4 978	2 248	1 308

Year	Kuwait		Malaysia		Pakistan	
1965	41	306	75	263	104	27
1970	94	308	166	419	138	42
1974	279	2 132	708	979	226	75
1975	367	2 012	566	691	290	89

Year	Philippines		Saudi Arabia		Singapore	
1965	240	254	48	231	124	33
1970	454	533	84	435	423	87
1974	911	1 105	677	5 238	1 388	619
1975	1 026	1 121	1 351	6 135	1 524	399

Year	Thailand		Europe (total)		Belgium	
1965	219	131	1 297	1 002	49	25
1970	449	190	3 363	2 555	154	74
1974	951	686	10 276	6 930	483	230
1975	959	724	10 346	5 778	510	161

Year	France		Germany, Fed. Rep. of		Italy	
1965	49	62	215	223	52	38
1970	127	186	550	617	192	134
1974	736	592	1 498	1 454	416	462
1975	699	501	1 661	1 139	334	365

Year	Netherlands		Norway		Spain	
	Exports	Imports	Exports	Imports	Exports	Imports
1965	119	43	79	9	22	20
1970	277	104	184	34	104	28
1974	1 055	222	471	89	239	127
1975	726	214	523	76	302	115

Year	Sweden		Switzerland		United Kingdom	
1965	61	34	62	70	205	163
1970	99	89	168	177	480	395
1974	336	250	373	453	1 530	878
1975	384	199	348	417	1 473	810

Year	North and Central America (total)		Canada		Cuba	
1965	2 933	3 040	214	357	3	29
1970	7 095	6 886	563	929	39	111
1974	16 578	16 312	1 587	2 676	203	444
1975	14 697	14 929	1 151	2 499	439	343

Year	Mexico		United States		South America (total)	
1965	41	145	2 479	2 366	248	391
1970	94	151	5 940	5 560	596	976
1974	305	308	12 799	12 682	2 875	1 759
1975	348	212	11 149	11 608	2 368	1 701

Year	Argentina		Brazil		Africa (total)	
1965	44	48	27	50	818	353
1970	96	154	167	218	1 423	1 099
1974	440	229	1 389	657	4 930	2 935
1975	363	213	927	883	5 557	2 320

Year	Liberia		South Africa		Oceania (total)	
1965	371	17	137	120	404	652
1970	588	32	329	314	802	1 812
1974	2 345	36	959	763	2 689	4 888
1975	2 585	16	872	868	2 295	4 788

Year	Australia		New Zealand		USSR	
1965	313	552	61	61	168	240
1970	589	1 508	114	158	341	481
1974	1 998	4 025	485	402	1 096	1 418
1975	1 739	4 156	393	367	1 626	1 170

(Tables on pages 230 and 231 reproduced from the *Statistical Handbook of Japan 1977* by kind permission of the Japanese Bureau of Statistics, Office of the Prime Minister.)

JAPAN'S TRADE WITH THE UNITED KINGDOM

Exports to Japan (£ thousand)	1977	1978
Live animals excluding zoo animals, cats and dogs	263	1,588
Dairy products and eggs	39	340
Cereals and cereal preparations	4,819	4,467
Sugar, sugar preparations and honey	1,789	2,061
Coffee, tea, cocoa, spices and manufacturers thereof	14,064	10,120
Beverages	41,339	50,574
Tobacco and tobacco manufactures	1,406	1,987
Crude rubber including synthetic and reclaimed	1,265	2,420
Textile fibres not manufactured and their waste etc	8,840	10,819
Crude fertilisers and minerals excluding fuels etc	891	867
Metalliferous ores and metal scrap	1,400	1,301
Petroleum and petroleum products	518	797
Dyeing, tanning and colouring materials	8,888	8,328
Medicinal and pharmaceutical products	23,938	27,532
Essential oils and perfume materials etc	5,839	7,839
Plastic materials and artificial resins	3,240	3,630
Chemical materials and products n.e.s.	14,010	16,902
Leather, leather manufactures n.e.s. and dressed furskins	4,601	5,338
Rubber manufactures n.e.s.	760	1,330
Paper, paperboard and manufactures thereof	2,823	3,133
Textile yarns, fabrics, made up articles etc	34,648	48,141
Non-metallic mineral manufactures n.e.s.	17,837	17,189
Iron and steel	1,130	1,516
Non-ferrous metals	27,851	37,017
Manufactures of metal n.e.s.	9,473	13,370
Electrical machinery, apparatus and appliances	21,652	14,933
Sanitary, plumbing, heating and lighting fixtures	459	382
Clothing, knitted articles etc	7,437	11,016
Miscellaneous manufactured articles n.e.s.	22,356	26,323

The classification of the above commodities is based on the Standard International Trade Classification (Revised) of the United Nations.

JAPAN'S TRADE WITH THE UNITED KINGDOM

Imports from Japan (£ thousand)

	1977	1978
Meat and meat preparations	8	4
Fish and fish preparations	15,227	12,388
Fruit and vegetables	485	466
Coffee, tea, cocoa, spices and manufactures thereof	290	25
Hides, skins and furskins undressed	851	607
Wood, lumber and cork	3,628	2,812
Textile fibres not manufactured and their waste, etc	2,917	2,809
Metalliferous ores and metal scrap	1,704	1,307
Crude animal and vegetable materials n.e.s.	1,090	1,589
Plastic materials and artificial resins	8,206	8,160
Chemical materials and products n.e.s.	2,732	4,569
Rubber manufactures n.e.s.	7,668	8,026
Wood and cork manufactures excluding furniture	2,072	2,065
Paper, paperboard and manufactures thereof	3,427	5,663
Textile yarns, fabrics, made up articles etc	23,430	34,128
Non-metallic mineral manufactures n.e.s.	9,764	10,781
Iron and steel	46,162	43,191
Non-ferrous metals	3,296	5,837
Manufactures of metal n.e.s.	20,498	21,990
Electrical machinery, apparatus and appliances	75,277	87,003
Travel goods, handbags and similar articles	1,616	1,573
Clothing, knitted articles etc	7,189	8,184
Footwear	806	674
Miscellaneous manufactured articles n.e.s.	51,222	61,709

(The trade figures on pages 232 and 233 are supplied by H.M. Customs & Excise Statistical Office.)

APPENDIX D

USEFUL ADDRESSES IN TOKYO

British Embassy, 1 Ichi-ban-cho, Chiyoda-ku. Tel. 265 5511

British Airways, Sanshin Building, Yuraku-cho, Chiyoda-ku. Tel. 591 1261 or Hibiya Park Building, Yuraku-cho, Chiyoda-ku. Tel. 214 4161

British Chamber of Commerce in Japan, 7-3 Marunouchi, 3-chome, Chiyoda-ku. Tel. 211 8070

Bank of Japan, Foreign Capital Centre, CPO Box 203 Tokyo. Tel. 279 1111 (Handles all matters of foreign capital venture approval)

Fair Trade Commission (Kosei Torihiki Iinkai) 2-2 Kasumigaseki, Chiyoda-ku. Tel. 581 5471 (regulates advertising, promotion and similar standards)

Japan Air Lines, Daini Tekko Building, Marunouchi 1-chome, Chiyoda-ku. Tel. 747 3111. (Also has Airport office and desks in all the major hotels. Has Executive Lounge and Business Information Centre in the Imperial Hotel.)

Japan National Tourist Office, Tourist Information Centre, 6-6 Yurako-chu, 1-chome, Chiyoda-ku. Tel. 502 1461/3 (also at Airport).

Japan External Trade Organisation, 2 Aio-cho, Akasaka, Minato-ku. Tel. 582 5511

Japanese Chamber of Commerce & Industry, 2-2 Marunouchi, 3-chome, Chiyoda-ku. Tel. 211 4411 (Same address and telephone number for the Tokyo Chamber of International Commerce & Industry.)

Ministry of International Trade & Industry, 1, 3-chome, Kasumigaseki, Chiyoda-ku.

Ministry of Finance, 1-1, 3-chome, Kasumigaseki, Chiyoda-ku.

Tokyo Immigration Office, 3-20, 3-chome, Kokan, Minato-ku. Tel. 471 5111. (Must be approached if you want to extend your 60-day residence permit, allowing 10 to 14 days notice.)

FOREIGN EMBASSIES IN TOKYO

Australia: 1-14, Mita 2-chome, Minato-ku. Tel. 453-0251
Canada: 3-38 Akasaka 7-chome, Minato-ku. Tel. 408-2101
France: 11-44 Minami Azabu 4-chome, Minato-ku. Tel. 473-0171
Germany (West): 5-10 Minami Azabu 4-chome, Minato-ku. Tel. 473-0151
Great Britain: 1 Ichiban-cho, Chiyoda-ku. Tel. 265-5511
India: 2-11 Kudan Minami 2-chome, Chiyoda-ku. Tel. 262-2391
Italy: 5-4 Mita 2-chome, Minato-ku. Tel. 453-5291
New Zealand: 26 Sanban-cho, Chiyoda-ku. Tel. 263-0611
Pakistan: 14-9 Moto Azabu 2-chome, Minato-ku. Tel. 451-8386
Portugal: Olympia Annexe, Jingu-mae 6-chome, Shibuya;ku. Tel. 400-7907
United States: Tameike Tokyu Building, 1-14 Akasaka 1-chome, Minato-ku. Tel. 583-7141

JAPANESE MEDIA ADDRESSES

Advertising in Japan is anything but cheap if effective coverage is to be obtained. Any company entering the market for the first time should consider the comparatively inexpensive coverage both in copy and in advertisements that can be obtained through the services of the British Embassy Information Department in Tokyo. This department publishes two excellent journals to assist the British exporter. These are *British Industrial News*, a monthly in Japanese for the capital goods market and *New from Britain*, a quarterly magazine in Japanese devoted to new cunsumer goods. News items for either should be sent first to the Central Office of Information, Hercules Road, London SE1., while advertisements should be placed through the British Embassy in Tokyo.

The three main national daily papers in Japanese all have circulations in the 5 to 6 million range and advertising space is accordingly highly priced. These journals are the *Asahi, Mainichi* and *Yomiuri* newspapers at the following addresses:-
Asahi Shimbun Publishing Co. Ltd., 3 Yuraku-cho, 2 chome, Chiyoda-ku, Tokyo. London Representative: Room 420, The Times, Printing House Square EC4.
Mainichi Shimbun Sha, 1 Hitotsubashi 1 chome, Chiyoda-ku, Tokyo. London Representative: 8 Bouverie Street, EC4.

Yomiuri Shimbun Sha, 1 Ginza Nishi 3 chome, Chuo-ku, Tokyo. London Representative: c/o Daily Mail, Room 45, Northcliffe House, EC4.

There is also the *Japan Times,* 5-4 Shibaura 4-chome, Minato-ku, Tokyo 108. Central PO Box 144.352.

There are two important daily business papers with circulations in the half million region, comparable with the *Financial Times* except that one is primarily economic while the other has a more industrial slant. (Keizai = economics; Kogyo = industry). The journals are:

Nihon Keizai Shimbun Sha, 5 1 chome, Ote-machi, Chiyoda-ku, Tokyo. London Representative: c/o The Financial Times, Bracken House, Cannon Street, EC4.

Nihon Kogyo Shimbun Sha, 7-2 Ote-machi, 1-chome, Chiyoda-ku, Tokyo.

The number of radio and television channels which handle advertising is so large that specialist advice is necessary for the prospective advertiser. The same applies to the many weekly and monthly magazines published, the more important of which have circulation figures of around 750,000. As there are over 3000 advertising agencies in Japan, mostly small and usually specialising in one section of the media, an approach to Dentsu Advertising in London (32 St James's Street, SW1. Tel. 01-930 0878) is advisable. Alternatively, the Exports to Japan Unit of the B.O.T.B. may be able to suggest a suitable agency, if your needs are explained to them.

LAWYERS PRACTISING IN TOKYO

The following firms, among others, are experienced in handling foreign business. There is no guarantee of the competence or probity of any particular firm nor is any responsibility taken whatsoever for the consequences of accepting legal advice or initiating legal action. Those marked with an asterisk are members of the English Bar.

*Adachi,
409-415 Sumitomo Building,
1-2 Marunouchi,
Chiyoda-ku, Tokyo.
Telephone: 281-5389/6173.

Anderson, Mori & Rabinowitz,
Central P.O. Box 1195
Chiyoda-ku, Tokyo.
Telephone: 214-1371-80.

Thomas L. Blakemore,
Room 912, Iino Building,
1-1, 2-chome,
Uchisaiwai-cho,
Chiyoda-ku, Tokyo.
Telephone: 503-5571.

Furness, Capron, Sato &
Matsui, 311 Fukoku Building,
2-2, 2-chome, Uchisaiwai-cho,
Chiyoda-ku, Tokyo.
Telephone: 591-4124/7.

*Braun Moriya & Hoashi,
Room 911, Iino Building,
1-1, 2-chome, Uchisaiwai-cho,
Chiyoda-ku, Tokyo.
Telephone: 501-0251.

*Hill, Betts, Yamaoka,
Freehill & Longscope,
8th Floor, Yamaguchi Building,
1-1, 2-chome, Shinbashi,
Minato-ku, Tokyo.
Telephone: 503-2407/9 and
503-2400.

Logan Bernhard & Okamoto,
330 New Otemachi Building,
4 Ote-machi, 2-chome,
Chiyoda-ku, Tokyo.
Telephone: 211-1721/3.

McIvor,
Kauffman & Christensen,
Suite 729, New Tokyo Building,
2, 3-chome, Marunouchi,
Chiyoda-ku, Tokyo.
Telephone: 211-8871

*Takashima, Fumio,
Marunouchi-Yaesu Building,
Room 322,
2-6, Marunouchi,
Chiyoda-ku, Tokyo.
Telephone: 281-0683.

*Usami Law Office,
Room 319, Sanshin Building,
10, 1-chome, Yurako-cho,
Chiyoda-ku, Tokyo.
Telephone: 591-4716/7620
3776.

*Yuasa, Sakamoto, Kawai &
Ikenaga,
Room 206,
New Otemachi Building,
4, 2-chome, Ote-machi,
Chiyoda-ku, Tokyo.
Telephone: 270-6641.

LAWYERS PRACTISING IN OSAKA AND KOBE

OSAKA
Mr Seiichi Wada,
53 Funadaiku-cho,
Dojima,
Kita-ku,
Osaka.

Mr Hideo Tameike,
Kawanishi Building,
4th floor, No 55,
25 Nishino-cho,
Unagidani,
Minami-ku,
Osaka.

KOBE
Mr Shinichi Hirabayshi,
Room 605,
Shosen Building,
5 Kaigan-dori,
Ikuta-ku,
Kobe.

Mr Hiroyuki Matsui,
153 Shimoyamate-dori,
8-chome,
Ikuta-ku,
Kobe.

TAXATION IN JAPAN

Taxes are levied in Japan both on individuals and corporations in much the same way as in the UK, ie as Income Tax and Corporation Tax. There are both national and local (prefectural and municipal) taxes on personal and company income, as well as various taxes on property, on consumption and on the transfer of goods and assets. Most of these have their equivalents in our own tax system.

Personal Taxation
Short-stay visitors (those on a 60 day permit) are not subject to direct taxes. Indirect taxes such as Liquor Tax (5.5% of national tax income) and Tax on Consumption at Hotels and Restaurants (2.9% of Local Tax Revenue) are likely to be more painful and irksome than Hunter's Licence or Bathing Tax!

Income tax payers are divided into 'resident' and 'non resident' categories. The former are those who have a 'jusho' (domicile) or have had a residence for a year or more in Japan and such citizens must pay income tax on all their income from both within and outside Japan. An exception is made in the case of 'non-permanent residents', ie those who do not intend to reside in Japan permanently and have resided there uninteruptedly for not more than five years. Such people are taxed only on their total income derived from sources within Japan and from other sources paid in Japan or remitted to Japan from abroad.

Non-resident taxpayers are those who have no 'jusho' and have lived in Japan for less than a year. For them tax is only due on their income derived from sources in Japan.

Rates of income tax are typically progressive with the level of income and range from 10% to 75%. Income is assessed by deducting 'necessary expenses' from gross receipts. The interpretation of these expenses is not unlike that of the Inland Revenue department in the UK, though perhaps slightly more liberal. However, if you win on the horses or on a television quiz, 50% of the net income over 500,000 Yen is taxable! 'Reasonable travel expenses' for getting to work and back are not subject to tax (nor for that matter is a Nobel Prize!). As in the UK, assessments for personal income tax are based on the taxpayer's own declaration though, if the correct return is not filed in time, the tax authorities may make an assessment through what they term 'the processes of correction or determination'. The accounting period for personal taxation is January 1st to December 31st. Conventions for the Avoidance of Double Taxation (and Prevention of Tax Evasion) exist between Japan and twenty-nine other countries including the USA, Canada, Australia and New Zealand as well as most countries in Europe. The honest British businessman will doubtless be glad to know that the United Kingdom is among these countries.

Business Taxation
All companies and corporations engaging in trade of any kind are liable to taxation though, as mentioned elsewhere, a foreign company may set up an office in Japan for liaison with local agents or for their own market research etc. and, so long as it does not actually engage in any commercial transactions, no tax will be levied on it except, of course, local taxation which in the UK we would consider under the general heading of 'rates'. This includes both Prefectural and Municipal taxes.

The main tax on companies engaging in trade of whatever kind is Corporation Tax, which is calculated on the basis of both the company's capital and its turnover as shown below. The accounting period is generally the calendar year but companies may choose their own periods if they wish. Taxable income is considered to be the excess of gross revenue over the total of its cost and business expenses. Every company is required to file a Corporation Tax Return with a balance sheet and a profit and loss statement with the District Tax Office in principle within two months of the end of each accounting period and must pay the tax due as reported in the return. Failure to do so may result in reassessment through 'correction' or 'determination' by the tax authorities. You may be interested to note, as I was when studying Japanese Tax Laws, that 'social and entertainment expenses include secret service money ...' I have not yet been able to interpret this one!

To revert to the basis on which tax is calculated for companies, there are three basic categories according to the scale of the company's operations. These are (1) Income of 1.5 million Yen or less per annum and capital of 100 million Yen or less. (2) Income between 1.5 and 3 million Yen and the same limit of capitalisation. (3) Income of over 3 million Yen and/or capital of over 100 million Yen. Corporation tax for the first two categories is levied at 22% and 28% respectively for income distributed as dividends and for undistributed income. For companies in the third category the rates are 26% and 36.7% respectively. All companies must pay Municipal tax at the rate of 9.1% of the amount of corporation tax payable while Prefectural tax is at three rates for the three categories, 6%, 9% and 12% respectively.

If you are going to get personally or corporately involved in taxation in Japan, an experienced accountant is essential and may possibly save you in more than the usual way as certain standards of accounting qualify the taxpayer for appreciable concessions. I can do no more than skim the surface here and would defy even my own accountant to explain UK Income Tax in under a thousand words!

APPENDIX E

HOTELS IN JAPAN

Japanese hotels fall broadly into two categories, Western style or the traditional Japanese style or 'ryokan'. The former differ little from their Western counterparts except that, depending somewhat on the rating, service in the Japanese hotel is likely to be a good deal better and really is covered by the service charge on the bill. Service is a tradition, too, in the ryokan but can be carried to the extent that it becomes embarrassing to some Western visitors. Most don't mind taking off their shoes on entering or changing into a cotton yukata. They are not put out by the lack of furniture in their rooms or having their meals served there. Many can accustom themselves to the attentions they receive in the communal bath but still jib at other aspects of the 'service'. I remember a friend who spent an almost sleepless night in a ryokan at one of the 'onsen' or hot springs. The kimonoed young maid allotted to his room laid out the 'futon' on the floor and saw him undressed and safely into bed. When he put out the light, she curled up on the bare floor at the foot of his mattress. He found her proximity kept him from going to sleep but he was too much of a gentleman to risk hurting her feelings by telling her to get out, even if he could find the right words for it. About three o'clock in the morning, he could bear it no longer and in sign language he got her to leave. Drawing the paper 'shoji' door to with a smile, she quite happily curled up and went to sleep on the corridor floor outside. Lost opportunity, are you thinking? Maybe but she was only there to ensure his comfort!

In recent years, at least out of the cities, a third style of hotel seems to be spreading which is a cross between the other two types, combining perhaps the best elements of both but sometimes the worst! I don't know how one finds or recognises this sort of hotel. I've only stayed in one, The Miyahama Seaside hotel on the coast of the Inland Sea between Hiroshima and Kintai. Japanese decor combined with Western beds, my own 'rest room' or bathroom and a well-stocked fridge. No doubt your Japanese friends can find this sort of accommodation but, as I say, it's not to be found in the industrial and business centres so far as I know.

The best source of information on hotels is the *Japan Hotel Guide* with up-to-date prices put out by the Japanese National Tourist Organisation and available from their London office. There is also a special guide to ryokan hotels published by their own Association.

It is impossible to know the reader's tastes and the depth of his pocket and, in this changing world, it is of little use to quote prices, as they become out-of-date as soon as they are printed if not before. The following hotels in the main industrial and commercial cities, however, can be quoted as giving value for the money they charge. For full addresses, telephone and telex numbers, see the *Japan Hotel Guide* (Japan National Tourist Organisation).

Tokyo
Okura Hotel, Minato-ku
Tokyo Hilton, Chiyoda-ku
Tokyo Prince, Shiba, Minato-ku
Palace Hotel, Marunouchi
New Otani Hotel, Akasaka
Keio Plaza Intercontinental, Shinjuku-ku
Pacific Hotel, Minato-ku
Imperial Hotel, Hibiya Park, Chiyoda-ku
Hotel New Japan, Chiyoda-ku
Marunouchi Hotel, Chiyoda-ku
Akasaka-tokyu Hotel, Minato-ku
Ginza-Tokyu Hotel (Convenient for Harumi exhibition halls)
Haneda-Tokyu Hotel (Near airport)

Osaka
Osaka Royal Hotel
Plaza Hotel
Osaka Grand Hotel
Hanshin Hotel
New Osaka Hotel
International Hotel

Nagoya
Nagoya Castle Hotel
Intercontinental Hotel
New Nagoya Hotel
Nagoya Hotel
Nagashima Hotel
Nagoya Kanko Hotel

Kobe
New Port Hotel
Kobe International Hotel
Rokkosan Hotel
Oriental Hotel

ENTERTAINMENT

The lesser nightspots of the major Japanese cities tend to be as ephemeral as dragonflies and, for advice on them, it is best to ask locally when you are there. Most hotel desks are cooperative and helpful, as are the Japan National Tourist Organisation who will go to any lengths to see happy smiling visitors. On the other hand there are some very permanent entertainment centres which are worth while mentioning. While they are generally in the field of 'traditional' entertainment, this now extends to the inclusion of up-to-date spectacular review-type shows with all-female casts. Tokyo and Osaka, as the top two cities, are naturally best endowed with all forms of entertainment.

Tokyo
Kabuki-za Theatre, Ginza. Traditional Kabuki drama.
Kokusai Theatre, Asakusa (also the Takarazuki Theatre). All-girl review shows.
National Theatre. In two halls various types of traditional drama — Noh, Kabuki and Bunraka are shown.
Nichigeki Theatre, Yurako-cho. Reviews and Musicals often with many Western elements.
Nissei Theatre. Opera.
Metropolitan Festival Hall, Ueno and the Hibiya Public Hall. Orchestral Music. Also ballet, a growing art in Japan.

Osaka
Asahi Theatre, Doton-bori. Bunraku puppet plays.

Shin Kabuki-za, Naba-Shinchi. Kabuki drama.
Takarazuka Theatre, Takarazuka (some 14 miles from Osaka).
All-girl shows. Both opera and review.
Festival Hall, Nakanoshima and the Mainichi Hall in the same
area: orchestral music etc.

In spite of television, the Japanese cinema industry flourishes
and is probably second only to that of India in popularity. Any
hotel will advise on local films showing. Foreign films are often
shown with original dialogue and Japanese sub-titles.

RESTAURANTS

Apart from eating in your hotel, the following can be recom-
mended:

Tokyo
For Sukiyaki: Zakuro, Rangetsu and Suehiro.
For Tempura: Ten-ichi, Inagiku, Hige-no-Tenpei and Hashizen.
For Tenpanyaki: Akasaka Misono, Beliere, Mikasa Kaikan.

These are traditional Japanese cuisine restaurants but food
from almost every other country in the world is available for the
gourmet. Naturally Chinese and Korean restaurants abound, but
you may go to the Swiss 'Chalet', the German 'Ketel's
Lohmeyer' or the 'Rosenkeller', the Italian 'Al Chianti' or the
'San Marino'. There is the Russian 'Manos' restaurant, the
Indian 'Ashoka', the Greek 'Double Ax' ... the list is endless and
the hungry visitor is well advised to consult the Tokyo weekly
Tour Companion paper previously mentioned.

Among the more reputable and well-established clubs with
cabaret are Copacabana, New Latin Quarter, Golden Akasaka
and Crown and Mikado.
Osaka
Here the cuisine is a little different. As in Tokyo, each restaurant
tends to specialise in one type of cooking and the following are
well-known:
For Sukiyaki: Hanafusa, Hiriju, Suehiro.
For Tempura: Shori and Hanayagi.
Hanafusa and Suehiro are also good for steaks.
For Kaminabe, a dish of fish stewed in paper pots, try Rogetsu.
Cabaret is to be experienced at the Metro, Bel Ami, Club Yudo,
Crown and Club Arrow among many others. Seek local advice.

For similar information on other major cities such as

Yokohama, Nagoya, Kyoto, Hiroshima, Sendai, Fukuoka and Sapporo, ask the Japan National Tourist Organisation or Japan Airlines.

GOURMET'S GLOSSARY

I have yet to find a Japanese host who was not at pains to explain the arcana of the Japanese cuisine, though there have been times when the problems of language have prevented communication at a satisfactory level. A Tokyo friend who speaks fluent English spent his early childhood in China where his father was a diplomat and, having a great liking for the food of that country, took me out to the best Chinese restaurant in Tokyo where the menu listed, if I remember rightly, 399 different dishes. As he suggested, I let him choose our meal. The exercise that my jaw went through in masticating what looked like a bowlful of small translucent rubber coil-springs was only compensated for by my pride in the way I managed to manipulate these improbable morsels with my chopsticks. I later learnt that I had been chomping on fried, shredded, jellyfish and then we went on to plough through a special delicacy, little rolls of rice, seaweed and some delicious crunchy brown outer integument. Replete, I asked what they were. Perhaps it was the rice wine that affected my hearing but I could have sworn that Kawamura-san said, "Those were the skins of dogs," and I pictured Chinese butchers and chefs singeing the hair from the pelts of Pekingeses and Shih-tzus, with little enthusiasm and a sinking feeling in my well-filled stomach. Only after sleeping on it, did I realise that he had said 'the skins of ducks'. The famous Peking Duck of course!

I digress across the sea to China but similar misunderstandings can occur with Japanese food. The following brief summary may help to avoid similar troubles and be of use to the 'gaijin' visitor if he wants to go out on his own and sample some of the most fascinating and tasteful food in the world.

The Main Styles of Japanese Cuisine
Fish (Sakana)
Sashimi   Sliced raw fish.
Sushi   Sashimi in balls of rice.
Tempura   Various fishes and fish portions with vegetables fried in batter.

Meat (Niku)

Shabu Shabu   (Pronounced Shab-shab from the sound of the cooking chopsticks in the pot.) Thin-sliced beef and vegetables cooked in a simmering broth, later drunk as soup.

Sukiyaki   Thin-sliced beef grilled with vegetables, bean curd and noodles.

Teppanyaki   Beef Steak chopped, with onions, bean-shoots and possibly other vegetables, fried on a hot steel plate which forms the centre of the table.

Teriyaki   Meat (or sometimes fish) marinated in soya sauce and sweet saké and charcoal grilled.

Tonkatsu   Pork cutlet, grilled with various garnishings.

Okoribayaki   Game cooked in the same way as Sukiyaki.

Yakatori   Chicken (and/or other meats) with onions, peppers etc., charcoal-grilled on skewers. Similar to kebabs.

Some Japanese Specialities

Vegetables (Yasai-mono)

Daikon   Giant Japanese radish.

Ginnan   Gingko nuts.

Go-han   Rice cooked. (Uncooked rice is kome.)

Kombu   Kelp seaweed.

Matsutake   The so-called 'phallic' mushroom from its shape. A great delicacy.

Menrui   Noodles. Different types are Soba, Uden and Somen.

Miso   Soya bean paste.

Nori   Purple seaweed.

Shoga   Ginger.

Shiitake   Mushrooms.

Shoyu   Soya sauce which accompanies almost everything.

Shungiku   Chrysanthemum leaves, like mild spinach, and served fried or boiled.

Renkon.   Lotus root.

Tofu   Bean curd.

Wakame   Green seaweed.

Wasabi   Japanese horseradish.

Fish (Sakana)

Ebi   Shrimp.

Ise-ebi   Lobster.

Kuruma-ebi   Prawn.

Fugu   Blowfish (only eaten in restaurants licensed to serve it).
Kaki   Oysters.
Sake   Salmon.
Unagi   Eel.

Drinks (Nomimono)
Biiru   Beer.
Budoshu   Grape wine.
Gyunyu   Milk.
Ko-cha   Indian or 'black' tea.
Mizu   Water.
Kohi   Coffee.
O-Cha   Japanese or green tea.
Saké   Rice wine.
Uisiki   Whisky, Scotch or Japanese.
(Note: Saké comes in four grades. 'Tokkyu' is the best, followed by Ikkyu, Nikyu and Shochu. The last is definitely to be avoided at all costs!)

Some Common Requirements

Bata   butter
Chizu   cheese
Kosho   pepper
Kudamono   fruit
Pan   bread
Sarada   salad
Sato   sugar
Shio   salt
Su   vinegar
Tamago   egg
(*Note*: A great number of terms on the menu are English words transmogrified into Japanese as butter, cheese and salad above. Similarly, you may come across 'aisukurimu' (ice-cream), 'bifubaga', (beefburger) or 'hanbaga', and 'hottu doggu' for hot dog. Likewise you may ask for 'keki', 'appurapai' (apple pie), an 'omoretsu' (omelette) or just settle for a plain 'sandoithchi' with 'oranjiedo' or 'pepushi kora' (Pepsi Cola if you hadn't guessed). Most comestibles that are not indigenous to Japan have this type of name. If in doubt try the English word, substituting 'ru-' for l and adding -u, -i or -o at the end.

Eating Equipment

Chawan   cup
Foku   fork
Haizara   ashtray
Hashi   chopsticks
Koppu   glass or cup
Naifu   knife
Sara   plate
Supun   spoon
Isu   chair
Teburu   table (Western style)
Habakari   toilet (or o-benjo, colloquial for 'gents')
o-Bento   a packed lunchbox for the traveller

It is polite to say 'Itadaki imasu' ('imasu' pronounced 'mass')
before starting your meal, much as the French say 'bon appetit'.

APPENDIX F

ANNUAL HOLIDAYS

As already mentioned, Japan is a land of festivals, some local and some national. The local ones are too numerous to be included here but a list of the major events in different centres can be obtained from the Japanese National Tourist Organisation. If you are going to Japan purely for business it is wise to check on the local festival holidays while the national 'days off' are listed below:

Public Holidays are:

1 January	New Year's Day
15 January	Adults' Day
11 February	National Foundation Day
21 March	Spring Equinox
29 April	The Emperor's Birthday
3 May	Constitution Day
5 May	Children's Day
15 September	Old People's Day
23 September	Autumn Equinox
10 October	Physical Education Day
3 November	Cultural Day
23 November	Labour Thanksgiving Day

Should one of these holidays fall on a Sunday, the following day is taken as a holiday instead.

APPENDIX G

GLOSSARY OF BUSINESS WORDS

Boeki: trade, commerce, merchant
Bussan: product, production, commodity
Denshin: telegram
Denwa: telephone
Eigyoman: businessman
Eikoku no: British
Eiyaku: English translation
Funani-shoken: Bill of Lading
Funazumi: shipment
Funazumi-sashizusho: shipping order
Funazumi-shorui: shipping documents
Ginko: bank
Gishi: engineer
Hoken: insurance
Horitsu: law
Jimusho: office
Kabushiki Kaisha (K.K.): Limited Company
Kai: meeting
Kaiun: marine transport, merchant shipping
Kake: credit
Kanjo: bill, account
Kanzei: customs duty
Keizai: economy, economics
Koeki: trade, commerce
Kojo: factory
Kogyo: industry
Kokoku: advertisement
Meishi: business card
Minato: seaport
O-tokuisan: customer

Rishi: interest
Ryutsu: marketing
Sangyo: industry
Seiko: steel industry, precision machinery
Seisakusha: maker, manufacturer
Setsuritsu: establishment, company
Sha: company, office
Shogyo: commerce
Shoji: commercial firm
Shoken-Gaisha: securities company
Shoko-Daijin: Minister of Trade & Industry
Sho-meisho: certificate (of authentication etc.)
Shoten: shop, small firm
Soroban: abacus
Tasetsu-na-hito: 'V.I.P.'
Tegami: letter
Tenran kaikan: exhibition hall
Tesuryo: commission, brokerage
Tsushin: correspondence
Tsuyaku: interpreter
Unchin: freight cost
Waribiki: discount
Yunyu: import
Yushutsu: export
Zaibatsu: 'big business'

GLOSSARY OF TOPOGRAPHICAL TERMS

Rural
Hanto: peninsula
Kaikyo, suido: channel, strait
Kawa, gawa: river
Ko: lake
Nada: open sea
Saki, Zaki, misaki: cape
Shima, jima, to: island
Shoto: islands
Toge: pass
Wan: gulf, bay
Yama, Zan, San, take, dake: mountain

Urban

Bashi, hashi: bridge
Chome: city block
Chuo: centre, central
Eki: railway station
Fu: urban prefecture
Gun: district, county
Hon dori: high street
Hoteru: hotel
Keisatsu: police station
Ken: prefecture
Kuko: airport
Kogai: suburb
Ku: ward, district
Machi, michi, cho, dori, tori: street, road
Minato: seaport
Ryojikan: consulate
Shi: town, city, municipality
Taishikan: embassy
Tatemono: building

The compass

Higashi: East
Kita: North
Minami: South
Nishi: West

APPENDIX H

BIBLIOGRAPHY AND SUGGESTIONS FOR FURTHER READING

1. General and Travel Books
The Silent Traveller in Japan. Chiang Yee (W.W. Norton, 1972; Tuttle, 1974).
The Kimono Mind. Bernard Rudofsky (Tuttle, 1965).
The Land of the Rising Yen. George Mikes (Andre Deusch, 1970; Penguin, 1973).
The Chrysanthemum and the Sword. Ruth Benedict (Tuttle, 1954).
Japan: It's Not All Raw Fish. Don Maloney (The Japan Times, 1975).
Japan: Patterns of Continuity. Fosco Maraini (Kodansha International, 1971).
Japanese Society. Chie Nakane (Weidenfeld, 1970; Pelican, 1973).

2. History
Japan. Its History and Culture. W. Scott Morton (Readers Union, 1973).
A History of Modern Japan. Richard Storry (Pelican, 1960; revised, 1972).
The Samurai. H. Paul Varley with Ivan & Nobuko Morris (Penguin, 1974).
Japan in Transition: 100 Years of Modernisation. (Ministry of Foreign Affairs, Japan, 1975).
Britain and Japan 1600-1975. Vol. 1 *Historical Perspective.* Vol. 2 *British Personalities* (The Embassy of Japan, 1975).
Hiroshima. John Hersey (New Yorker, 1946; Penguin, 1973).

3. Religion
Zen Flesh, Zen Bones. Paul Reps (Tuttle, 1957; Penguin, 1976).

4. Language
Teach Yourself Japanese. C.J. Dunn & S. Yanada (Teach Yourself Books, 1958).
Japanese in Thirty Hours. Eiichi Kiyooka (Hokuseido Press, 1953).
Japanese in a Hurry. O. & E. Vaccari (Vaccari's Language Institute, 1968).
Japanese for Travellers. (Berlitz, 1974).
Read Japanese Today. Len Walsh (Tuttle, 1969).

5. Art
Japanese Colour Prints. J. Hillier (Phaidon, 1972).
Japanese Graphic Art. Lubor Hajek (Octopus, 1976).
Japanese Painting. Theo Lesoualc'h (Heron Books, 1970).
The Heibonsha Survey of Japanese Art. Jointly published with John Weatherill, New York. Contains thirty volumes of high quality and content. Apart from painting, such subjects as calligraphy, sculpture, ceramics, architecture temples and gardens are covered.

6. Business and Politics
The Emerging Japanese Superstate. Herman Kahn (The Hudson Institute, 1970; Pelican, 1973).
Japanese Manners and Ethics in Business. Boye de Menthe (Simpson-Doyle/Phoenix, 1975).
The International Businessman in Japan. Herbert Glazer (Sophia University/Tuttle, 1968).
Business Strategies for Japan. James E. Abegglen (Boston Consulting Group/Sophia University, 1970).
The World of Japanese Business. T.F.M. Adams & N. Kobayashi (Kodansha, 1970).
Japanese Imperialism Today. J. Halliday & G. McCormack (Pelican, 1973).
Business in Japan (Japan Air Lines) Originally a series of booklets published in the 1970's, this is now available in one volume from JAL and edited by Geoffrey Brownas, Director of the Centre of Japanese Studies, University of Sheffield and Paul Norbury, Editor of JAL's quarterly magazine, *Tsuru*.
Japan as an Export Market and other booklets in the JETRO Marketing Series. Obtainable from the Japan External Trade Organisation in all major cities.
Introduction to Doing Business in Japan and other booklets

obtainable from the British Overseas Trade Board.
Selling to Japan. Introduced by John Field, Special Adviser to the Exports to Japan Unit, this book of 32 case studies of successful British export companies was published in October 1978 and is obtainable from the B.O.T.B.
The Statistical Handbook of Japan. Published annually by the Bureau of Statistics, Office of the Prime Minister, Tokyo. Available from the Japanese Embassy Information Department in London.
Japan Company Handbook. Published biannually by Toyo Keizai Shinposha (The Oriental Economist).

7. Literature (Classical)
Anthology of Japanese Literature to the 19th Century. Donald Keene (Grove Press, 1955; Penguin, 1968).
The Penguin Book of Japanese Verse. Geoffrey Bownas and Anthony Thwaite (Penguin, 1974).
The Pillow Book of Sei Shonogon. Translated by Ivan Morris (Penguin, 1967).
As I Crossed a Bridge of Dreams. Translated by Ivan Morris (Penguin, 1975).
The Narrow Road to the Deep North. Basho. Translated by Nobuyuki Yuasa (Penguin, 1975).

8. Literature (Modern)
I am a cat. Natsume Suseki, 1904 (Tuttle, 1972).
Botchan. Natsume Soseki, 1904 (Tuttle, 1975).
Kokoro. Natsume Soseki, 1914 (Tuttle, 1971).
Snow Country. Kawabata Yasunari (Knopf, 1956; Tuttle 1957).
Thousand Cranes. Kawabata Yasunari (Knopf, 1958; Tuttle, 1967).
The Sound of the Mountain. Kawabata Yasunari (Knopf, 1970; Penguin, 1974).
The Temple of the Golden Pavilion. Mishima Yukio (Knopf, 1959; Tuttle, 1959).
Forbidden Colours. Mishima Yukio (Knopf, 1968; Tuttle, 1969; Penguin, 1971).
Runaway Horses. Mishima Yukio (Secker & Warburg, 1973; Penguin, 1977).
Death in Midsummer & Other Stories. Mishima Yukio (Secker & Warburg, 1967; Penguin, 1977).

The Face of Another. Abe Kobo (Weidenfeld, 1969; Penguin, 1972).
The Ruined Map. Abe Kobo (Knopf, 1969; Tuttle 1974).
Japanese Inn. Oliver Statler (Pyramid, 1968).
New Writing in Japan. Edited by Mishima Yukio and Geoffrey Bownas (Penguin, 1972).

9. Artefacts & General
Japanese Things. Basil Hall Chamberlain, 1904 (Tuttle, 1971).
Everyday Life in Traditional Japan. Charles J. Dunn (Batsford, 1969; Tuttle, 1972).
Japanese Homes & Their Surroundings. Edward S. Morse, 1886 (Tuttle, 1972).

All the above books are selected from the author's own library. As a postscript I would add a few I've borrowed from the local public library. *Tokyo* and *Japan Behind the Fan* by James Kirkup, both published by J.M. Dent are well worth reading for local colour, as is *This is Japan* by Colin Simpson (Angus & Robertson) which gives an Australian traveller's observations. *Japan — A Short Cultural History* by G.B. Sansom is a classic for anyone who wants to delve deeper into this side of the national heritage. Pat Barr's *The Coming of the Barbarians* and *The Deer Cry Pavilion*, both published by Macmillan, give a fascinating picture of the early years of Westernisation, from 1853 to 1870 and from 1868 to 1905 respectively. Lastly, *Fodor's Guide to Japan & Korea, 1977*, by Fodor, Fisher & Morse, published in the UK by Hodder & Stoughton, is an invaluable and comprehensive guidebook.

INDEX

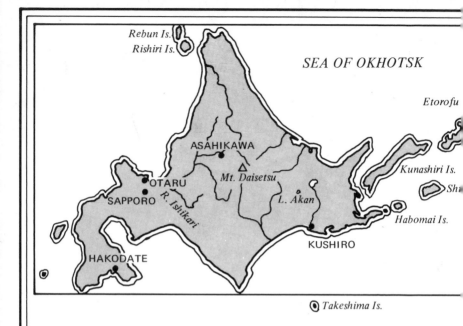

Rebun Is.
Rishiri Is.

SEA OF OKHOTSK

Etorofu

ASAHIKAWA

Mt. Daisetsu

Kunashiri Is.

OTARU

R. Ishikari

L. Akan

Sh

SAPPORO

Habomai Is.

KUSHIRO

HAKODATE

Takeshima Is.

SE.

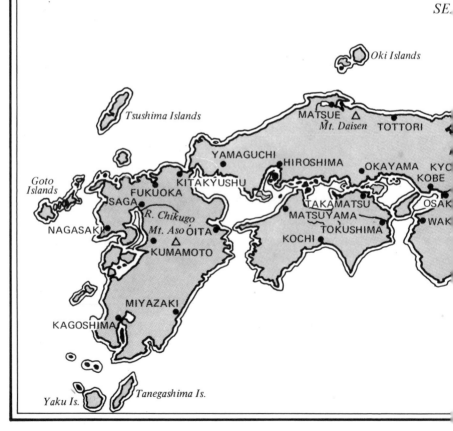

Oki Islands

Tsushima Islands

MATSUE

Mt. Daisen

TOTTORI

YAMAGUCHI

HIROSHIMA

OKAYAMA

KYO

KITAKYUSHU

KOBE

Goto Islands

FUKUOKA

SAGA

TAKAMATSU

OSAK

R. Chikugo

MATSUYAMA

WAK

Mt. Aso ÓITA

NAGASAKI

TOKUSHIMA

KUMAMOTO

KOCHI

MIYAZAKI

KAGOSHIMA

Yaku Is.

Tanegashima Is.